BE BEAUTIFUL • BE INTELLIGENT • BE HEALTHY • BE IMMORTAL

# BE SUPERIOR

# EXTREMIS 3.0

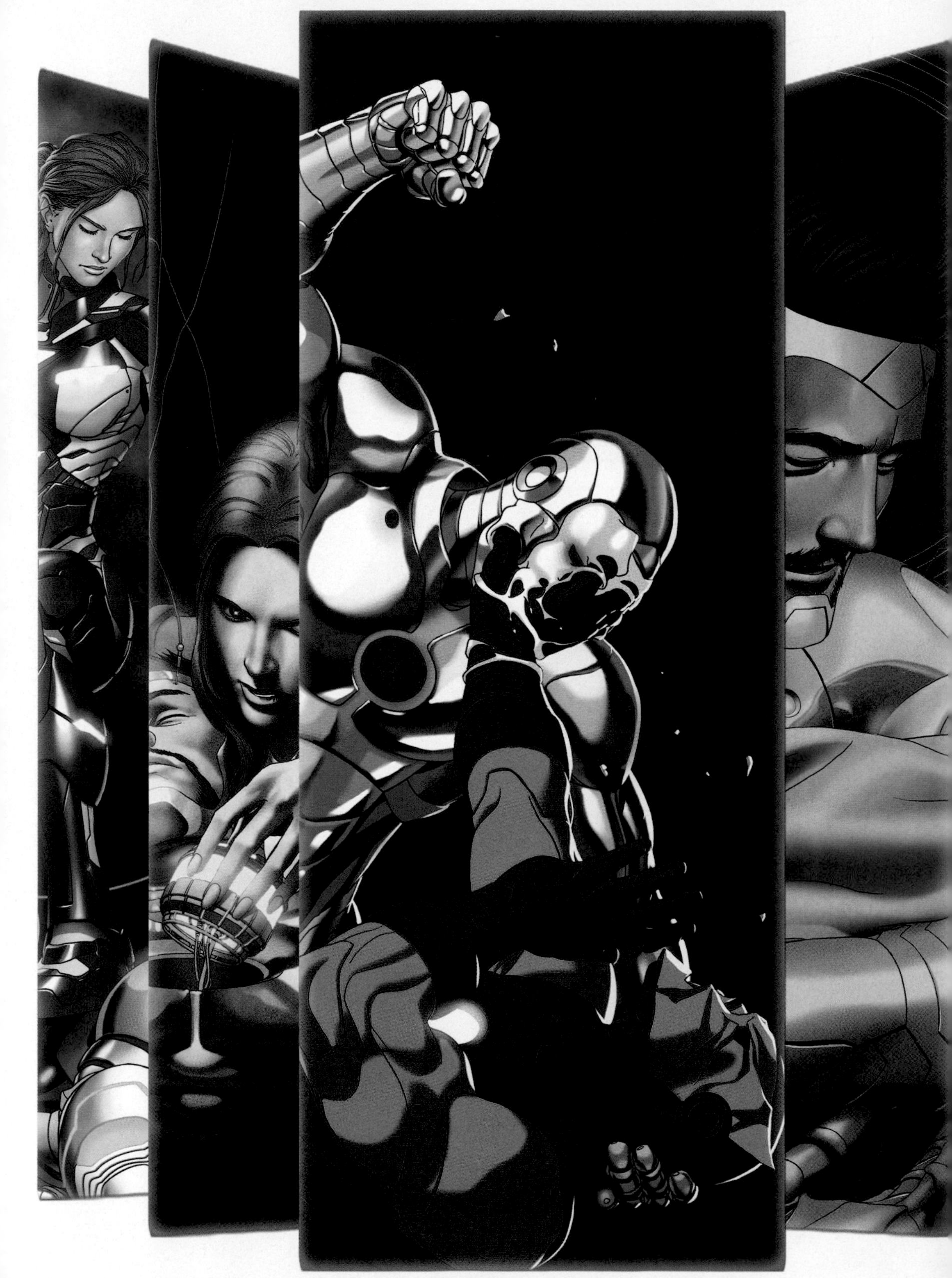

# SUPERIOR IRON MAN

# STARK CONTRAST

**Writer** Tom Taylor

***ISSUE #6***

**Artist** Laura Braga

***ISSUE #7***

**Pencilers** Yildiray Çinar & Felipe Watanabe

**Inkers** Yildiray Çinar & Ruy Jose

***ISSUE #8***

**Penciler** Felipe Watanabe

**Inkers** Ruy Jose, Jay Leisten & Walden Wong

***ISSUE #9***

**Artist** Yildiray Çinar

**Colorist** Guru-eFX

**Letterer** VC's Clayton Cowles

**Cover Art** Mike Choi

**Assistant Editor** Jon Moisan

**Editor** Mark Paniccia

**Iron Man created by** Stan Lee, Don Heck, Larry Lieber & Jack Kirby

**Collection Editor** Jennifer Grünwald **Assistant Editor** Sarah Brunstad
**Associate Managing Editor** Alex Starbuck **Editor, Special Projects** Mark D. Beazley
**Senior Editor, Special Projects** Jeff Youngquist **SVP Print, Sales & Marketing** David Gabriel

**Editor in Chief** Axel Alonso **Chief Creative Officer** Joe Quesada
**Publisher** Dan Buckley **Executive Producer** Alan Fine

**SUPERIOR IRON MAN VOL. 2: STARK CONTRAST.** Contains material originally published in magazine form as SUPERIOR IRON MAN #6-9 and IRON MAN #182. First printing 2015. ISBN# 978-0-7851-9378-4. Published by MARVEL WORLDWIDE, INC., a subsidiary of MARVEL ENTERTAINMENT, LLC. OFFICE OF PUBLICATION: 135 West 50th Street, New York, NY 10020.  **Printed in the U.S.A.** ALAN FINE, President, Marvel Entertainment; DAN BUCKLEY, President, TV, Publishing and Brand Management; JOE QUESADA, Chief Creative Officer; TOM BREVOORT, SVP of Publishing; DAVID BOGART, SVP of Operations & Procurement, Publishing; C.B. CEBULSKI, VP of International Development & Brand Management; DAVID GABRIEL, SVP Print, Sales & Marketing; JIM O'KEEFE, VP of Operations & Logistics; DAN CARR, Executive Director of Publishing Technology; SUSAN CRESPI, Editorial Operations Manager; ALEX MORALES, Publishing Operations Manager; STAN LEE, Chairman Emeritus. For information regarding advertising in Marvel Comics or on Marvel.com, please contact Jonathan Rheingold, VP of Custom Solutions & Ad Sales, at jrheingold@marvel.com. For Marvel subscription inquiries, please call 800-217-9158. **Manufactured between 7/10/2015 and 8/24/2015 by R.R. DONNELLEY, INC., SALEM, VA, USA.**

10 9 8 7 6 5 4 3 2 1

Tony Stark is a technological visionary...a famous, wealthy and unparalleled inventor. With the world's most advanced and powerful suit of armor, Stark has valiantly protected the innocent as the golden Avenger known as IRON MAN.

A recent battle with a mentally powered villain has altered Stark's mind. With a more arrogant and aggressive personality surfacing, Stark used San Francisco to beta test his newest invention...THE EXTREMIS 3.0 APP. It can improve people's lives, making them more attractive, smarter and healthier.

Jamie Carlson, A.K.A. TEEN ABOMINATION, attacked the city in an effort to get Stark's attention. He'd taken Extremis 3.0 in hopes of curing his hideous disposition but the app had no effect. Tony took him in under his protection and promised to cure him. While studying the teen's DNA, he discovered the boy's biological father was Tony's deceased friend, Happy Hogan.

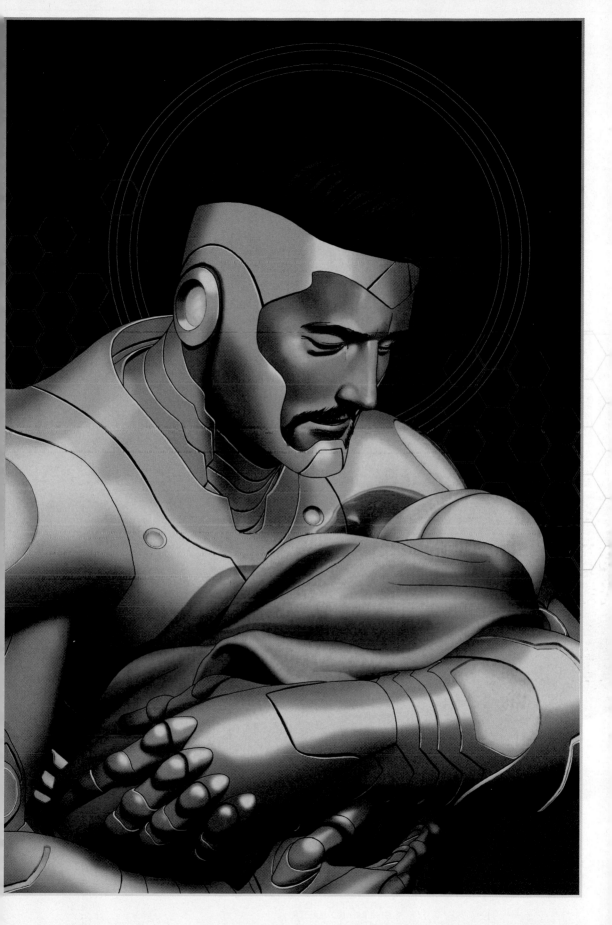

6: IN HIS OWN IMAGE

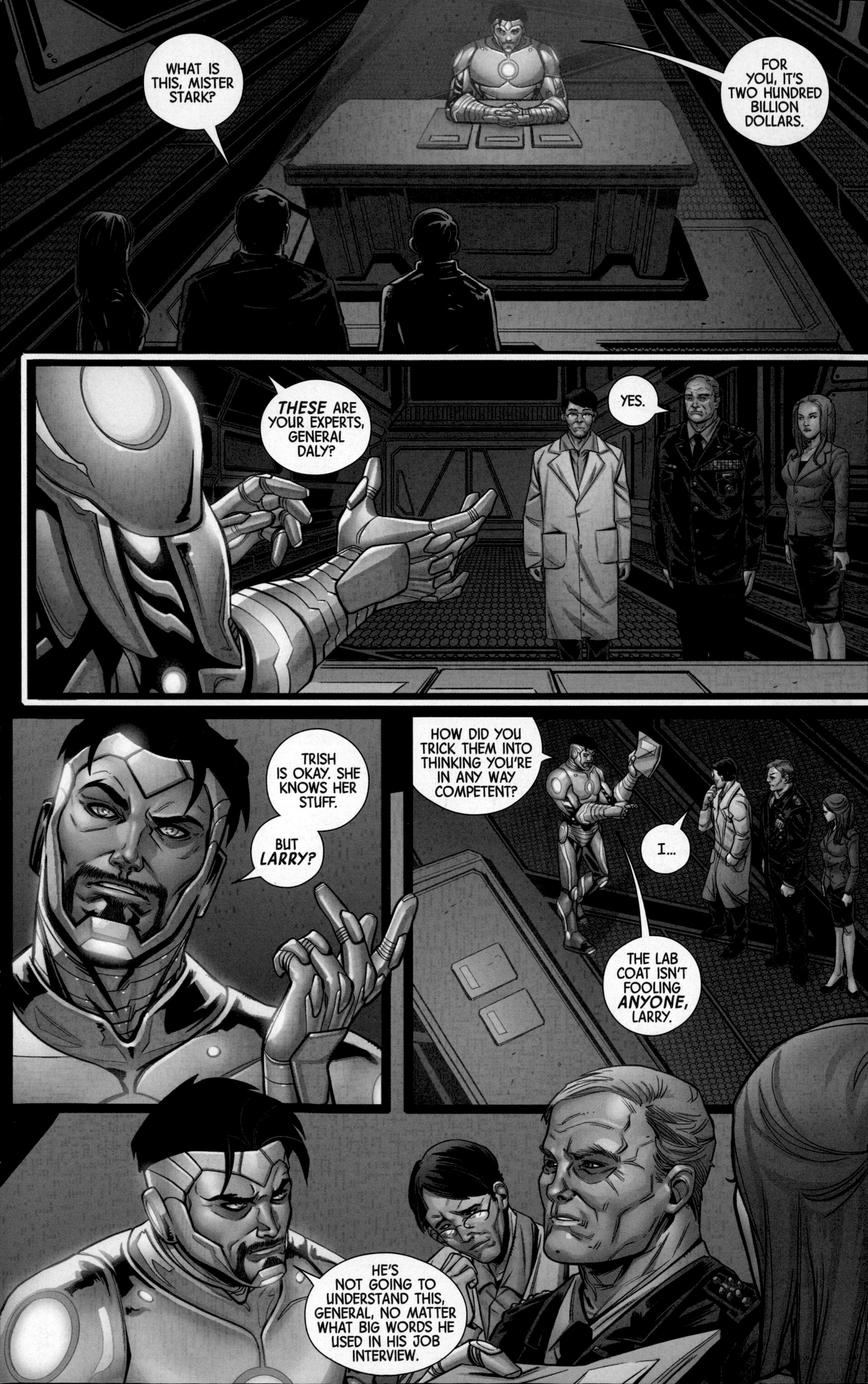
WHAT IS THIS, MISTER STARK?
FOR YOU, IT'S TWO HUNDRED BILLION DOLLARS.
THESE ARE YOUR EXPERTS, GENERAL DALY?
YES.
TRISH IS OKAY. SHE KNOWS HER STUFF.
BUT LARRY?
HOW DID YOU TRICK THEM INTO THINKING YOU'RE IN ANY WAY COMPETENT?
I...
THE LAB COAT ISN'T FOOLING ANYONE, LARRY.
HE'S NOT GOING TO UNDERSTAND THIS, GENERAL, NO MATTER WHAT BIG WORDS HE USED IN HIS JOB INTERVIEW.

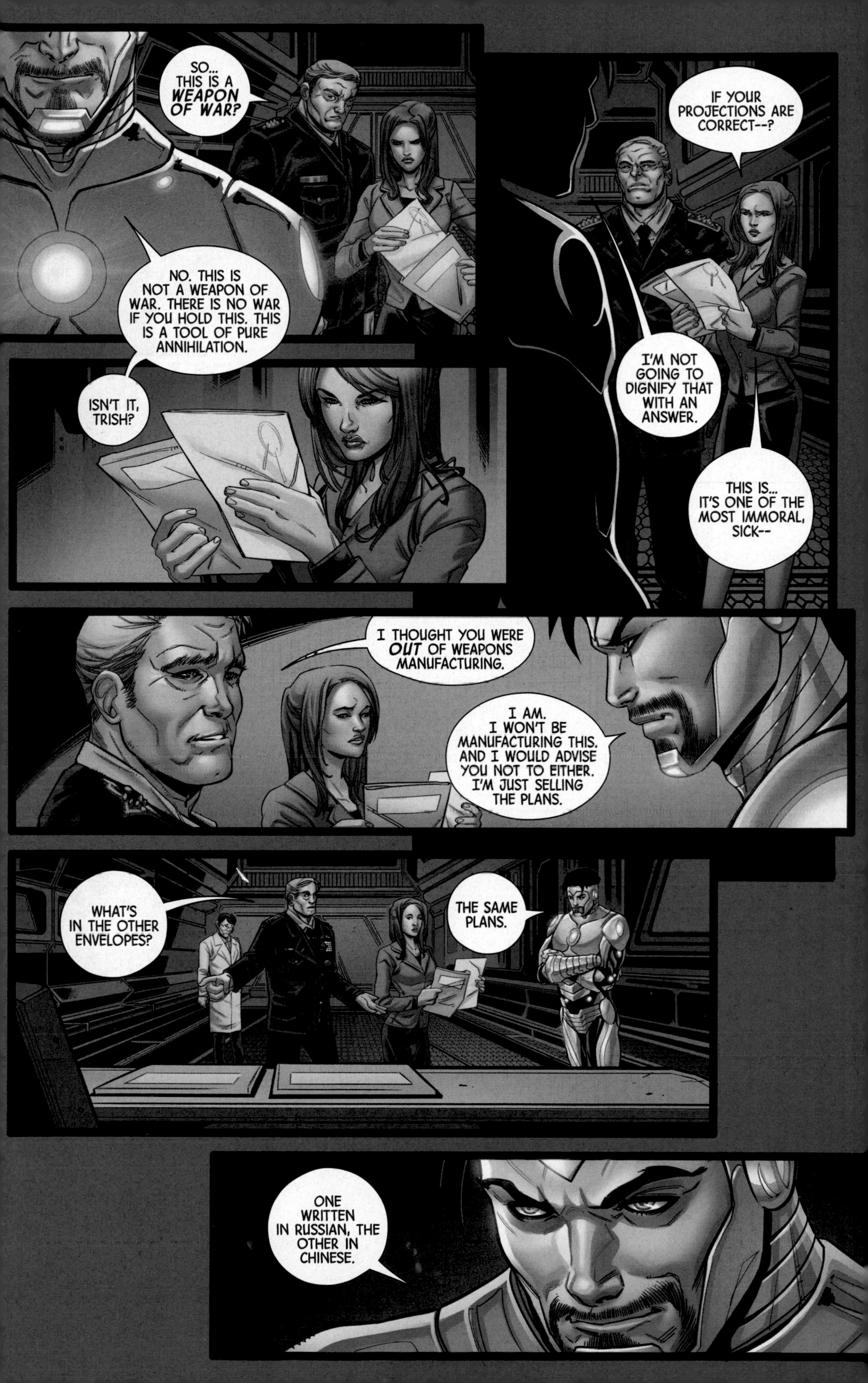
SO... THIS IS A WEAPON OF WAR?
NO. THIS IS NOT A WEAPON OF WAR. THERE IS NO WAR IF YOU HOLD THIS. THIS IS A TOOL OF PURE ANNIHILATION.
ISN'T IT, TRISH?
IF YOUR PROJECTIONS ARE CORRECT--?
I'M NOT GOING TO DIGNIFY THAT WITH AN ANSWER.
THIS IS... IT'S ONE OF THE MOST IMMORAL, SICK--
I THOUGHT YOU WERE OUT OF WEAPONS MANUFACTURING.
I AM. I WON'T BE MANUFACTURING THIS. AND I WOULD ADVISE YOU NOT TO EITHER. I'M JUST SELLING THE PLANS.
WHAT'S IN THE OTHER ENVELOPES?
THE SAME PLANS.
ONE WRITTEN IN RUSSIAN, THE OTHER IN CHINESE.

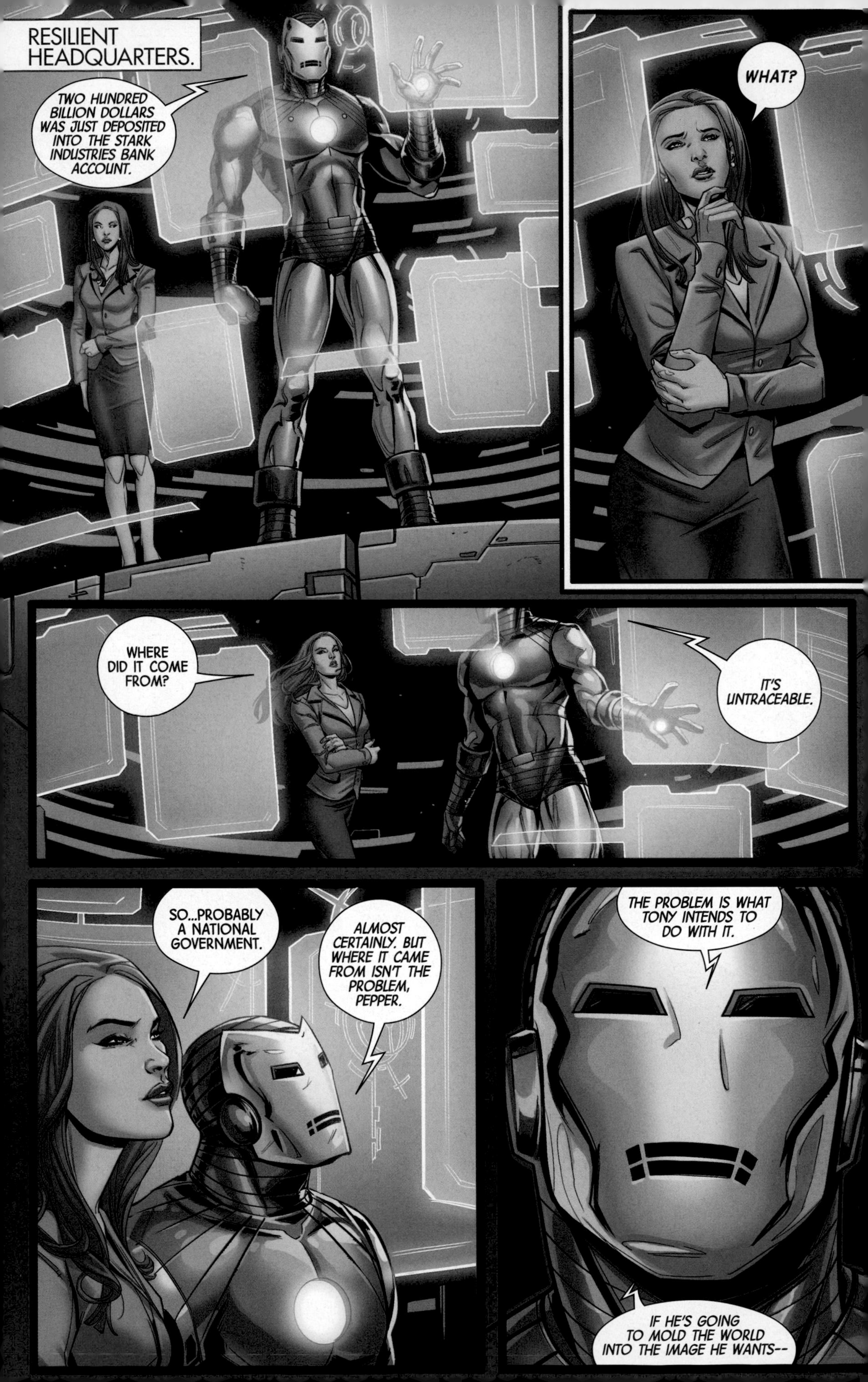
RESILIENT HEADQUARTERS.
TWO HUNDRED BILLION DOLLARS WAS JUST DEPOSITED INTO THE STARK INDUSTRIES BANK ACCOUNT.
WHAT?
WHERE DID IT COME FROM?
IT'S UNTRACEABLE.
SO...PROBABLY A NATIONAL GOVERNMENT.
ALMOST CERTAINLY. BUT WHERE IT CAME FROM ISN'T THE PROBLEM, PEPPER.
THE PROBLEM IS WHAT TONY INTENDS TO DO WITH IT.
IF HE'S GOING TO MOLD THE WORLD INTO THE IMAGE HE WANTS--

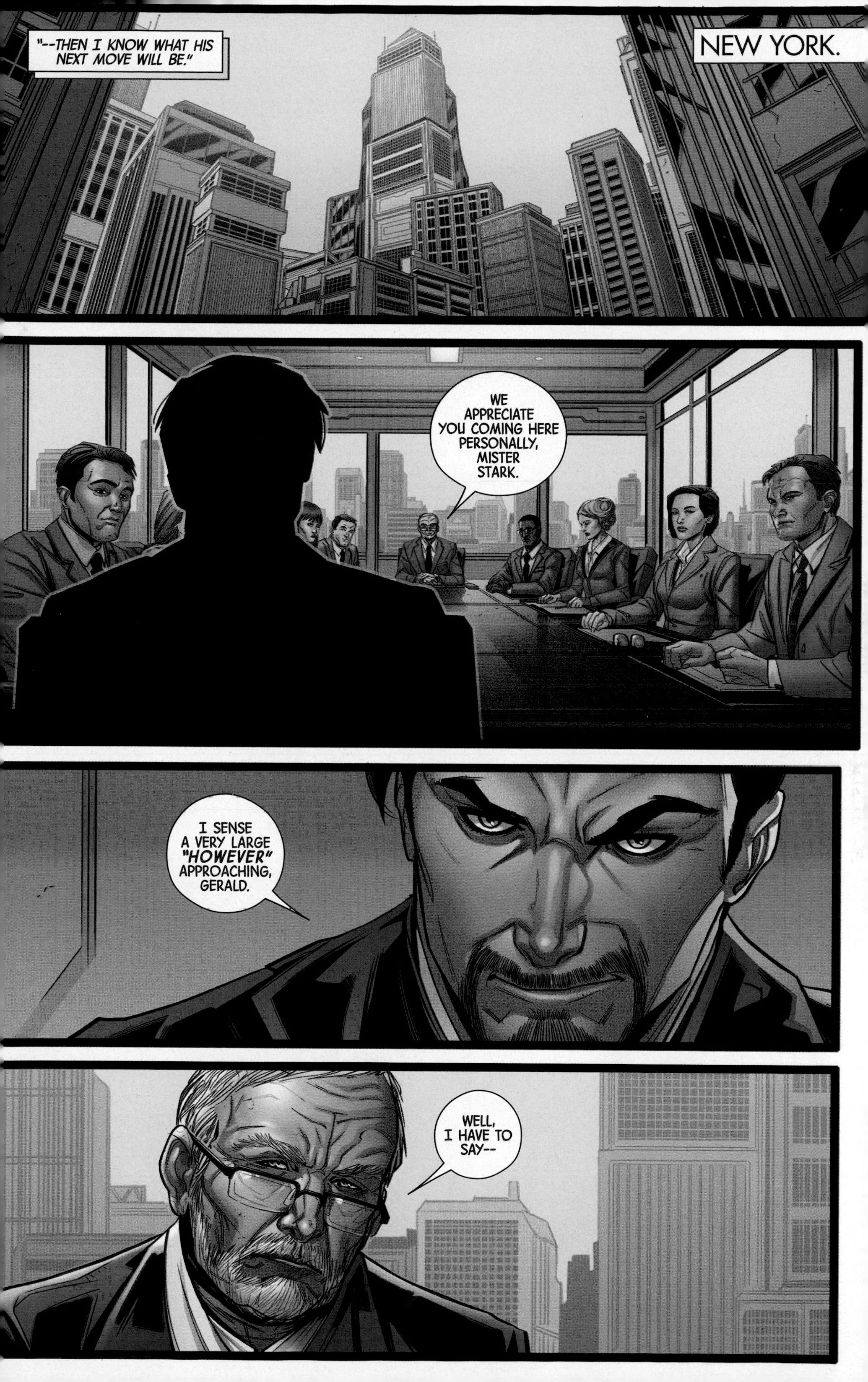
"--THEN I KNOW WHAT HIS NEXT MOVE WILL BE."
NEW YORK.
WE APPRECIATE YOU COMING HERE PERSONALLY, MISTER STARK.
I SENSE A VERY LARGE "HOWEVER" APPROACHING, GERALD.
WELL, I HAVE TO SAY--

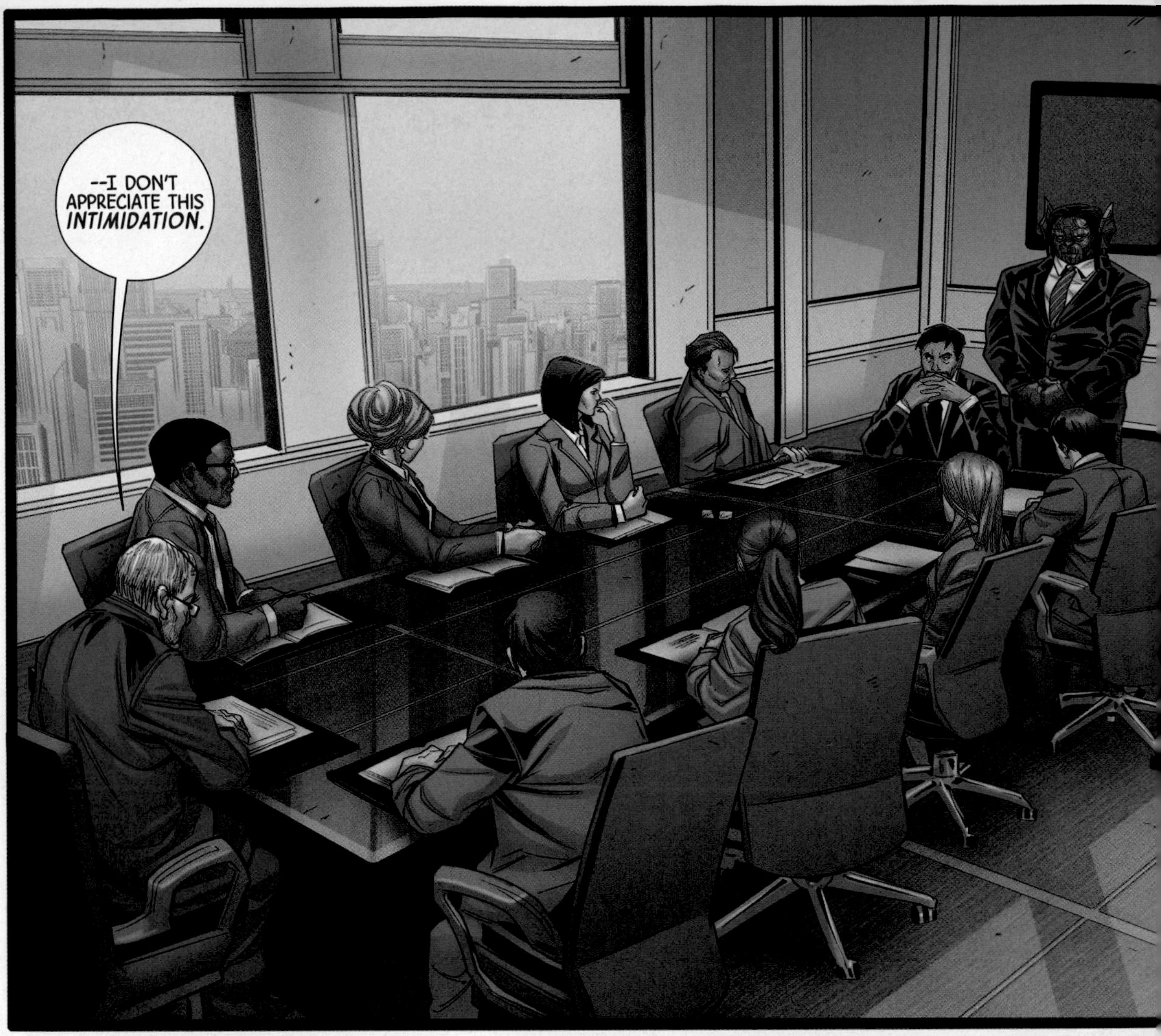
--I DON'T APPRECIATE THIS *INTIMIDATION.*

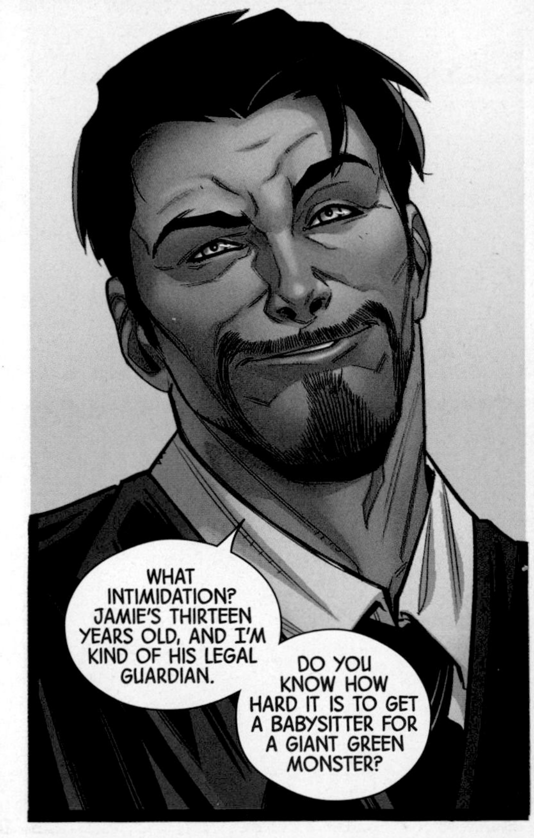
WHAT INTIMIDATION? JAMIE'S THIRTEEN YEARS OLD, AND I'M KIND OF HIS LEGAL GUARDIAN.
DO YOU KNOW HOW HARD IT IS TO GET A BABYSITTER FOR A GIANT GREEN MONSTER?

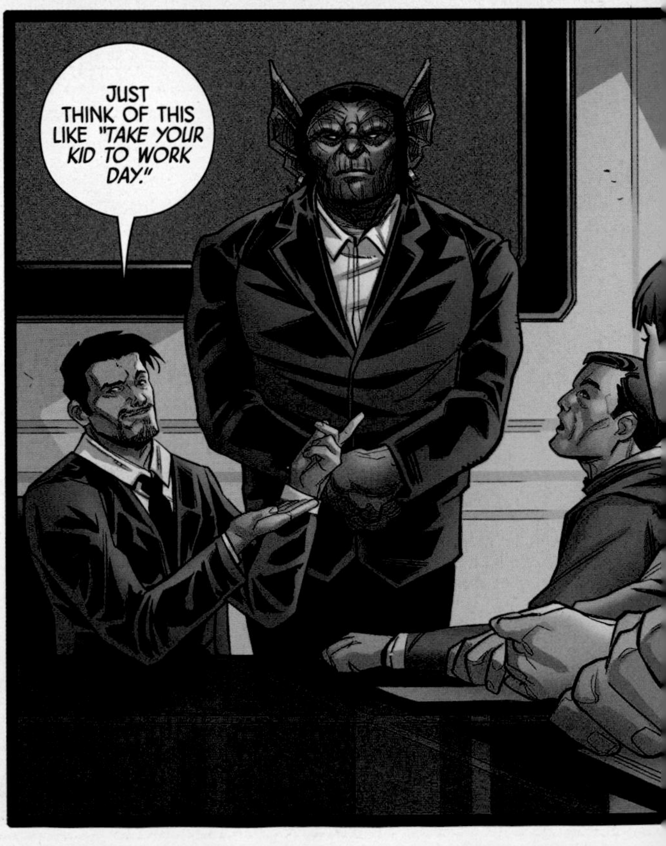
JUST THINK OF THIS LIKE *"TAKE YOUR KID TO WORK DAY."*

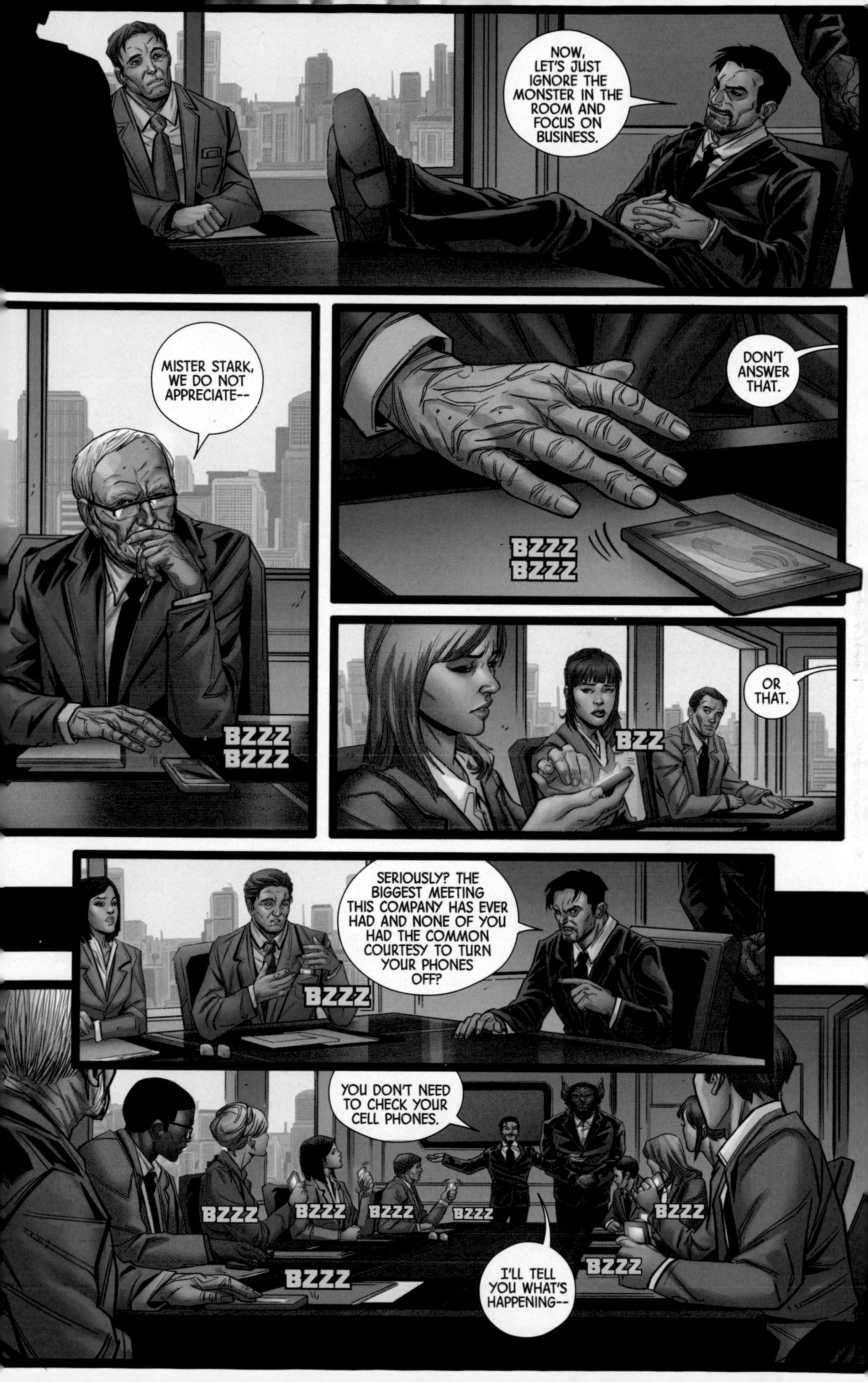
NOW, LET'S JUST IGNORE THE MONSTER IN THE ROOM AND FOCUS ON BUSINESS.
MISTER STARK, WE DO NOT APPRECIATE--
BZZZ BZZZ
DON'T ANSWER THAT.
BZZZ BZZZ
OR THAT.
BZZ
SERIOUSLY? THE BIGGEST MEETING THIS COMPANY HAS EVER HAD AND NONE OF YOU HAD THE COMMON COURTESY TO TURN YOUR PHONES OFF?
BZZZ
YOU DON'T NEED TO CHECK YOUR CELL PHONES.
BZZZ
BZZZ
BZZZ
BZZZ
BZZZ
BZZZ
BZZZ
I'LL TELL YOU WHAT'S HAPPENING--

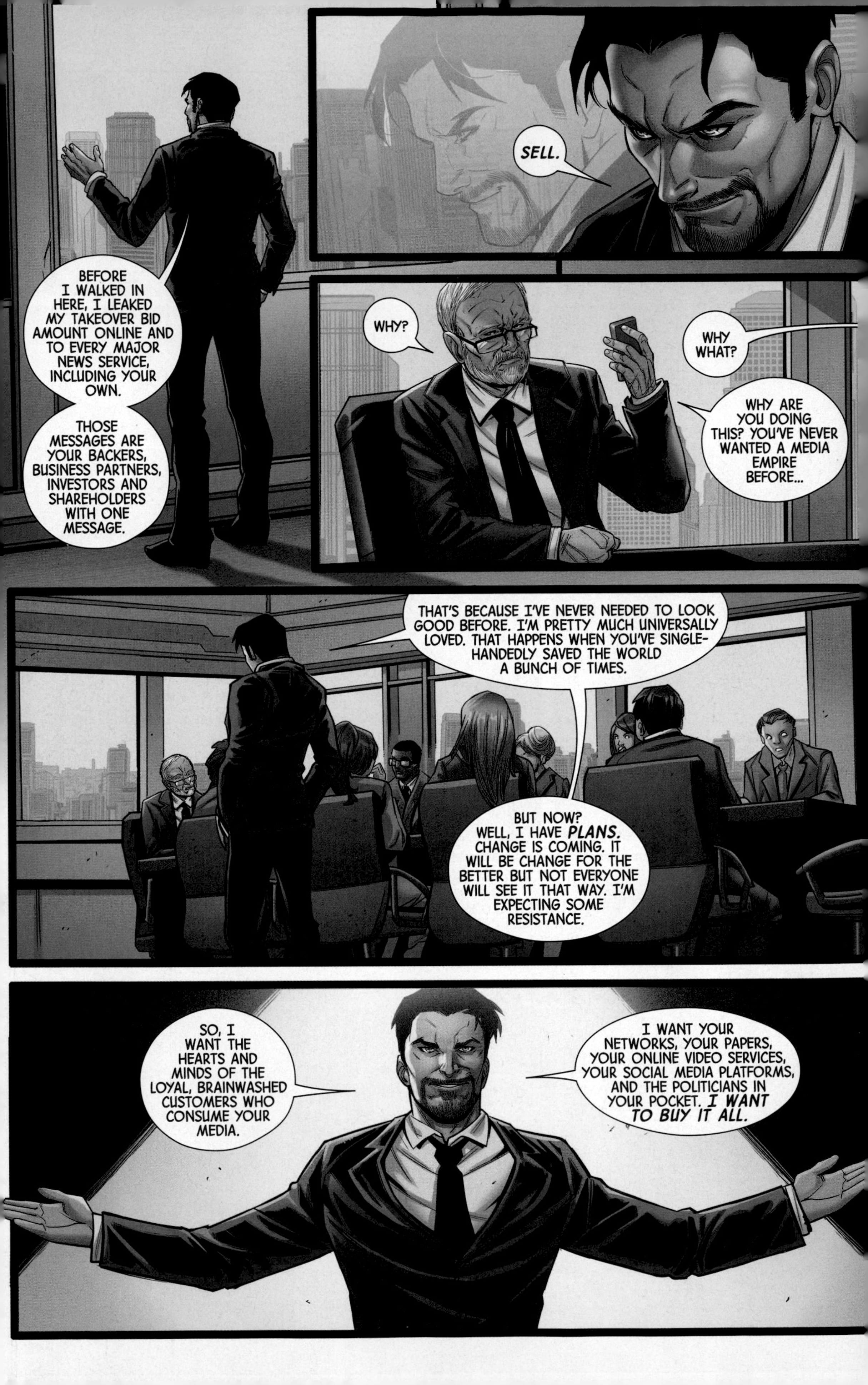
SELL.
BEFORE I WALKED IN HERE, I LEAKED MY TAKEOVER BID AMOUNT ONLINE AND TO EVERY MAJOR NEWS SERVICE, INCLUDING YOUR OWN.
THOSE MESSAGES ARE YOUR BACKERS, BUSINESS PARTNERS, INVESTORS AND SHAREHOLDERS WITH ONE MESSAGE.
WHY?
WHY WHAT?
WHY ARE YOU DOING THIS? YOU'VE NEVER WANTED A MEDIA EMPIRE BEFORE...
THAT'S BECAUSE I'VE NEVER NEEDED TO LOOK GOOD BEFORE. I'M PRETTY MUCH UNIVERSALLY LOVED. THAT HAPPENS WHEN YOU'VE SINGLE-HANDEDLY SAVED THE WORLD A BUNCH OF TIMES.
BUT NOW? WELL, I HAVE PLANS. CHANGE IS COMING. IT WILL BE CHANGE FOR THE BETTER BUT NOT EVERYONE WILL SEE IT THAT WAY. I'M EXPECTING SOME RESISTANCE.
SO, I WANT THE HEARTS AND MINDS OF THE LOYAL, BRAINWASHED CUSTOMERS WHO CONSUME YOUR MEDIA.
I WANT YOUR NETWORKS, YOUR PAPERS, YOUR ONLINE VIDEO SERVICES, YOUR SOCIAL MEDIA PLATFORMS, AND THE POLITICIANS IN YOUR POCKET. I WANT TO BUY IT ALL.

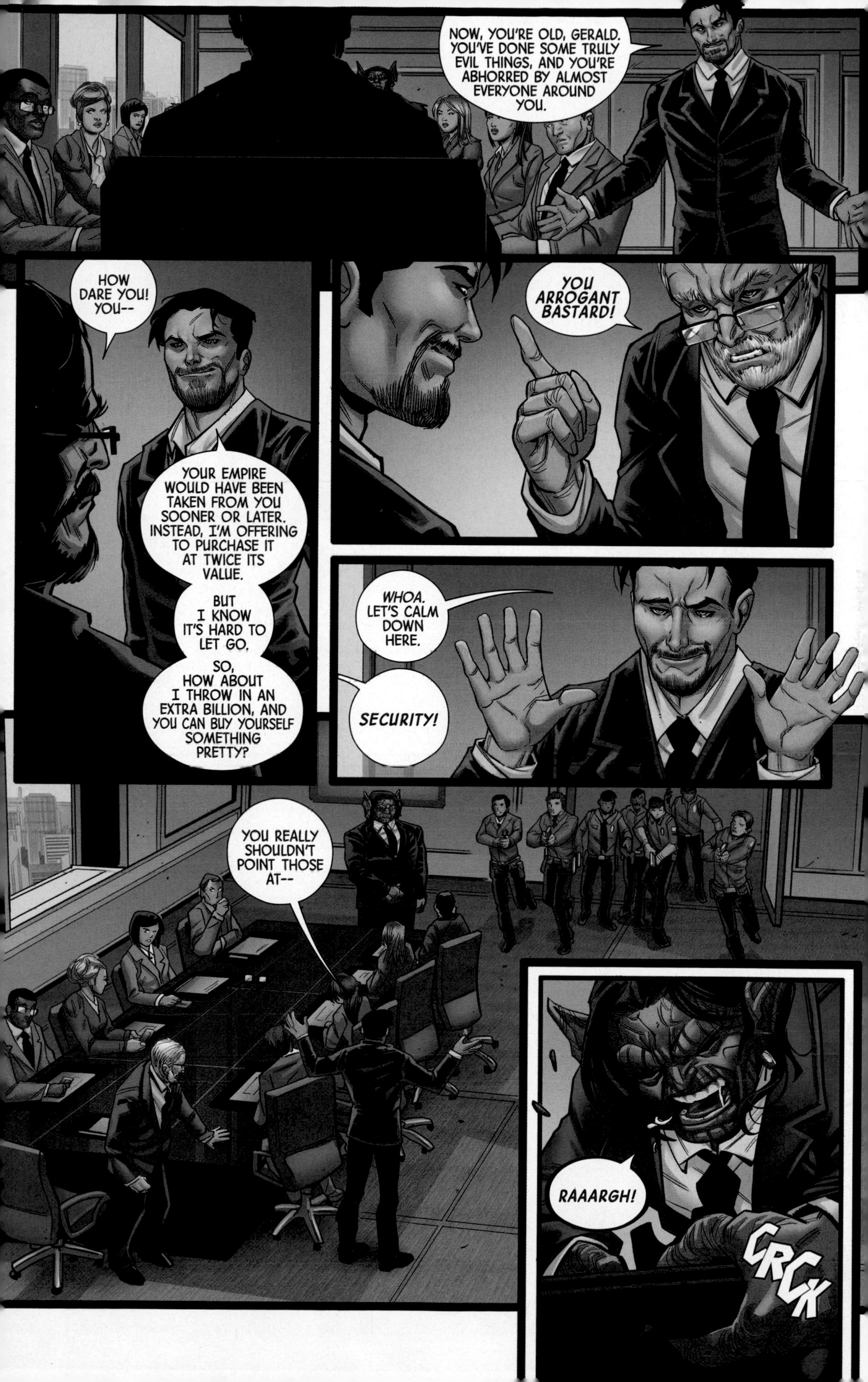
NOW, YOU'RE OLD, GERALD. YOU'VE DONE SOME TRULY EVIL THINGS, AND YOU'RE ABHORRED BY ALMOST EVERYONE AROUND YOU.
HOW DARE YOU! YOU--
YOUR EMPIRE WOULD HAVE BEEN TAKEN FROM YOU SOONER OR LATER. INSTEAD, I'M OFFERING TO PURCHASE IT AT TWICE ITS VALUE.
BUT I KNOW IT'S HARD TO LET GO.
SO, HOW ABOUT I THROW IN AN EXTRA BILLION, AND YOU CAN BUY YOURSELF SOMETHING PRETTY?
YOU ARROGANT BASTARD!
WHOA. LET'S CALM DOWN HERE.
SECURITY!
YOU REALLY SHOULDN'T POINT THOSE AT--
RAAARGH!
CRCK

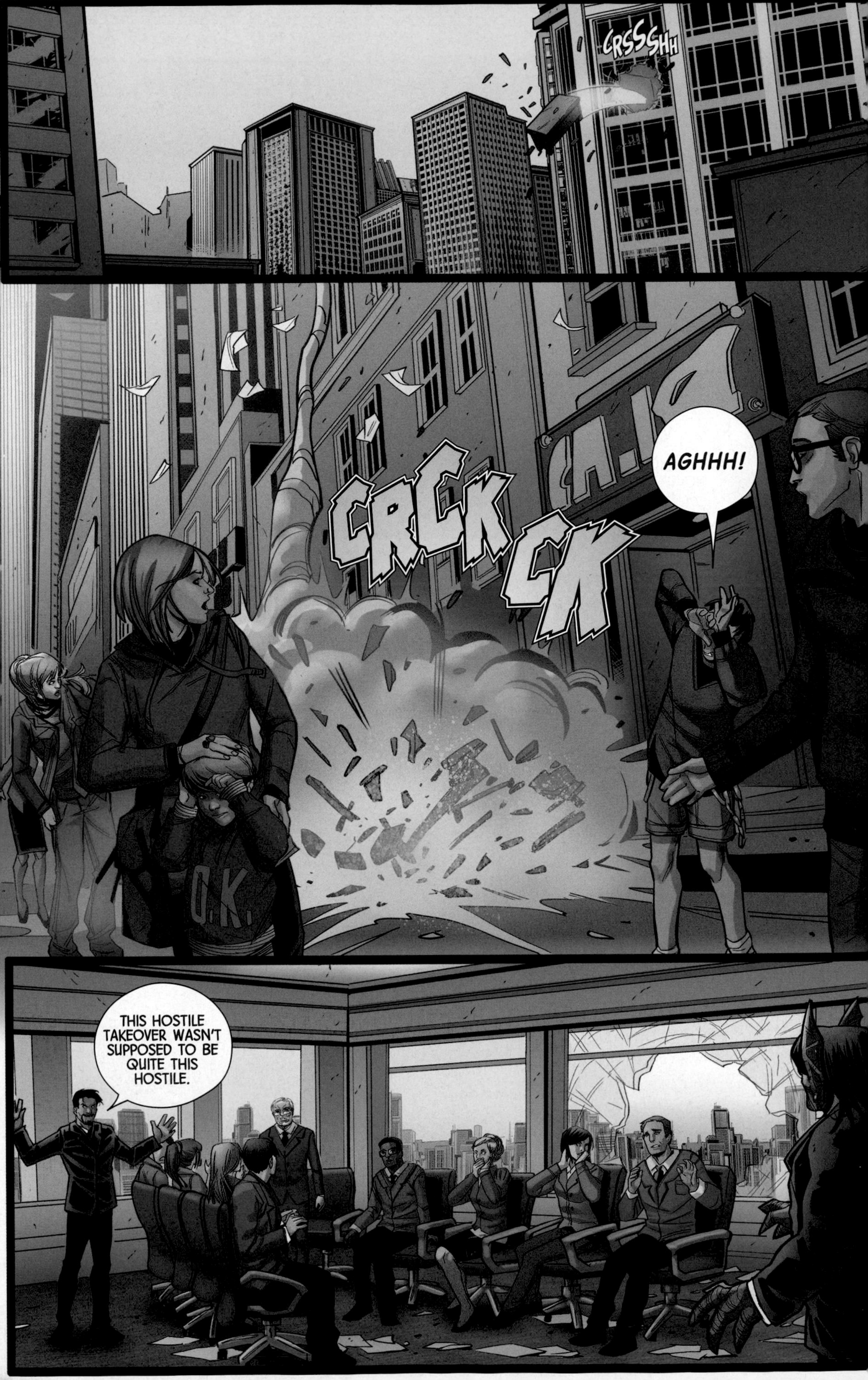
CRSSSHH
CRCK
CK
AGHHH!
THIS HOSTILE TAKEOVER WASN'T SUPPOSED TO BE QUITE THIS HOSTILE.

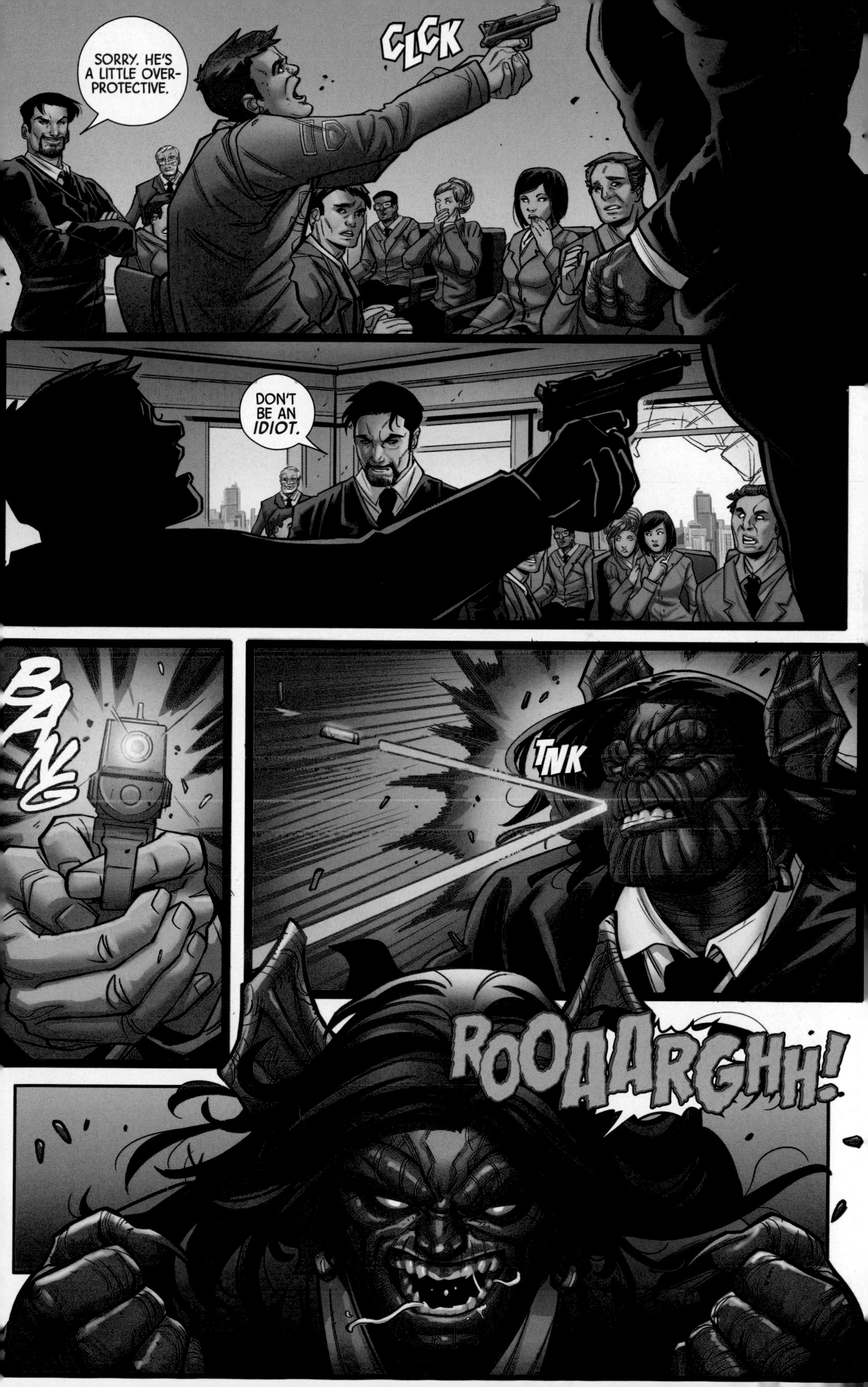
SORRY. HE'S A LITTLE OVER-PROTECTIVE.
CLCK
DON'T BE AN *IDIOT*.
BANG
TNK
ROOAARGHH!

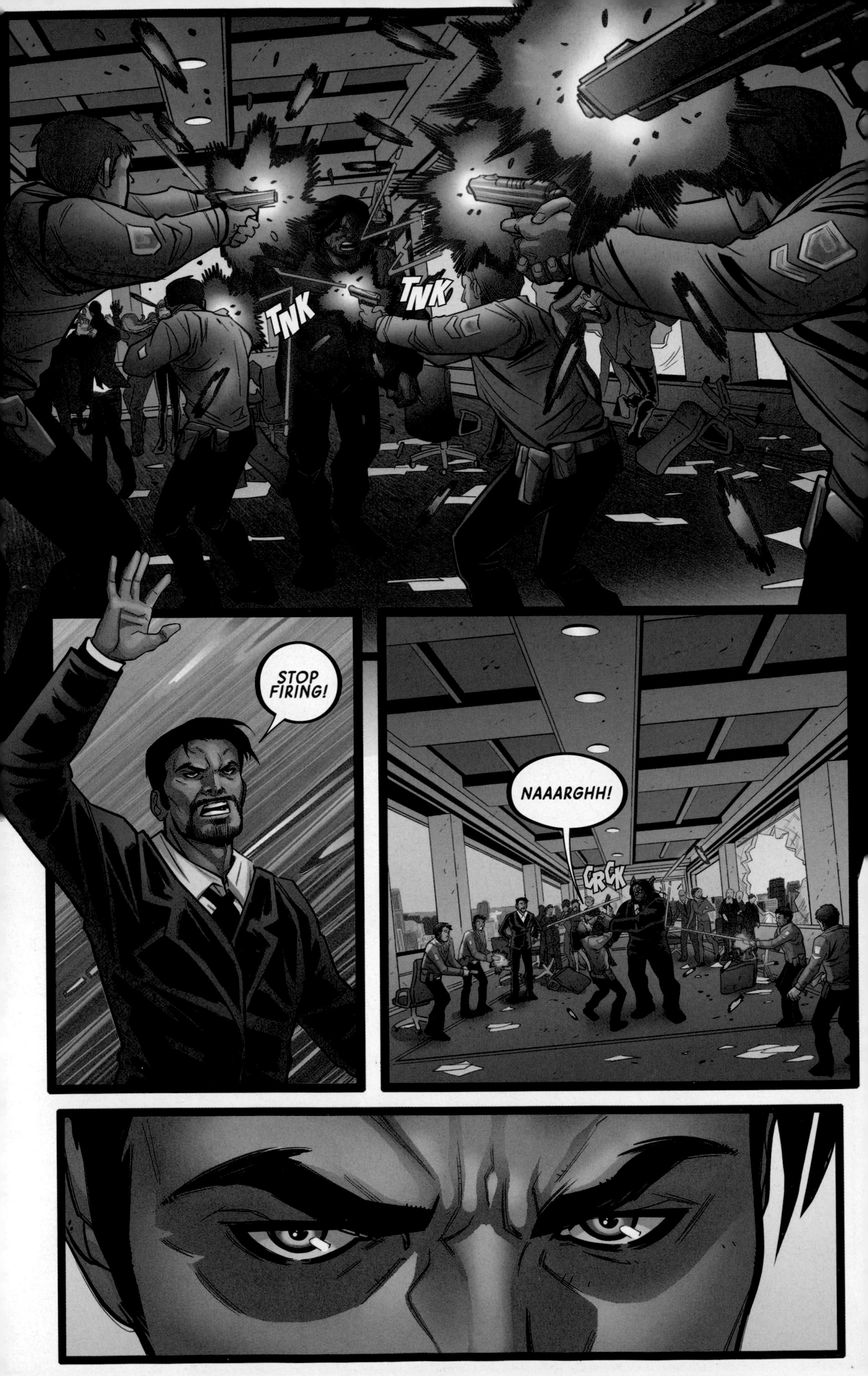
TNK
TNK
STOP FIRING!
NAAARGHH!
CRCK

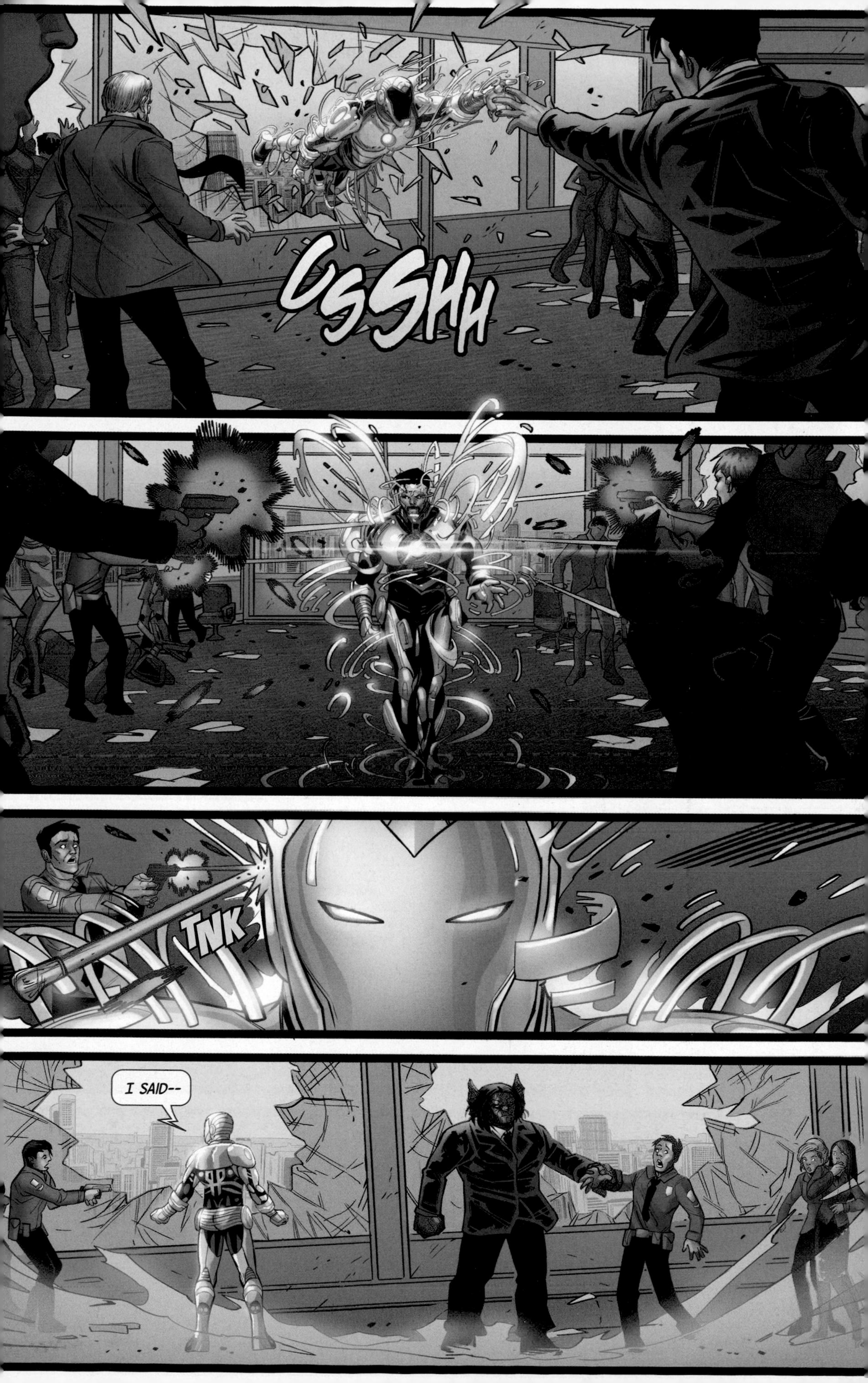
CSSHH
TNK
I SAID--

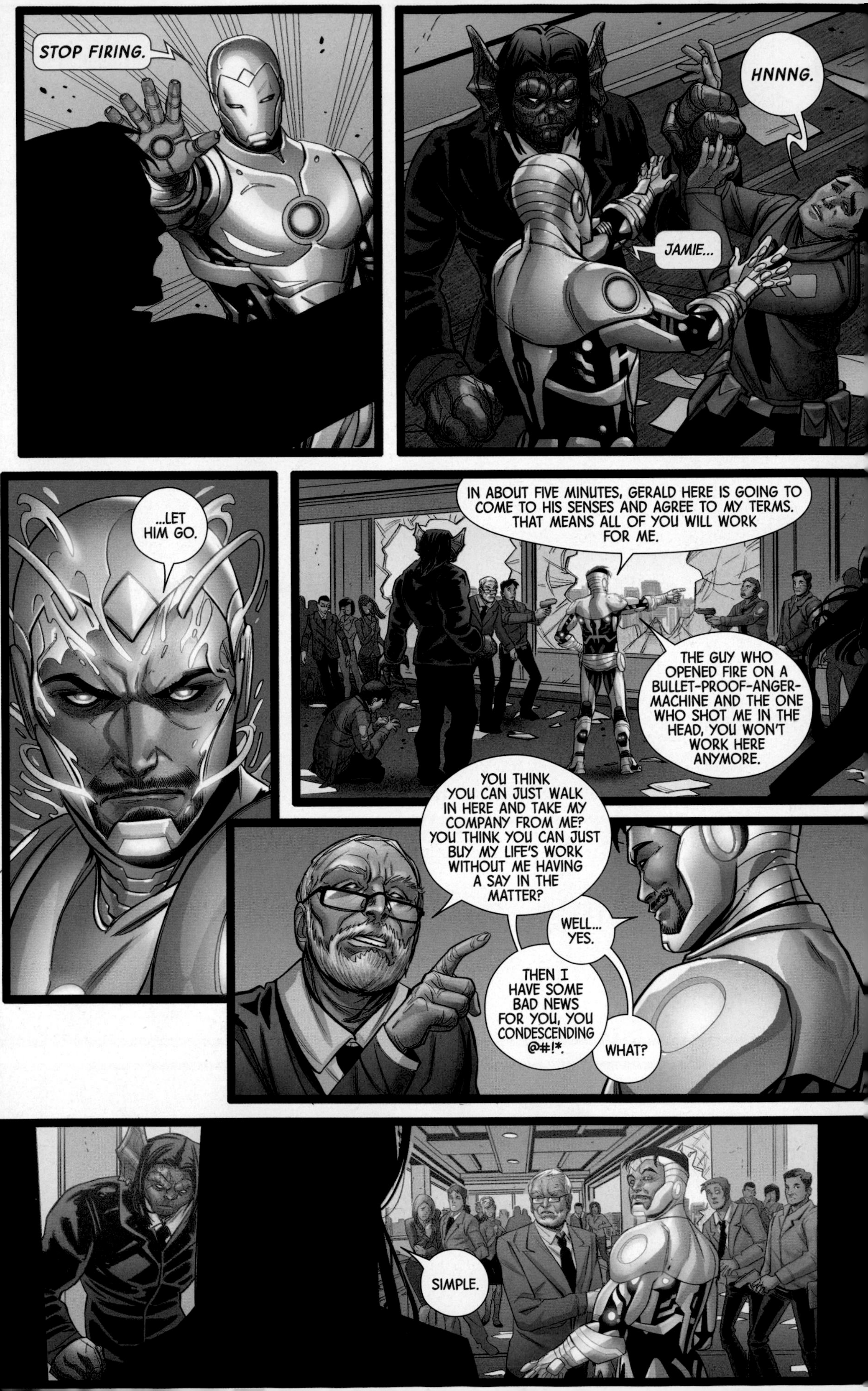
STOP FIRING.
HNNNG.
JAMIE...
...LET HIM GO.
IN ABOUT FIVE MINUTES, GERALD HERE IS GOING TO COME TO HIS SENSES AND AGREE TO MY TERMS. THAT MEANS ALL OF YOU WILL WORK FOR ME.
THE GUY WHO OPENED FIRE ON A BULLET-PROOF-ANGER-MACHINE AND THE ONE WHO SHOT ME IN THE HEAD, YOU WON'T WORK HERE ANYMORE.
YOU THINK YOU CAN JUST WALK IN HERE AND TAKE MY COMPANY FROM ME? YOU THINK YOU CAN JUST BUY MY LIFE'S WORK WITHOUT ME HAVING A SAY IN THE MATTER?
WELL... YES.
THEN I HAVE SOME BAD NEWS FOR YOU, YOU CONDESCENDING @#!*.
WHAT?
SIMPLE.

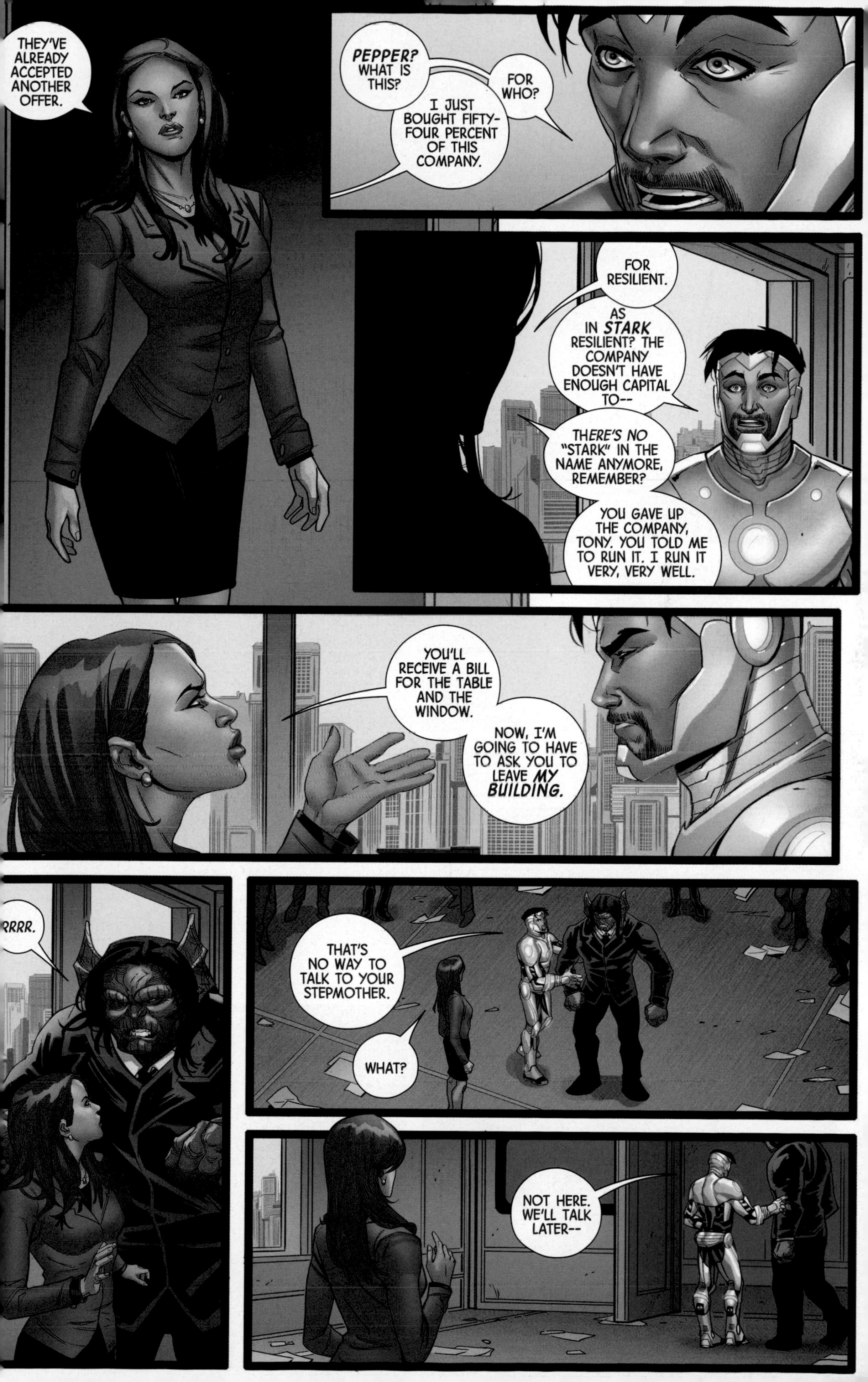

THEY'VE ALREADY ACCEPTED ANOTHER OFFER.
PEPPER? WHAT IS THIS?
I JUST BOUGHT FIFTY-FOUR PERCENT OF THIS COMPANY.
FOR WHO?
FOR RESILIENT.
AS IN STARK RESILIENT? THE COMPANY DOESN'T HAVE ENOUGH CAPITAL TO--
THERE'S NO "STARK" IN THE NAME ANYMORE, REMEMBER?
YOU GAVE UP THE COMPANY, TONY. YOU TOLD ME TO RUN IT. I RUN IT VERY, VERY WELL.
YOU'LL RECEIVE A BILL FOR THE TABLE AND THE WINDOW.
NOW, I'M GOING TO HAVE TO ASK YOU TO LEAVE MY BUILDING.
RRRR.
THAT'S NO WAY TO TALK TO YOUR STEPMOTHER.
WHAT?
NOT HERE. WE'LL TALK LATER--

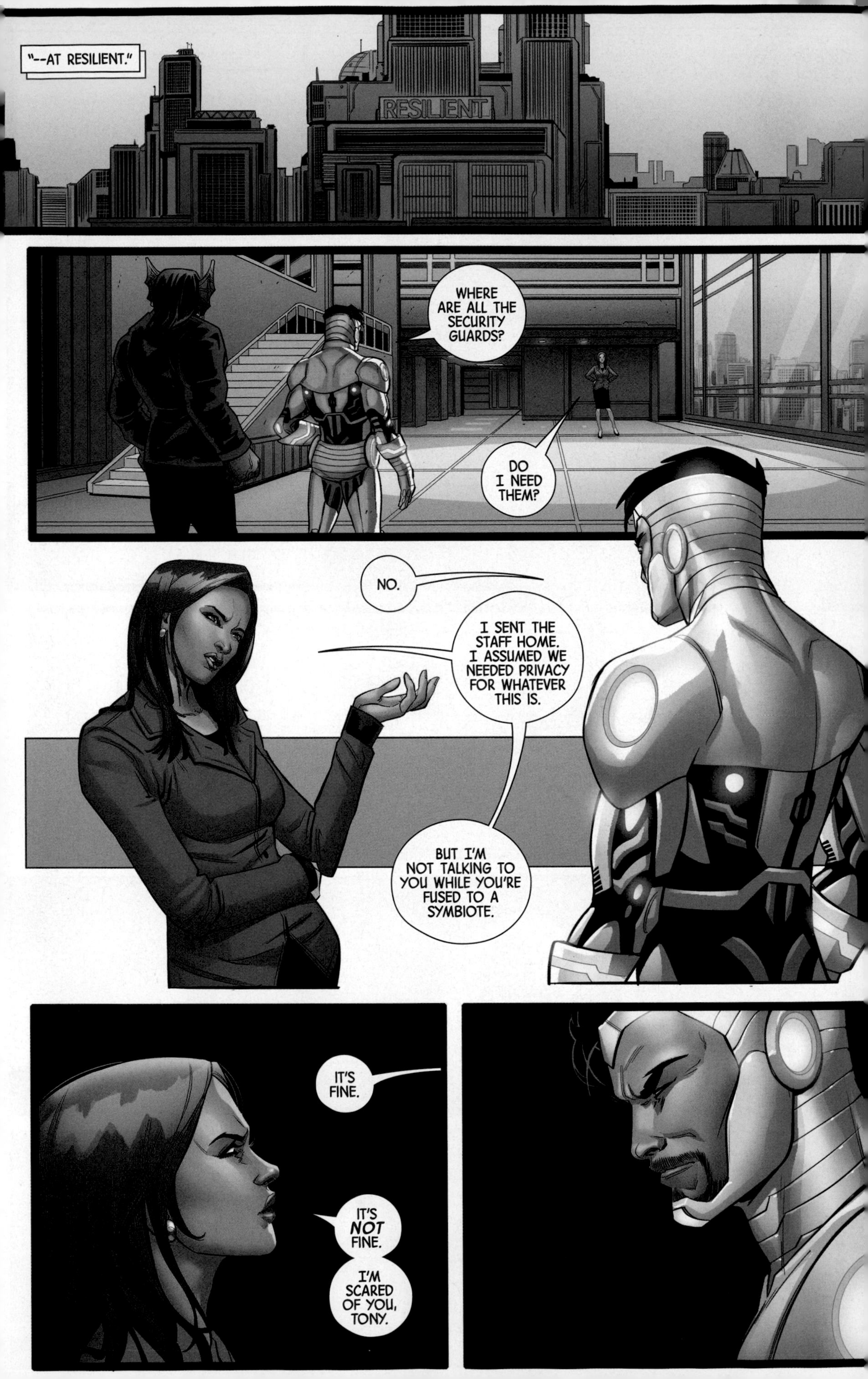
"--AT RESILIENT."
RESILIENT
WHERE ARE ALL THE SECURITY GUARDS?
DO I NEED THEM?
NO.
I SENT THE STAFF HOME. I ASSUMED WE NEEDED PRIVACY FOR WHATEVER THIS IS.
BUT I'M NOT TALKING TO YOU WHILE YOU'RE FUSED TO A SYMBIOTE.
IT'S FINE.
IT'S *NOT* FINE.
I'M SCARED OF YOU, TONY.

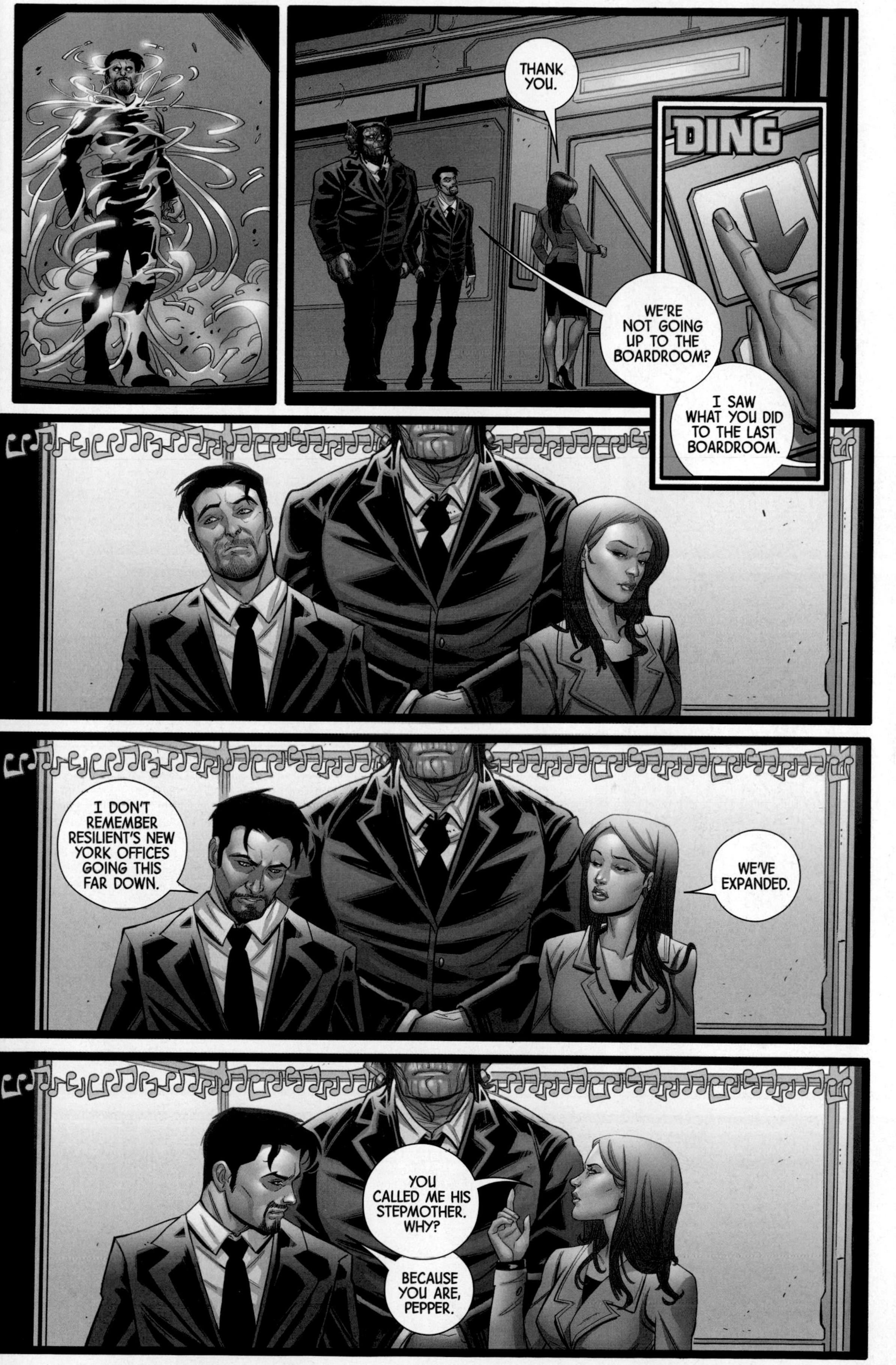
THANK YOU.
DING
WE'RE NOT GOING UP TO THE BOARDROOM?
I SAW WHAT YOU DID TO THE LAST BOARDROOM.
I DON'T REMEMBER RESILIENT'S NEW YORK OFFICES GOING THIS FAR DOWN.
WE'VE EXPANDED.
YOU CALLED ME HIS STEPMOTHER. WHY?
BECAUSE YOU ARE, PEPPER.

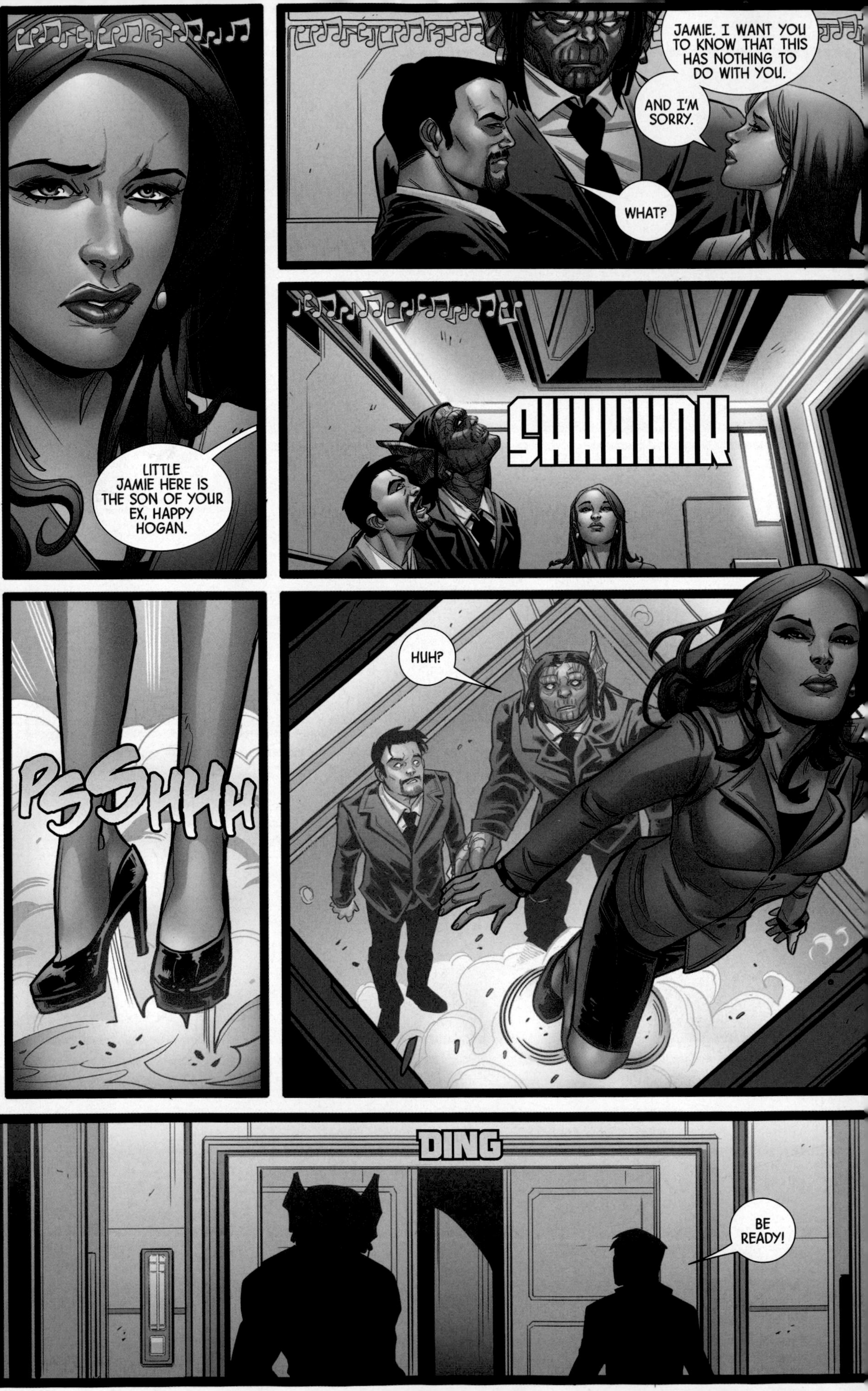

JAMIE. I WANT YOU TO KNOW THAT THIS HAS NOTHING TO DO WITH YOU.
AND I'M SORRY.
WHAT?
LITTLE JAMIE HERE IS THE SON OF YOUR EX, HAPPY HOGAN.
SHHHHNK
PSSHHH
HUH?
DING
BE READY!

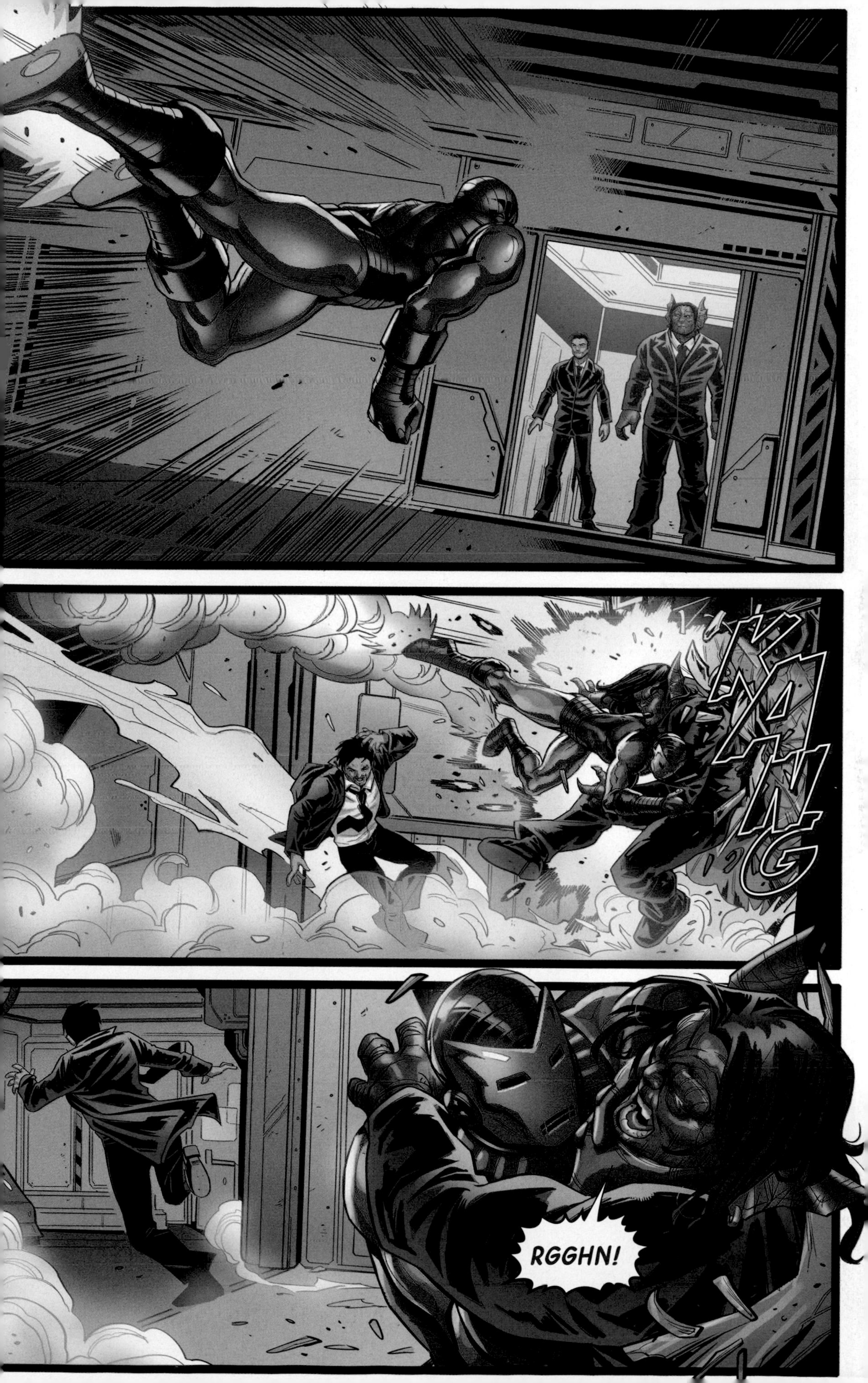
KRANG
RGGHN!

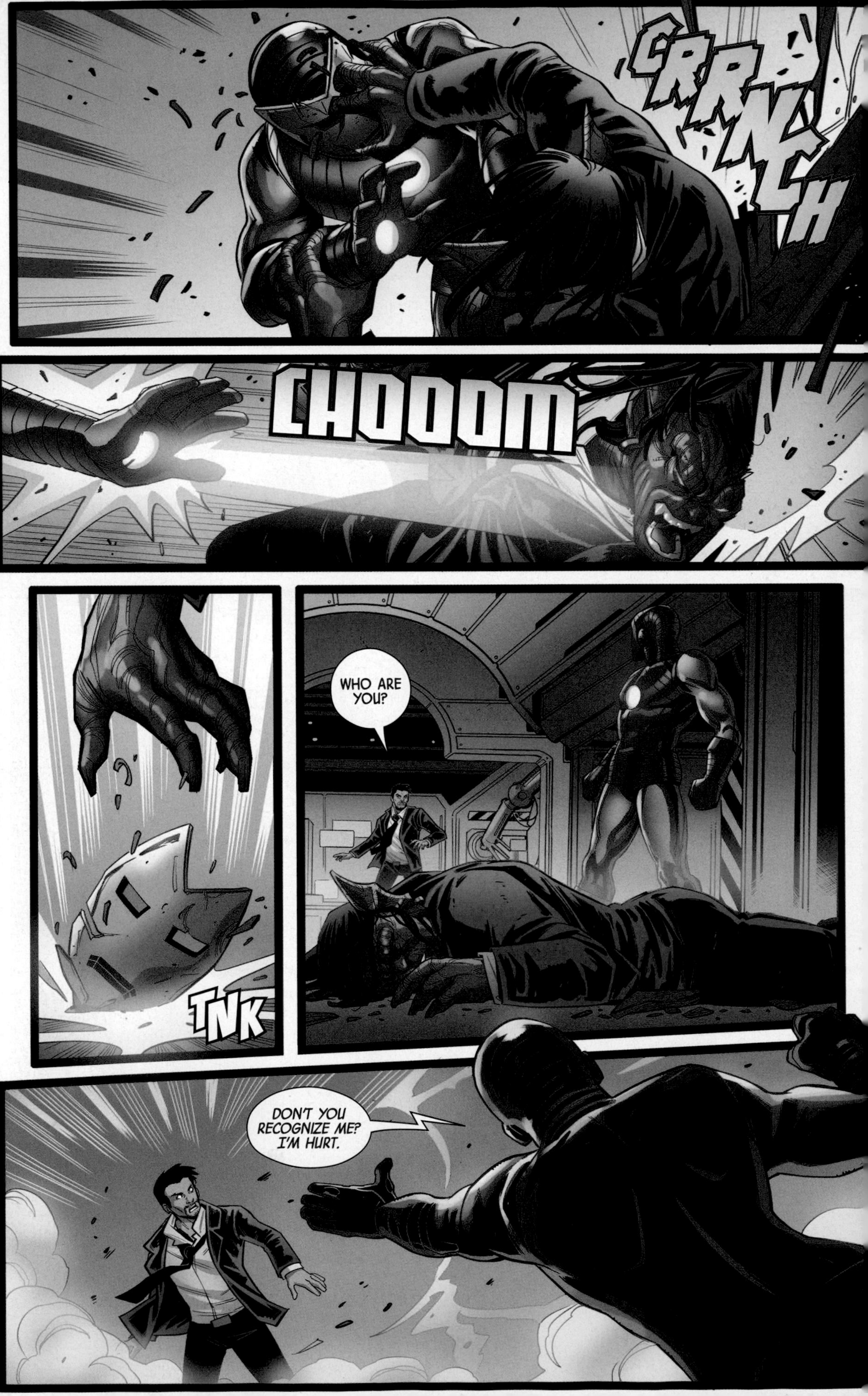
CRRNCH
CHOOOM
TNK
WHO ARE YOU?
DON'T YOU RECOGNIZE ME? I'M HURT.

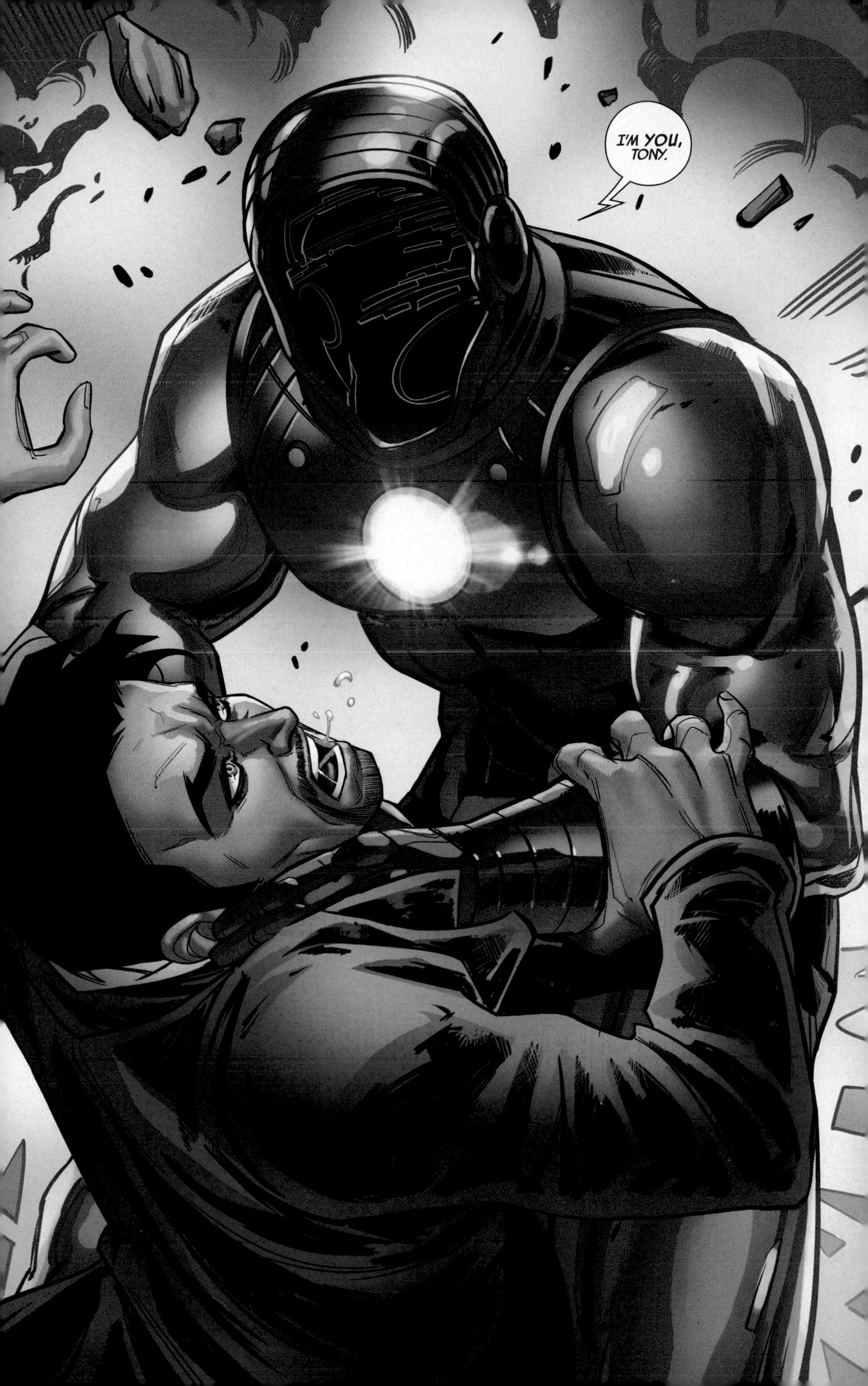
I'M YOU, TONY.

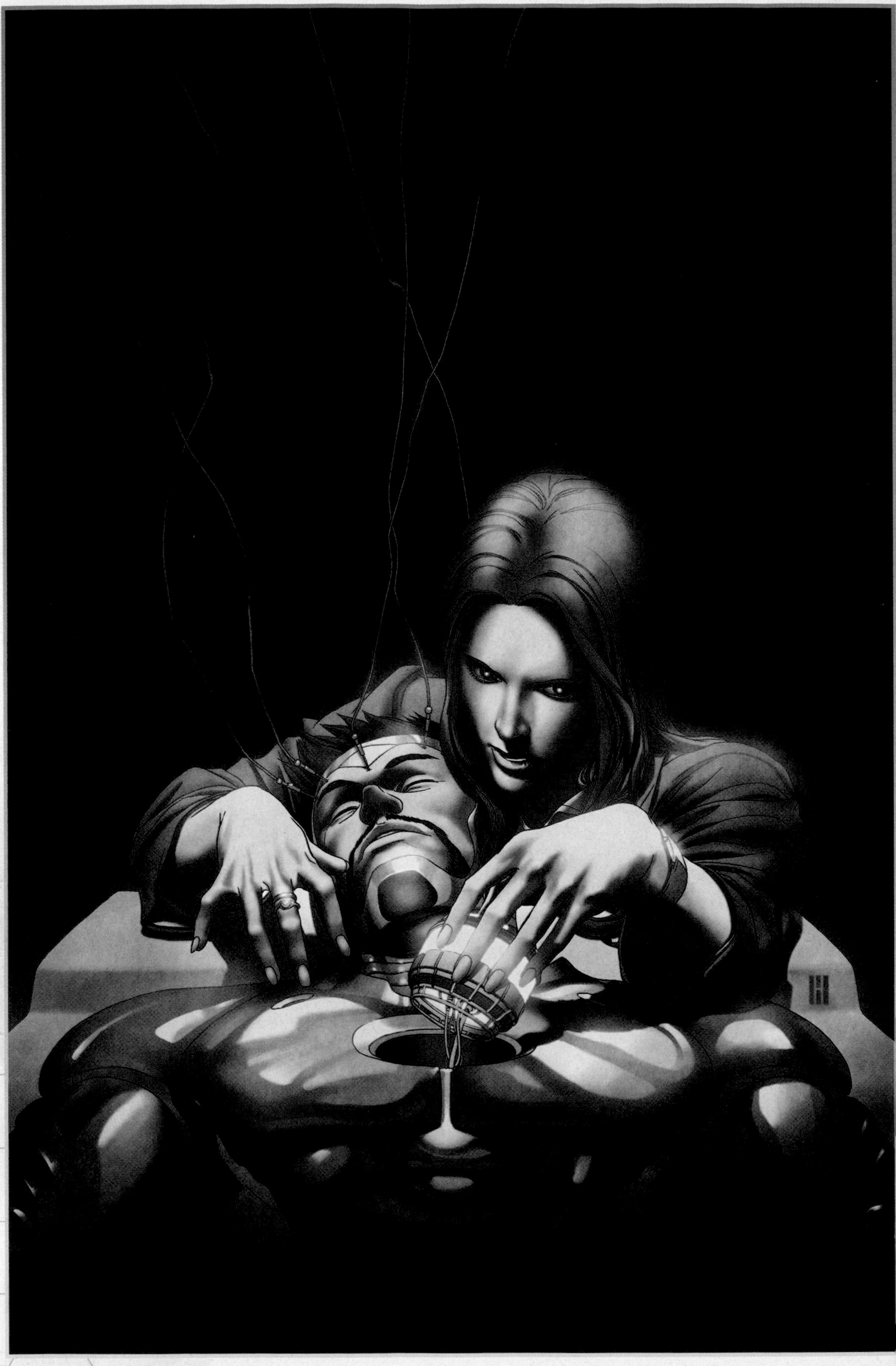

# 7: STARK CONTRAST

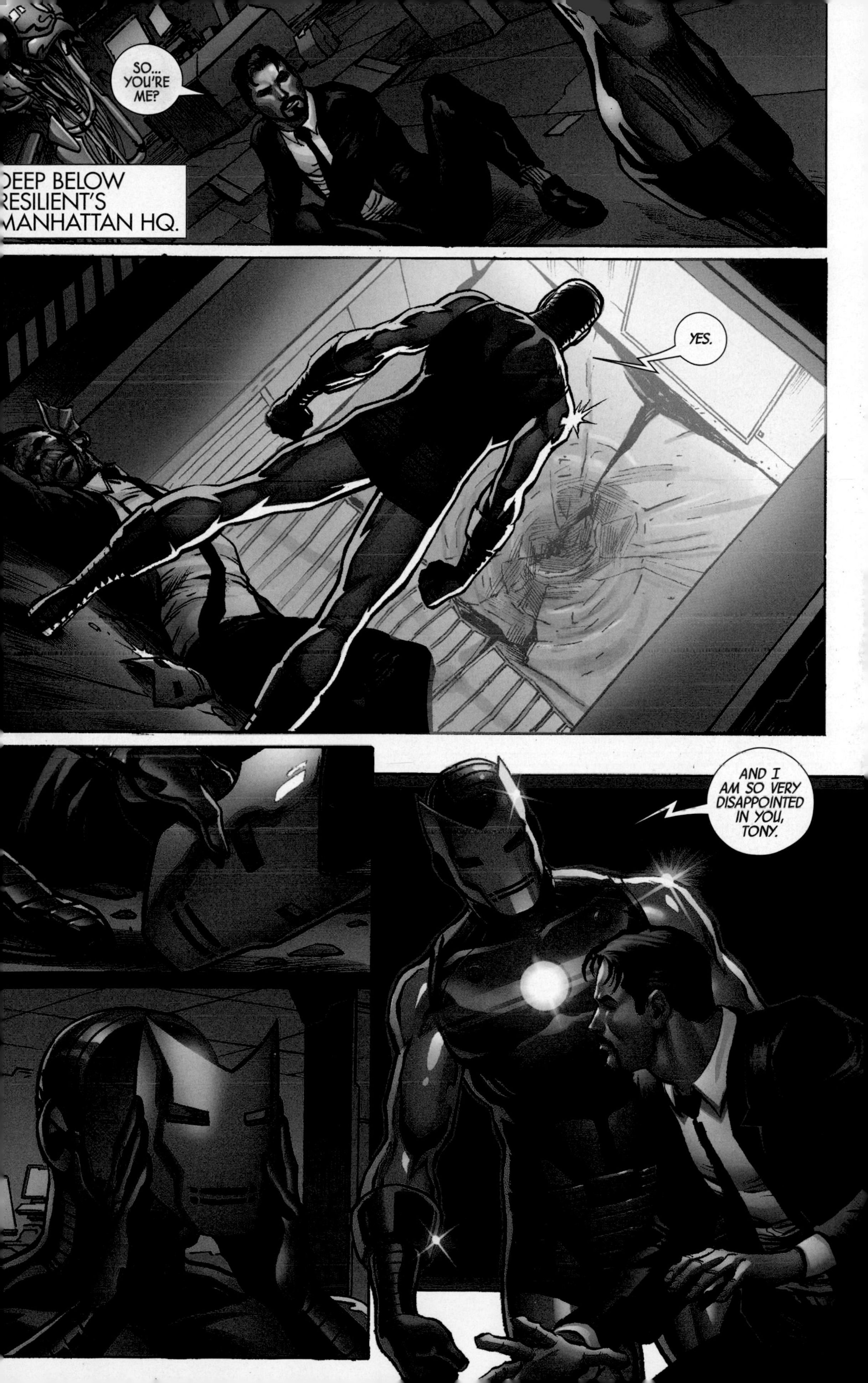
SO... YOU'RE ME?
DEEP BELOW RESILIENT'S MANHATTAN HQ.
YES.
AND I AM SO VERY DISAPPOINTED IN YOU, TONY.

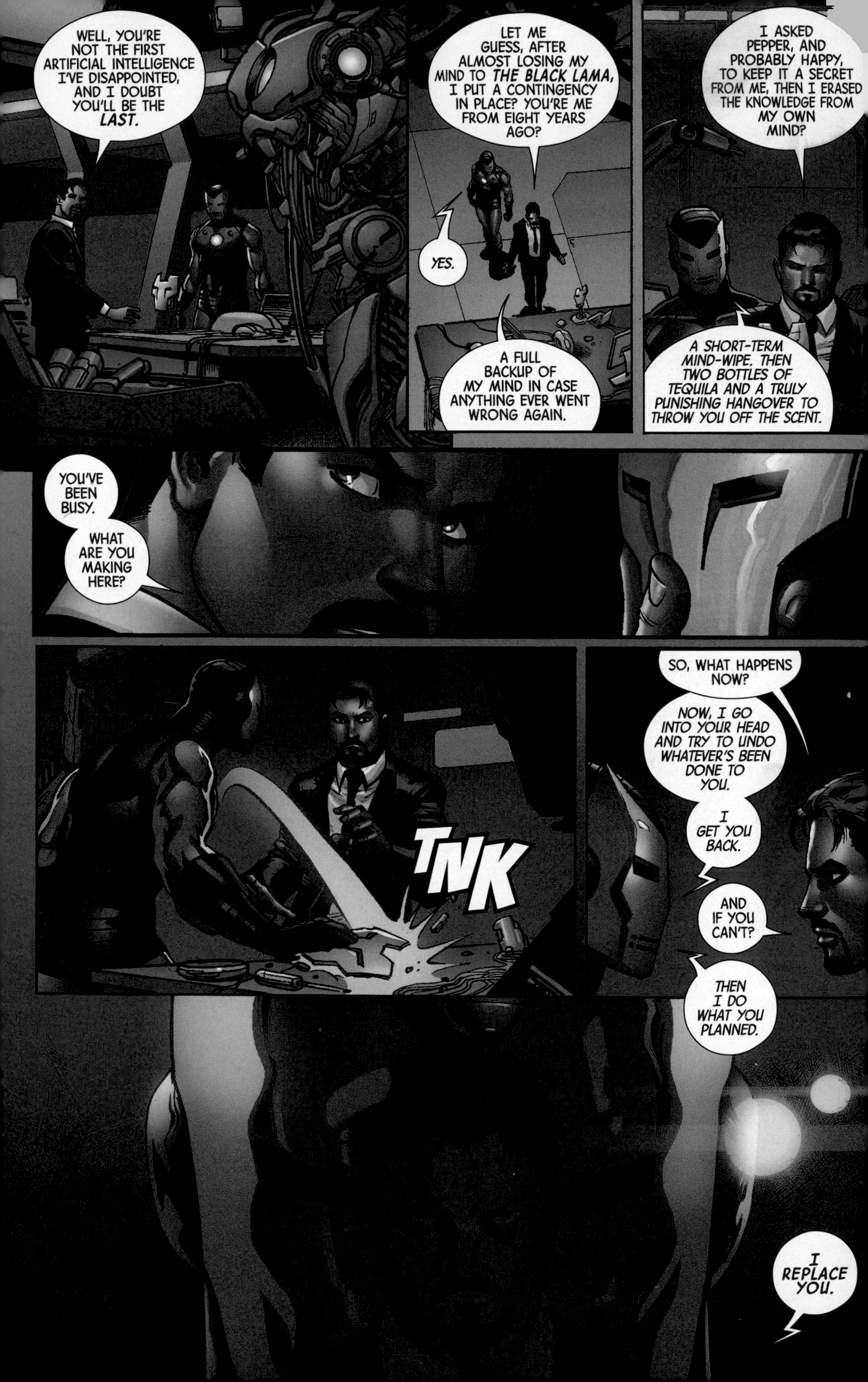
WELL, YOU'RE NOT THE FIRST ARTIFICIAL INTELLIGENCE I'VE DISAPPOINTED, AND I DOUBT YOU'LL BE THE *LAST.*
LET ME GUESS, AFTER ALMOST LOSING MY MIND TO *THE BLACK LAMA,* I PUT A CONTINGENCY IN PLACE? YOU'RE ME FROM EIGHT YEARS AGO?
YES.
A FULL BACKUP OF MY MIND IN CASE ANYTHING EVER WENT WRONG AGAIN.
I ASKED PEPPER, AND PROBABLY HAPPY, TO KEEP IT A SECRET FROM ME, THEN I ERASED THE KNOWLEDGE FROM MY OWN MIND?
A SHORT-TERM MIND-WIPE. THEN TWO BOTTLES OF TEQUILA AND A TRULY PUNISHING HANGOVER TO THROW YOU OFF THE SCENT.
YOU'VE BEEN BUSY.
WHAT ARE YOU MAKING HERE?
TNK
SO, WHAT HAPPENS NOW?
NOW, I GO INTO YOUR HEAD AND TRY TO UNDO WHATEVER'S BEEN DONE TO YOU.
I GET YOU BACK.
AND IF YOU CAN'T?
THEN I DO WHAT YOU PLANNED.
I REPLACE YOU.

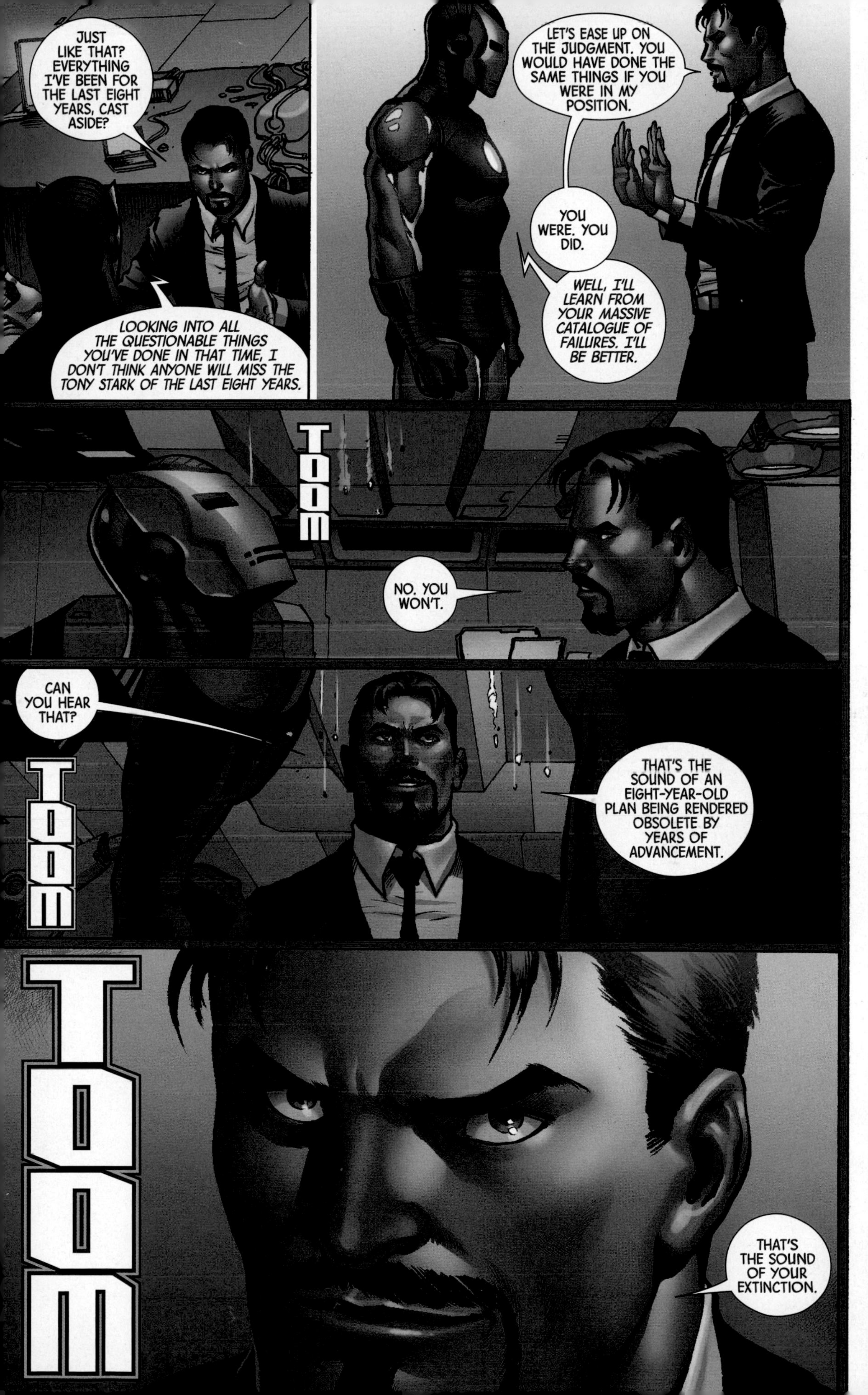
JUST LIKE THAT? EVERYTHING I'VE BEEN FOR THE LAST EIGHT YEARS, CAST ASIDE?
LOOKING INTO ALL THE QUESTIONABLE THINGS YOU'VE DONE IN THAT TIME, I DON'T THINK ANYONE WILL MISS THE TONY STARK OF THE LAST EIGHT YEARS.
LET'S EASE UP ON THE JUDGMENT. YOU WOULD HAVE DONE THE SAME THINGS IF YOU WERE IN MY POSITION.
YOU WERE. YOU DID.
WELL, I'LL LEARN FROM YOUR MASSIVE CATALOGUE OF FAILURES. I'LL BE BETTER.
TOOM
NO. YOU WON'T.
CAN YOU HEAR THAT?
TOOM
THAT'S THE SOUND OF AN EIGHT-YEAR-OLD PLAN BEING RENDERED OBSOLETE BY YEARS OF ADVANCEMENT.
TOOM
THAT'S THE SOUND OF YOUR EXTINCTION.

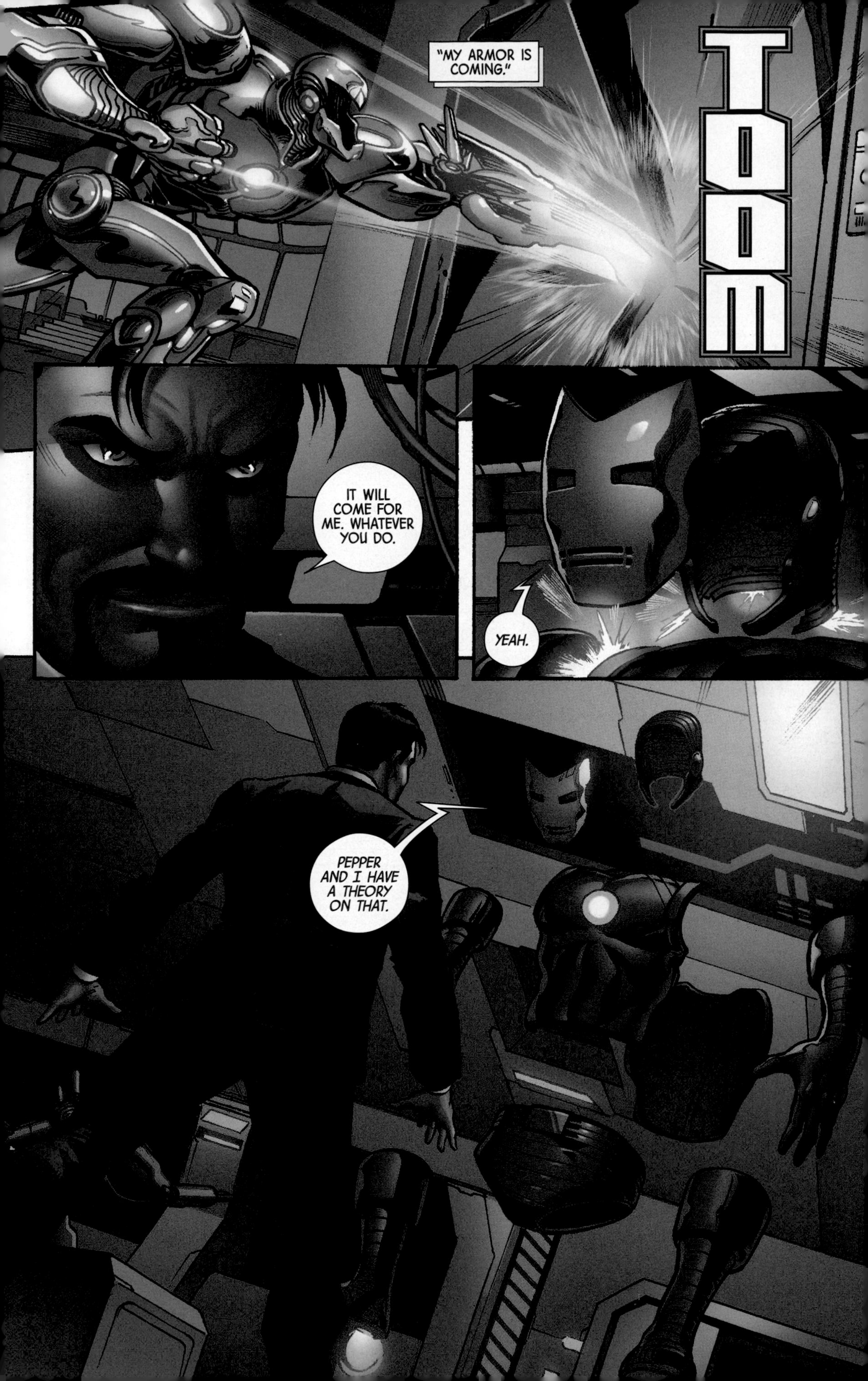
"MY ARMOR IS COMING."
TOOM
IT WILL COME FOR ME. WHATEVER YOU DO.
YEAH.
PEPPER AND I HAVE A THEORY ON THAT.

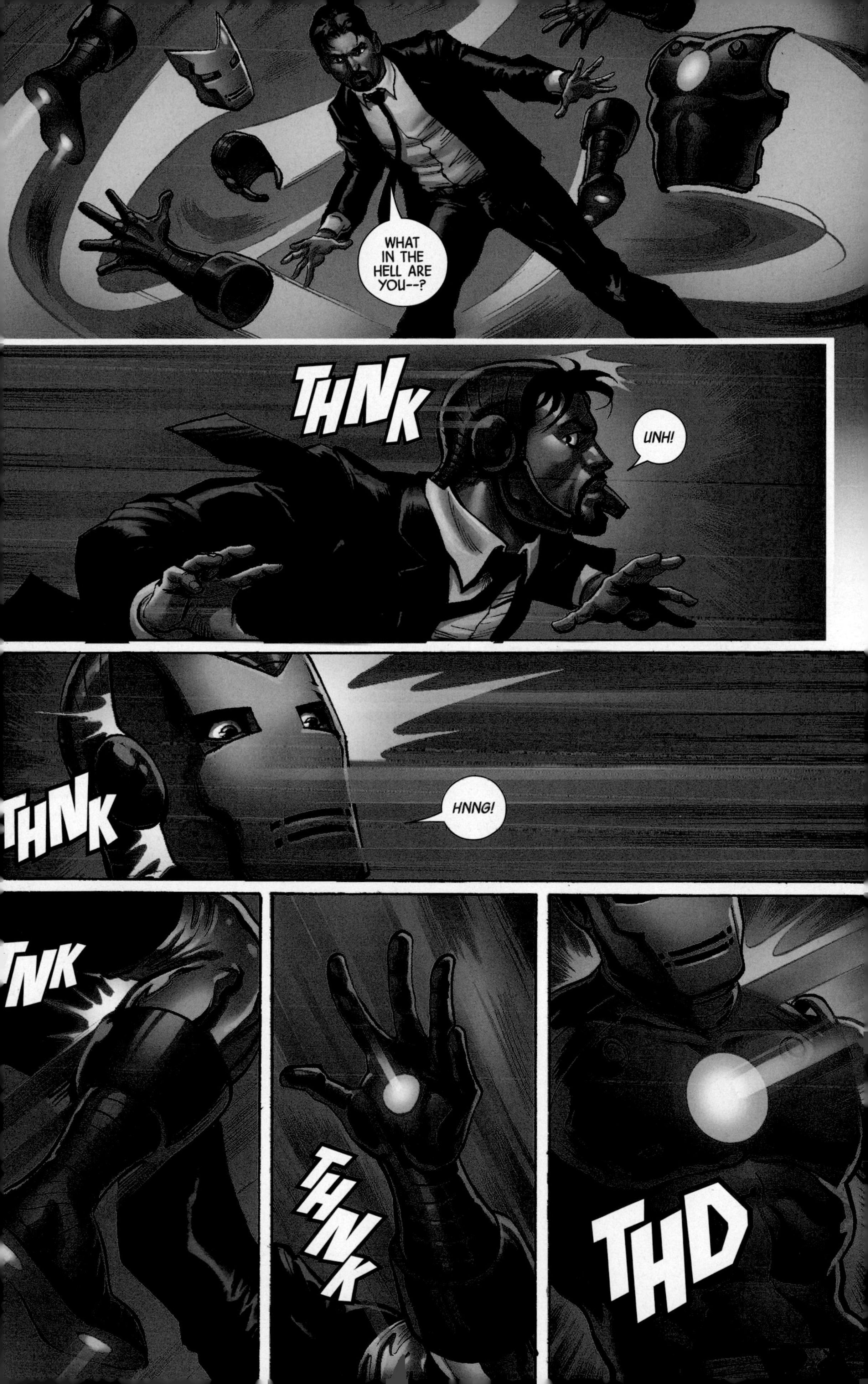
WHAT IN THE HELL ARE YOU--?
THNK
UNH!
THNK
HNNG!
TNK
THNK
THD

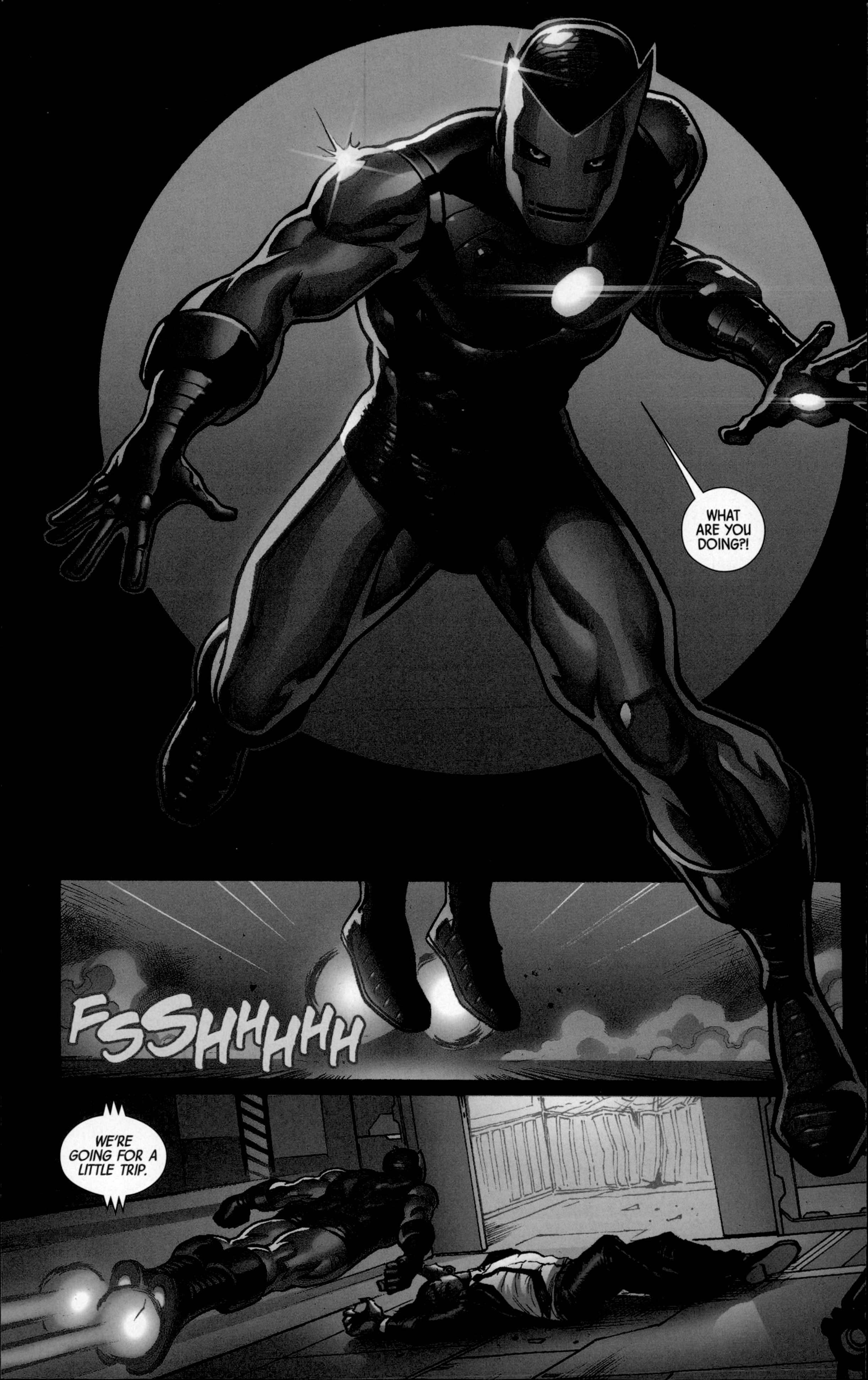
WHAT ARE YOU DOING?!
FSSHHHHH
WE'RE GOING FOR A LITTLE TRIP.

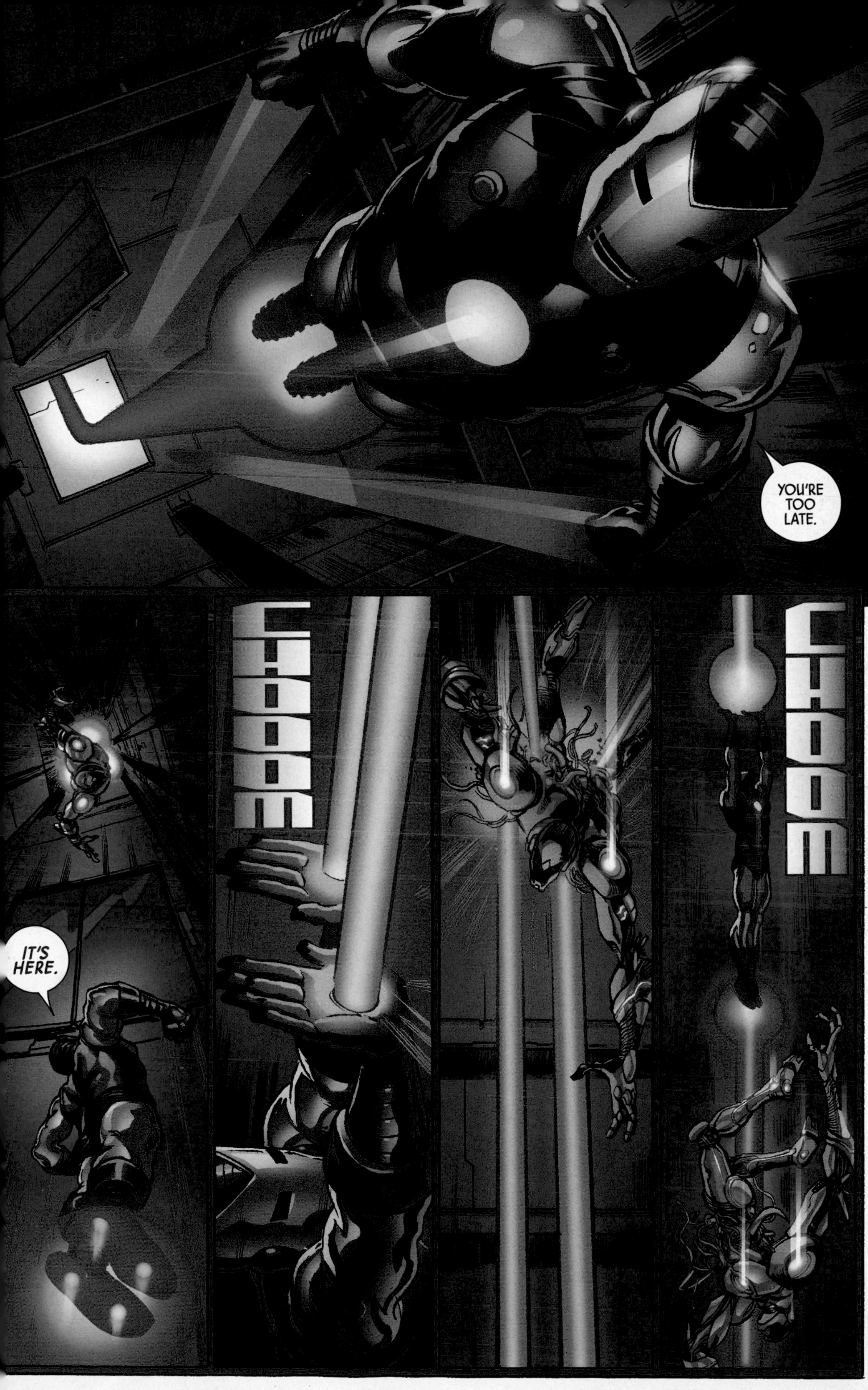
YOU'RE TOO LATE.
IT'S HERE.
CHOOM
CHOOM

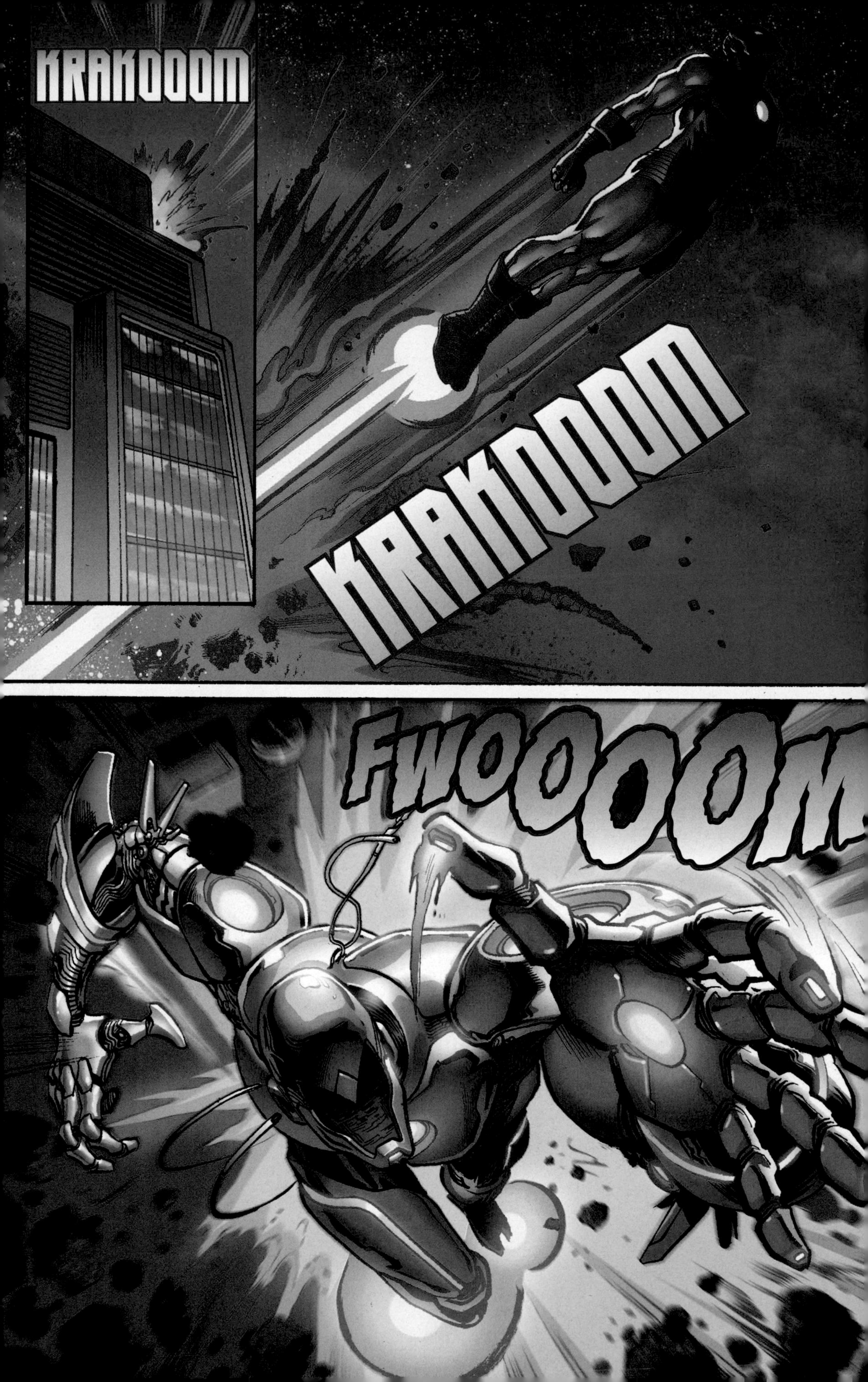
KRAKOOOM
KRAKOOOM
FWOOOOOM

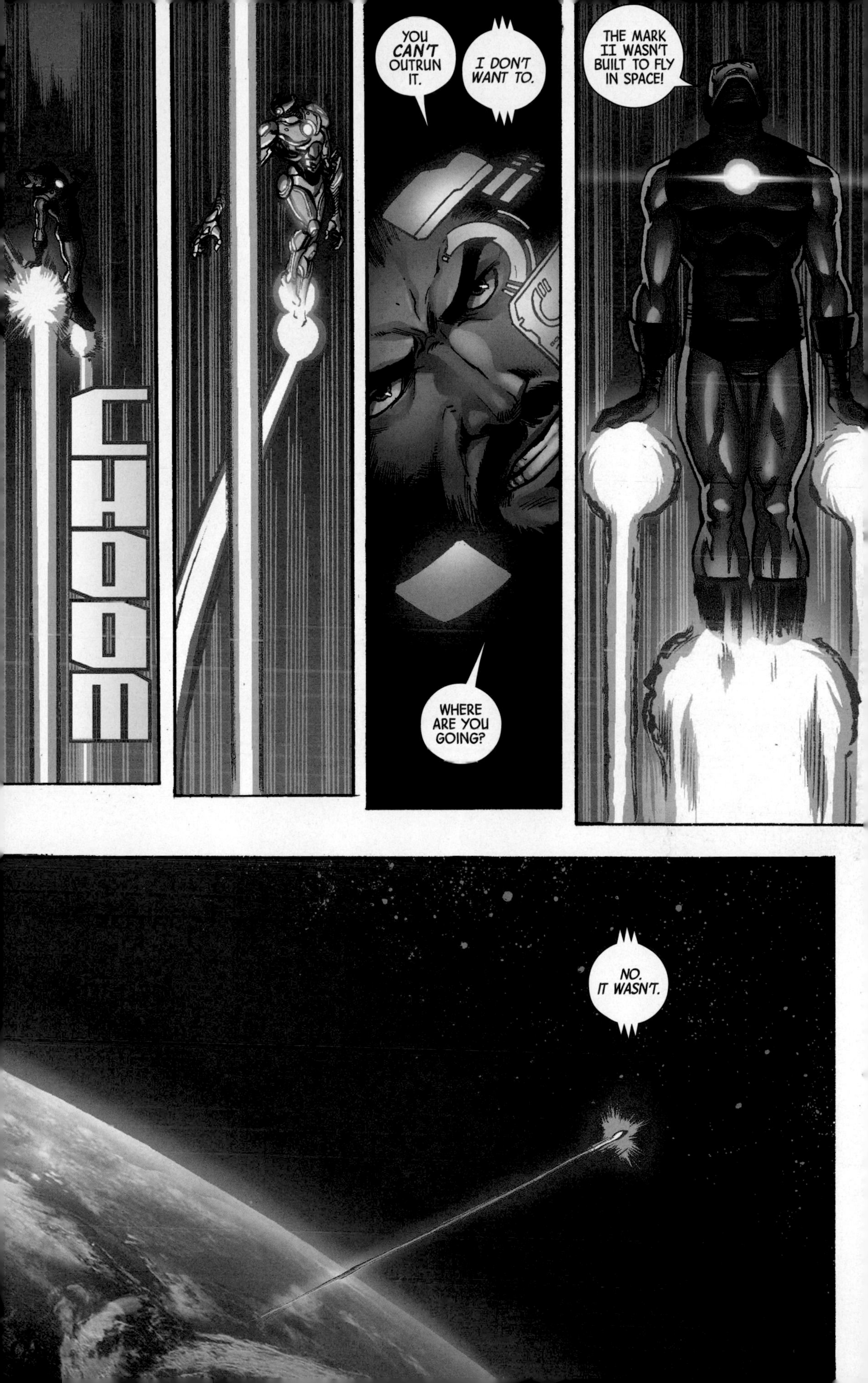
CHOOM
YOU CAN'T OUTRUN IT.
I DON'T WANT TO.
WHERE ARE YOU GOING?
THE MARK II WASN'T BUILT TO FLY IN SPACE!
NO. IT WASN'T.

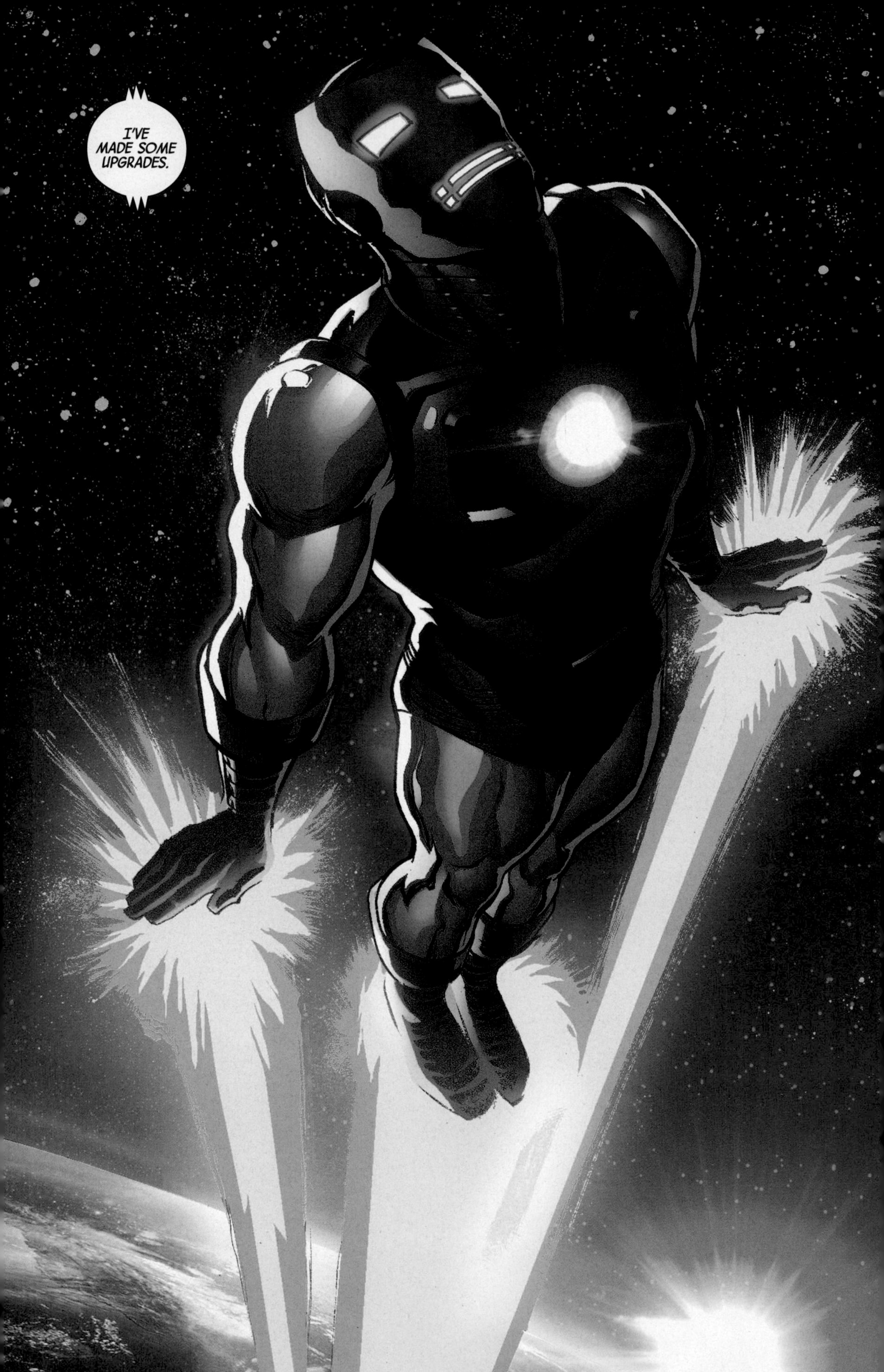
I'VE MADE SOME UPGRADES.

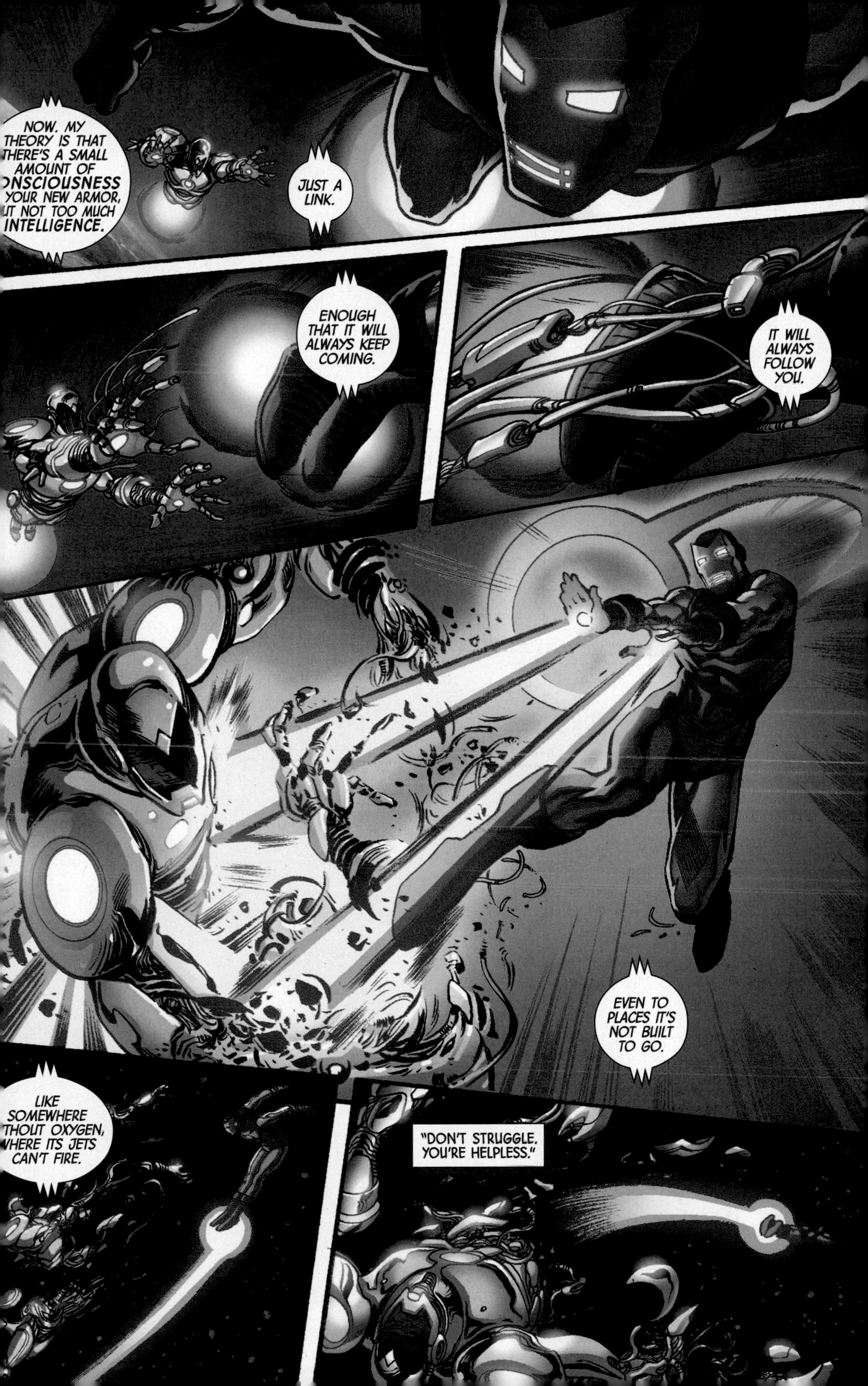
NOW. MY THEORY IS THAT THERE'S A SMALL AMOUNT OF ONSCIOUSNESS YOUR NEW ARMOR, UT NOT TOO MUCH INTELLIGENCE.
JUST A LINK.
ENOUGH THAT IT WILL ALWAYS KEEP COMING.
IT WILL ALWAYS FOLLOW YOU.
EVEN TO PLACES IT'S NOT BUILT TO GO.
LIKE SOMEWHERE THOUT OXYGEN, HERE ITS JETS CAN'T FIRE.
"DON'T STRUGGLE. YOU'RE HELPLESS."

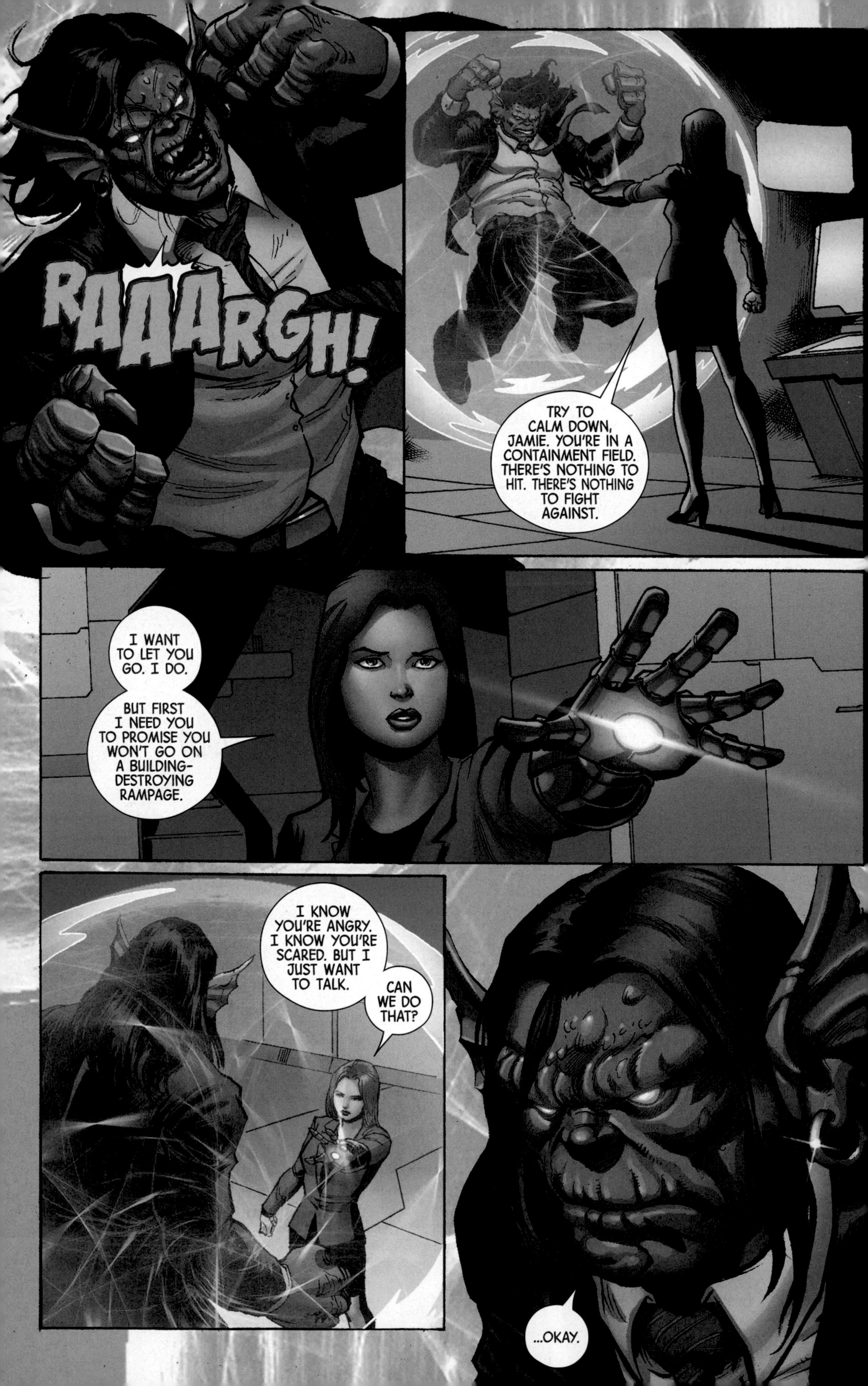
RAAAARGH!
TRY TO CALM DOWN, JAMIE. YOU'RE IN A CONTAINMENT FIELD. THERE'S NOTHING TO HIT. THERE'S NOTHING TO FIGHT AGAINST.
I WANT TO LET YOU GO. I DO.
BUT FIRST I NEED YOU TO PROMISE YOU WON'T GO ON A BUILDING-DESTROYING RAMPAGE.
I KNOW YOU'RE ANGRY. I KNOW YOU'RE SCARED. BUT I JUST WANT TO TALK.
CAN WE DO THAT?
...OKAY.

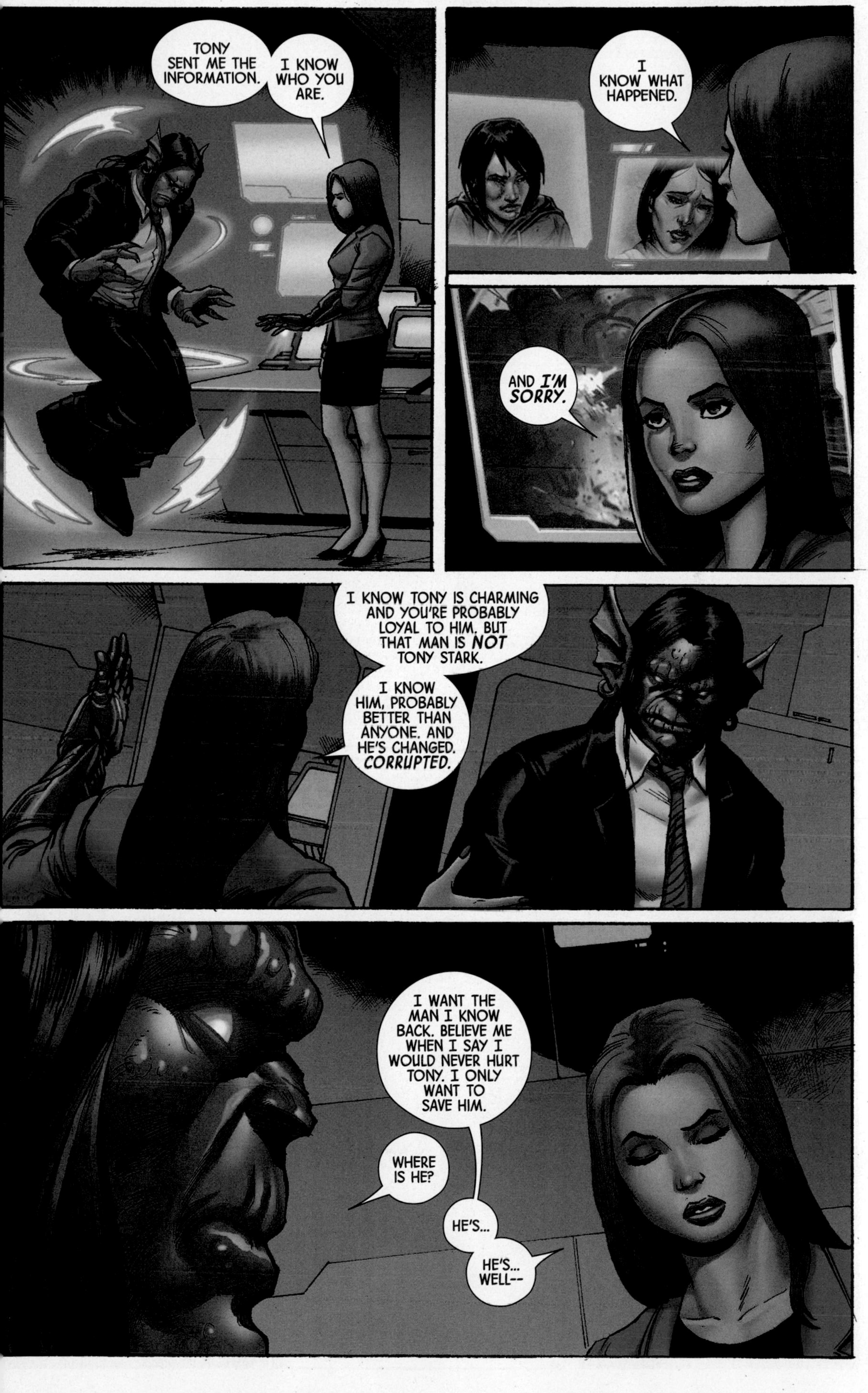
TONY SENT ME THE INFORMATION.
I KNOW WHO YOU ARE.
I KNOW WHAT HAPPENED.
AND I'M SORRY.
I KNOW TONY IS CHARMING AND YOU'RE PROBABLY LOYAL TO HIM. BUT THAT MAN IS NOT TONY STARK.
I KNOW HIM, PROBABLY BETTER THAN ANYONE. AND HE'S CHANGED. CORRUPTED.
I WANT THE MAN I KNOW BACK. BELIEVE ME WHEN I SAY I WOULD NEVER HURT TONY. I ONLY WANT TO SAVE HIM.
WHERE IS HE?
HE'S...
HE'S... WELL--

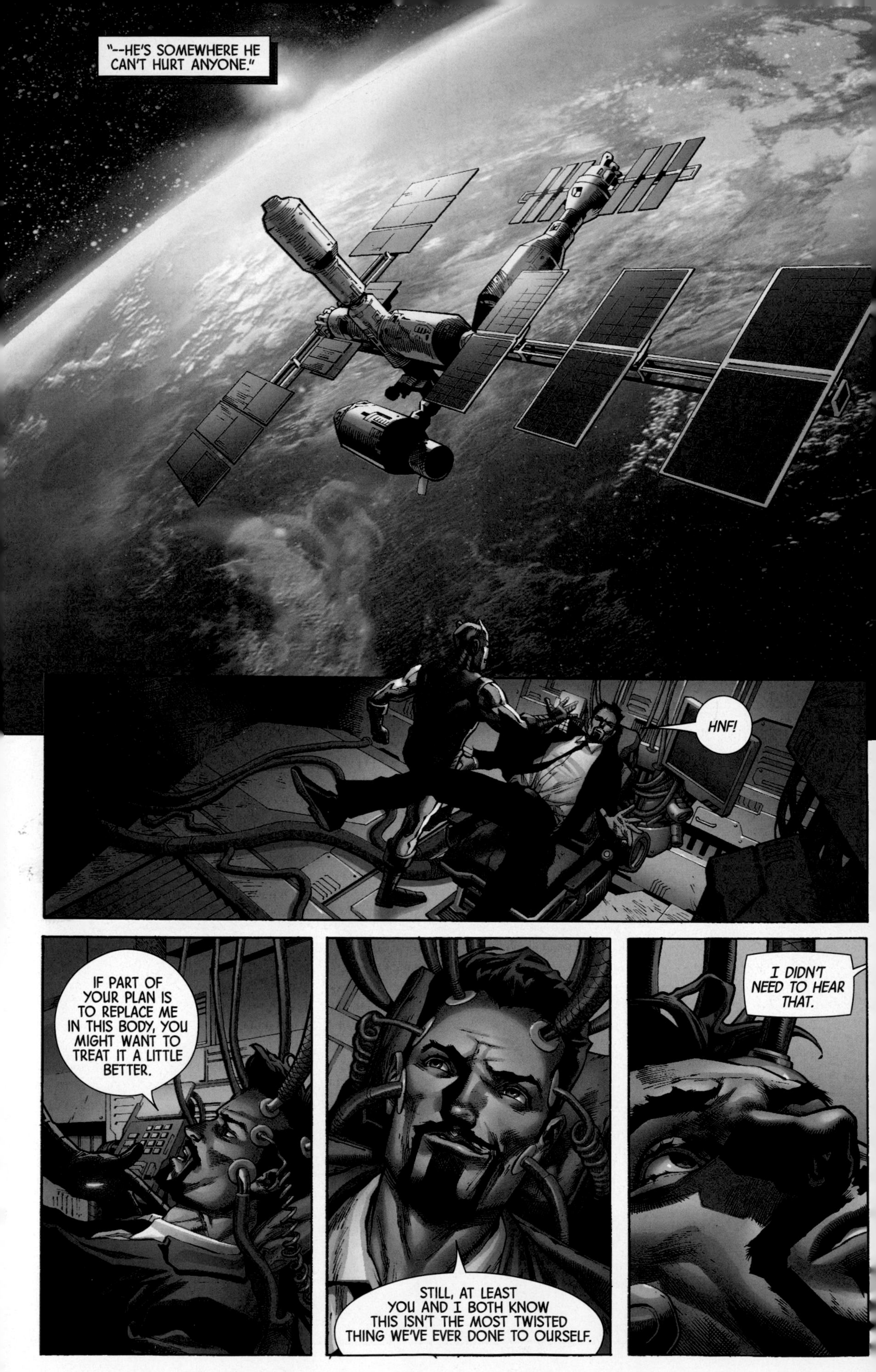
"--HE'S SOMEWHERE HE CAN'T HURT ANYONE."
HNF!
IF PART OF YOUR PLAN IS TO REPLACE ME IN THIS BODY, YOU MIGHT WANT TO TREAT IT A LITTLE BETTER.
STILL, AT LEAST YOU AND I BOTH KNOW THIS ISN'T THE MOST TWISTED THING WE'VE EVER DONE TO OURSELF.
I DIDN'T NEED TO HEAR THAT.

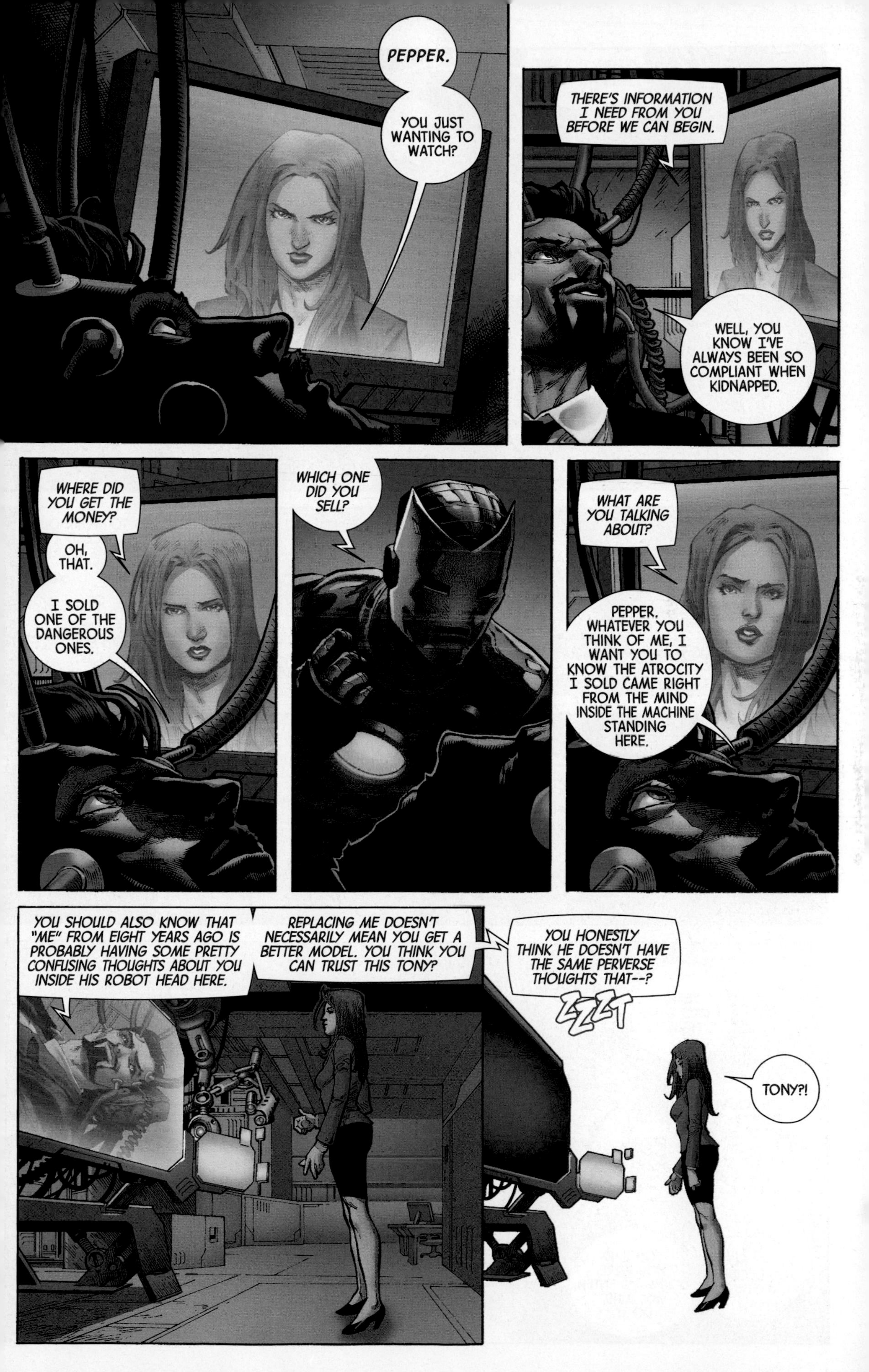
PEPPER.
YOU JUST WANTING TO WATCH?
THERE'S INFORMATION I NEED FROM YOU BEFORE WE CAN BEGIN.
WELL, YOU KNOW I'VE ALWAYS BEEN SO COMPLIANT WHEN KIDNAPPED.
WHERE DID YOU GET THE MONEY?
OH, THAT.
I SOLD ONE OF THE DANGEROUS ONES.
WHICH ONE DID YOU SELL?
WHAT ARE YOU TALKING ABOUT?
PEPPER. WHATEVER YOU THINK OF ME, I WANT YOU TO KNOW THE ATROCITY I SOLD CAME RIGHT FROM THE MIND INSIDE THE MACHINE STANDING HERE.
YOU SHOULD ALSO KNOW THAT "ME" FROM EIGHT YEARS AGO IS PROBABLY HAVING SOME PRETTY CONFUSING THOUGHTS ABOUT YOU INSIDE HIS ROBOT HEAD HERE.
REPLACING ME DOESN'T NECESSARILY MEAN YOU GET A BETTER MODEL. YOU THINK YOU CAN TRUST THIS TONY?
YOU HONESTLY THINK HE DOESN'T HAVE THE SAME PERVERSE THOUGHTS THAT--?
ZZZT
TONY?!

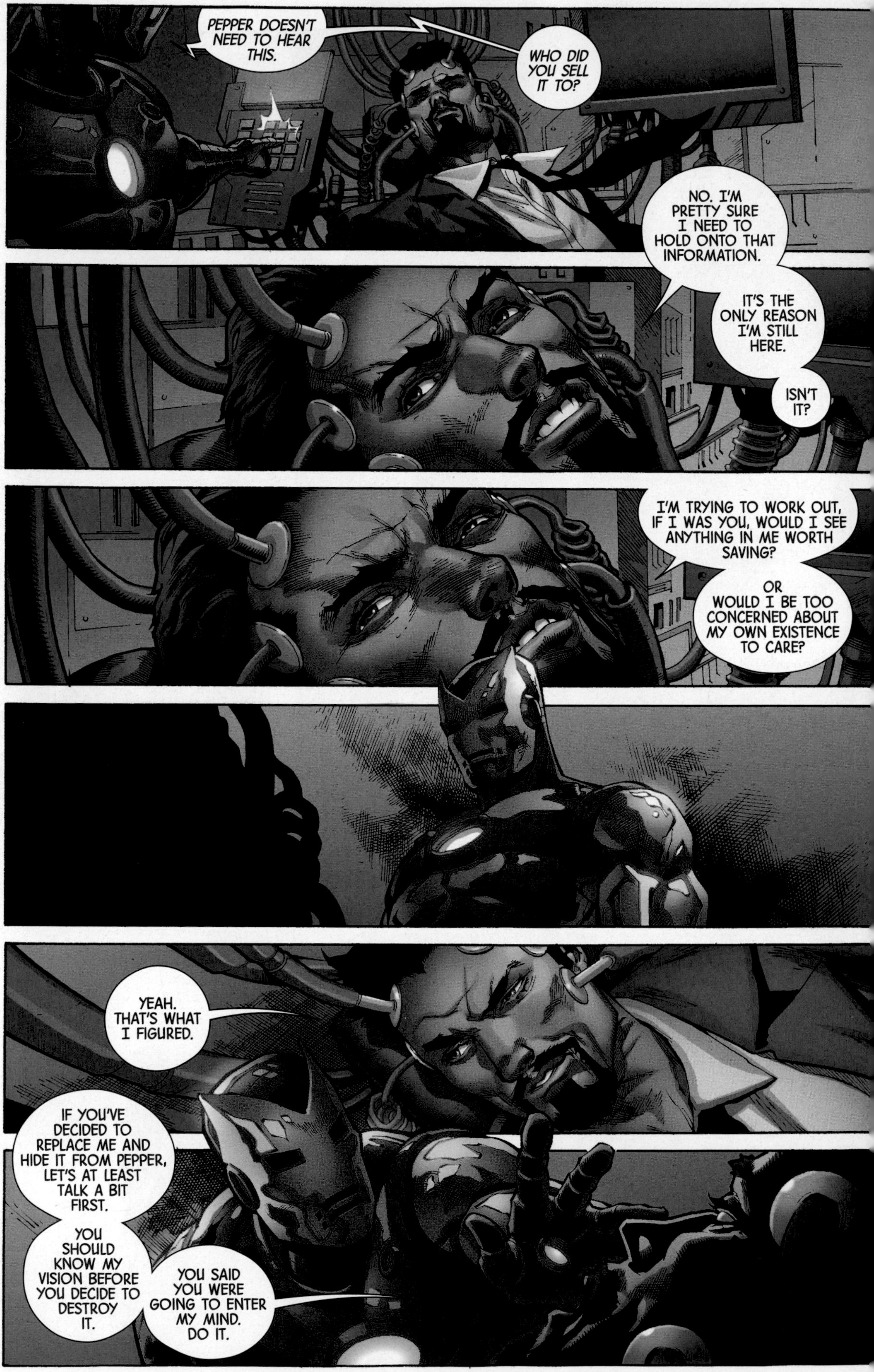
PEPPER DOESN'T NEED TO HEAR THIS.
WHO DID YOU SELL IT TO?
NO. I'M PRETTY SURE I NEED TO HOLD ONTO THAT INFORMATION.
IT'S THE ONLY REASON I'M STILL HERE.
ISN'T IT?
I'M TRYING TO WORK OUT, IF I WAS YOU, WOULD I SEE ANYTHING IN ME WORTH SAVING?
OR WOULD I BE TOO CONCERNED ABOUT MY OWN EXISTENCE TO CARE?
YEAH. THAT'S WHAT I FIGURED.
IF YOU'VE DECIDED TO REPLACE ME AND HIDE IT FROM PEPPER, LET'S AT LEAST TALK A BIT FIRST.
YOU SHOULD KNOW MY VISION BEFORE YOU DECIDE TO DESTROY IT.
YOU SAID YOU WERE GOING TO ENTER MY MIND. DO IT.

COME SEE THINGS FROM MY PERSPECTIVE.
THERE WE GO.
BE READY.
"I'M EXPECTING THIS TO GET A BIT WEIRD."

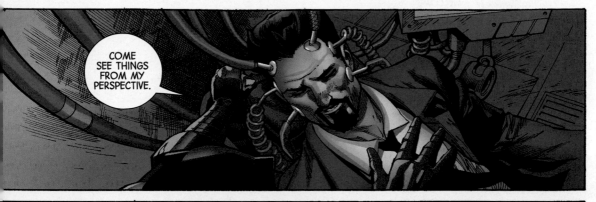

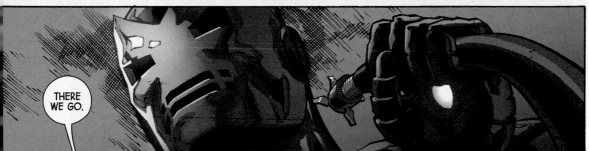

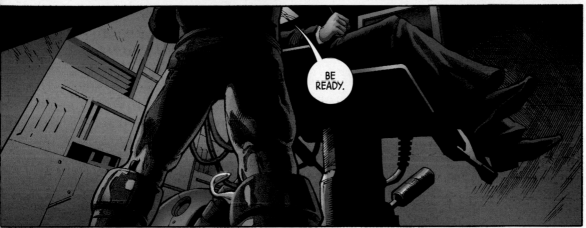

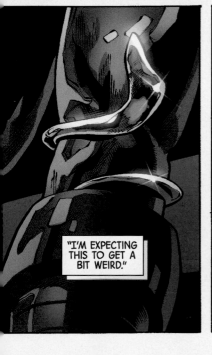

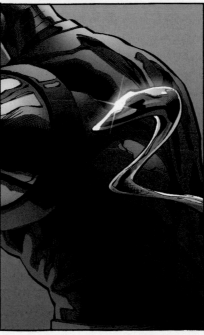

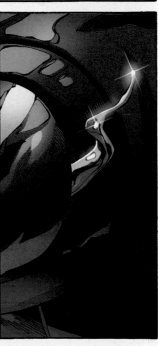

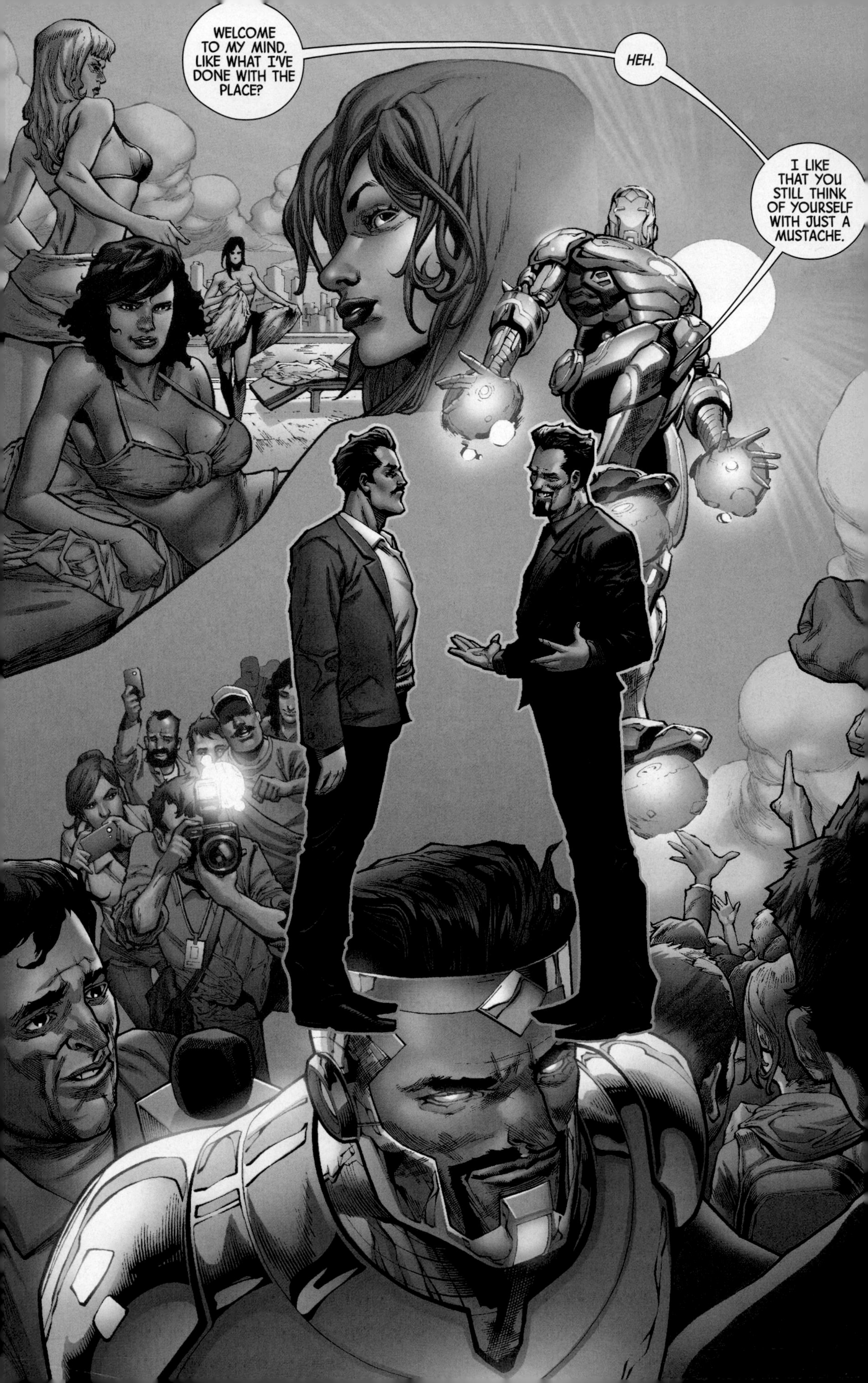
WELCOME TO MY MIND. LIKE WHAT I'VE DONE WITH THE PLACE?
HEH.
I LIKE THAT YOU STILL THINK OF YOURSELF WITH JUST A MUSTACHE.

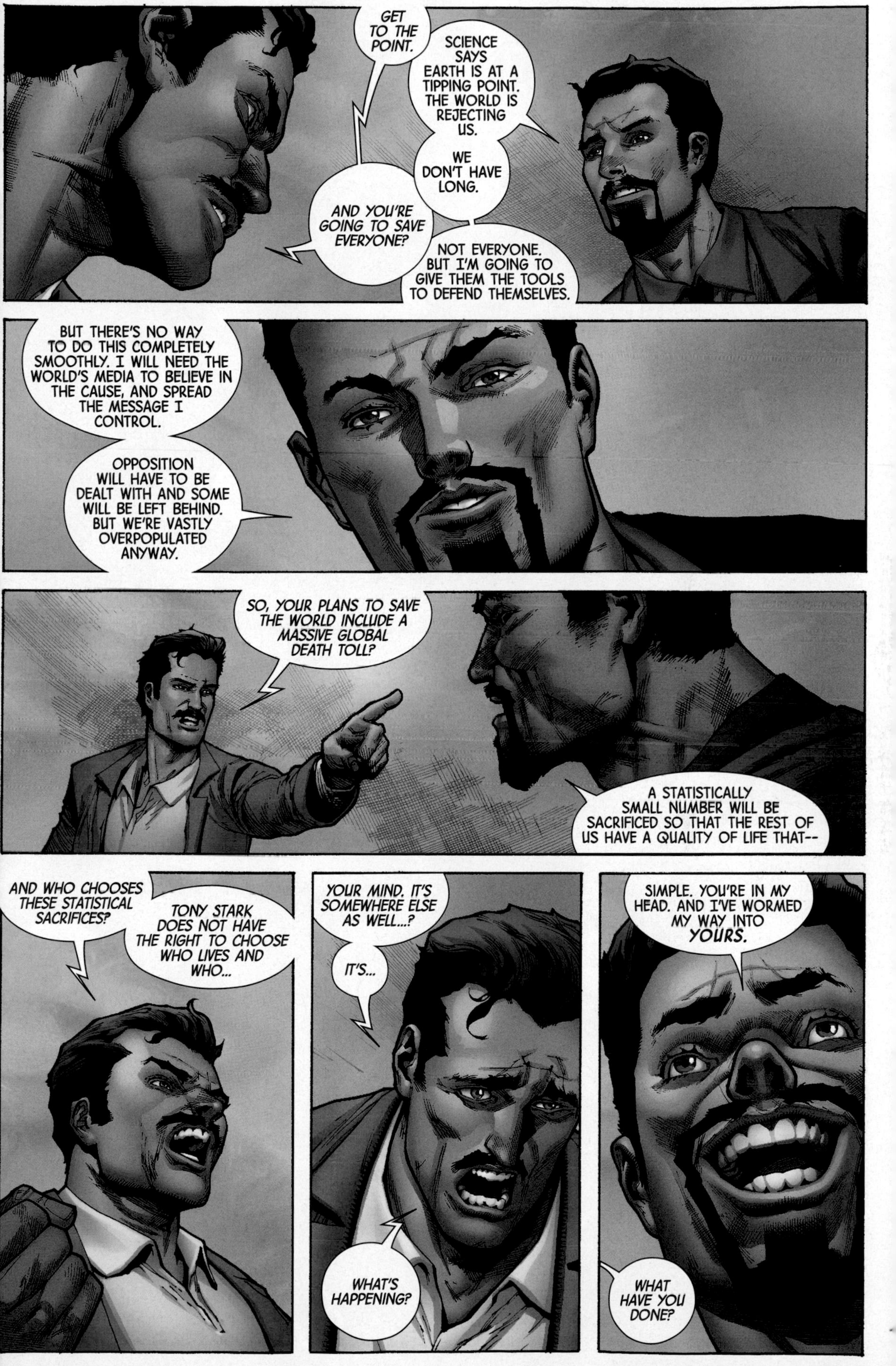
GET TO THE POINT.
SCIENCE SAYS EARTH IS AT A TIPPING POINT. THE WORLD IS REJECTING US.
WE DON'T HAVE LONG.
AND YOU'RE GOING TO SAVE EVERYONE?
NOT EVERYONE. BUT I'M GOING TO GIVE THEM THE TOOLS TO DEFEND THEMSELVES.
BUT THERE'S NO WAY TO DO THIS COMPLETELY SMOOTHLY. I WILL NEED THE WORLD'S MEDIA TO BELIEVE IN THE CAUSE, AND SPREAD THE MESSAGE I CONTROL.
OPPOSITION WILL HAVE TO BE DEALT WITH AND SOME WILL BE LEFT BEHIND. BUT WE'RE VASTLY OVERPOPULATED ANYWAY.
SO, YOUR PLANS TO SAVE THE WORLD INCLUDE A MASSIVE GLOBAL DEATH TOLL?
A STATISTICALLY SMALL NUMBER WILL BE SACRIFICED SO THAT THE REST OF US HAVE A QUALITY OF LIFE THAT--
AND WHO CHOOSES THESE STATISTICAL SACRIFICES?
TONY STARK DOES NOT HAVE THE RIGHT TO CHOOSE WHO LIVES AND WHO...
YOUR MIND. IT'S SOMEWHERE ELSE AS WELL...?
IT'S...
WHAT'S HAPPENING?
SIMPLE. YOU'RE IN MY HEAD. AND I'VE WORMED MY WAY INTO YOURS.
WHAT HAVE YOU DONE?

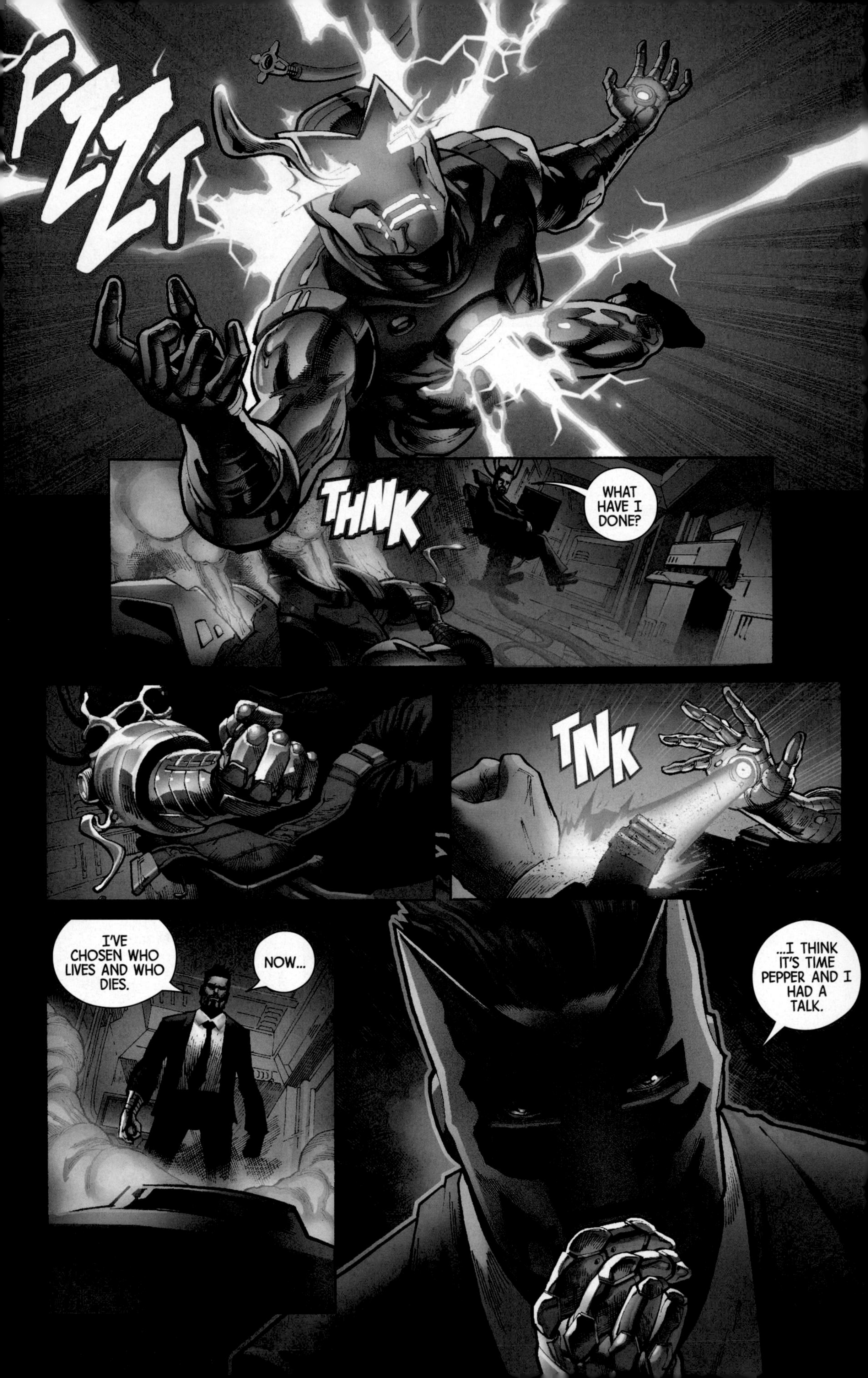
FZZT
THNK
WHAT HAVE I DONE?
TNK
I'VE CHOSEN WHO LIVES AND WHO DIES.
NOW...
...I THINK IT'S TIME PEPPER AND I HAD A TALK.

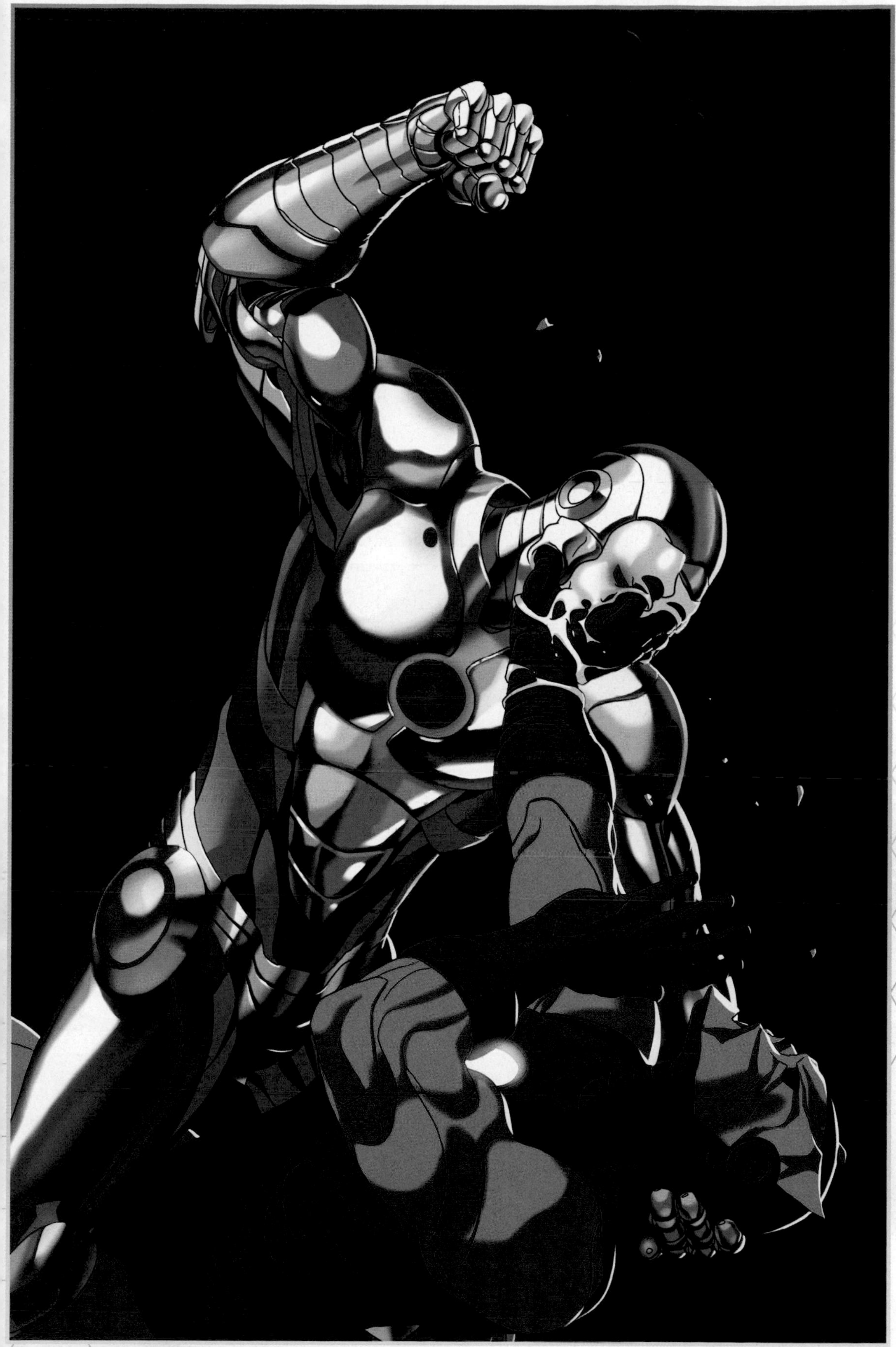

# 8: BIO-MARK-ONE

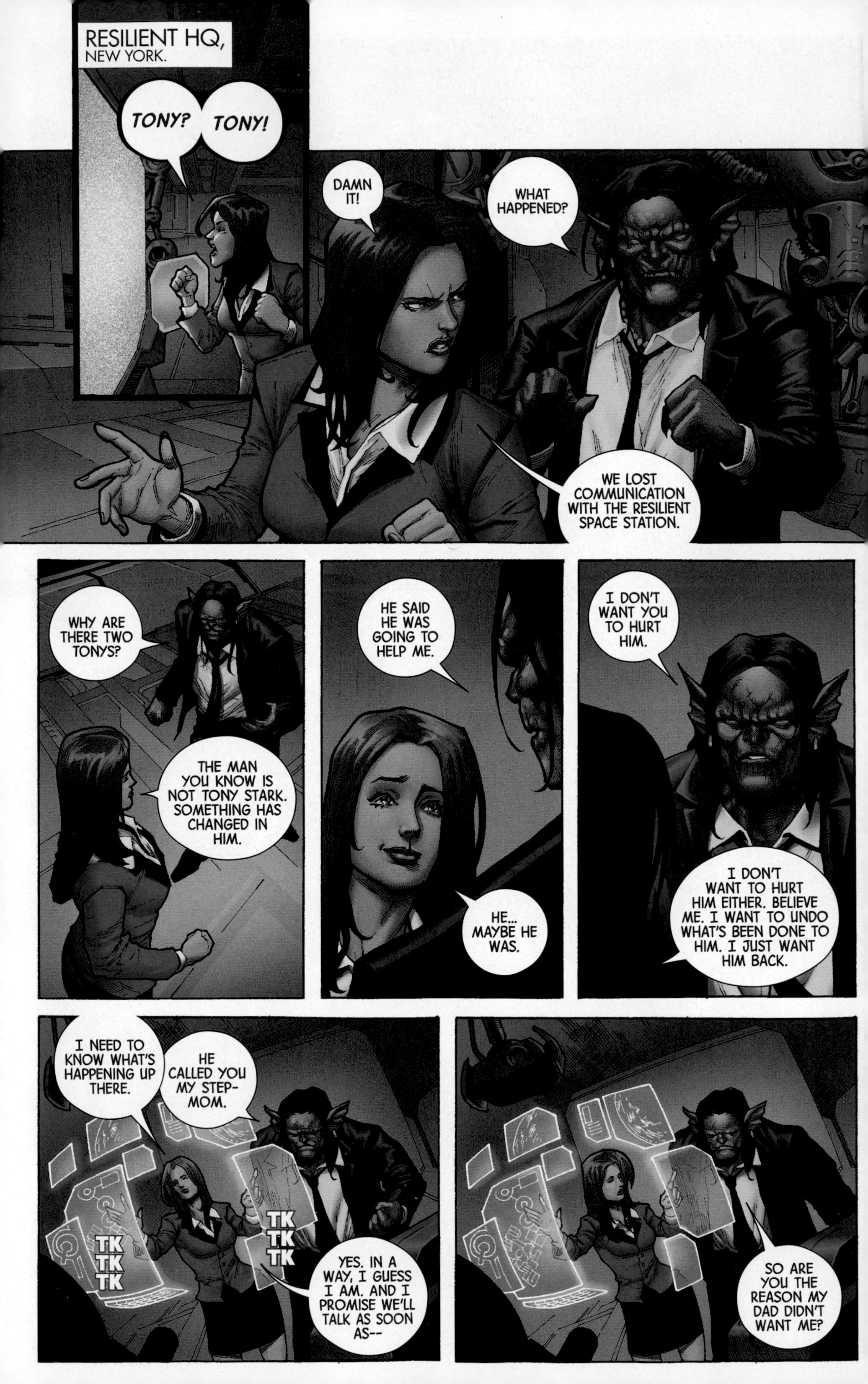
RESILIENT HQ, NEW YORK.
TONY?
TONY!
DAMN IT!
WHAT HAPPENED?
WE LOST COMMUNICATION WITH THE RESILIENT SPACE STATION.
WHY ARE THERE TWO TONYS?
THE MAN YOU KNOW IS NOT TONY STARK. SOMETHING HAS CHANGED IN HIM.
HE SAID HE WAS GOING TO HELP ME.
HE... MAYBE HE WAS.
I DON'T WANT YOU TO HURT HIM.
I DON'T WANT TO HURT HIM EITHER. BELIEVE ME. I WANT TO UNDO WHAT'S BEEN DONE TO HIM. I JUST WANT HIM BACK.
I NEED TO KNOW WHAT'S HAPPENING UP THERE.
HE CALLED YOU MY STEP-MOM.
TK TK TK
TK TK TK
YES. IN A WAY, I GUESS I AM. AND I PROMISE WE'LL TALK AS SOON AS--
SO ARE YOU THE REASON MY DAD DIDN'T WANT ME?

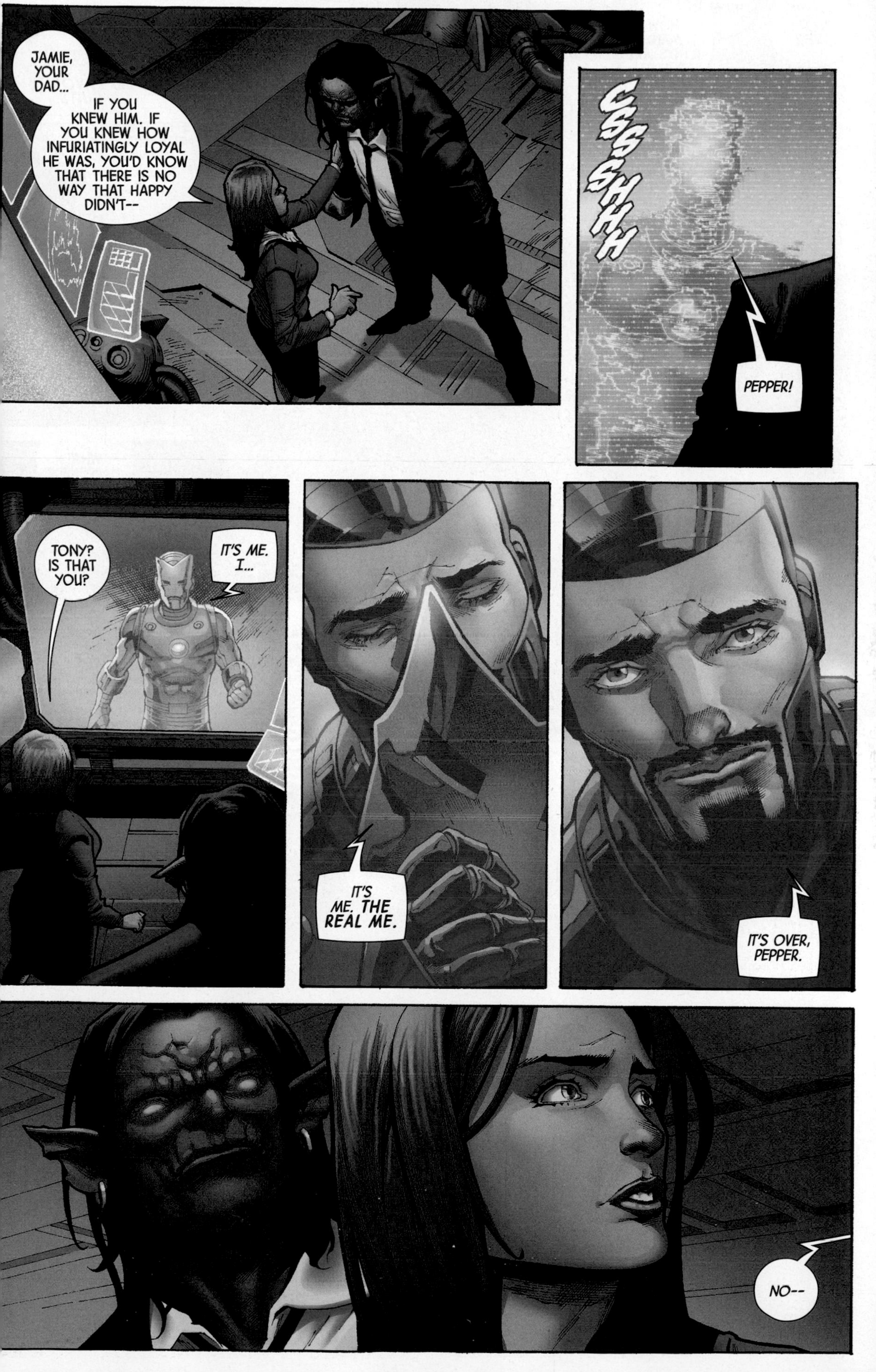
JAMIE, YOUR DAD...
IF YOU KNEW HIM. IF YOU KNEW HOW INFURIATINGLY LOYAL HE WAS, YOU'D KNOW THAT THERE IS NO WAY THAT HAPPY DIDN'T--
CSSSHHH
PEPPER!
TONY? IS THAT YOU?
IT'S ME. I...
IT'S ME. THE REAL ME.
IT'S OVER, PEPPER.
NO--

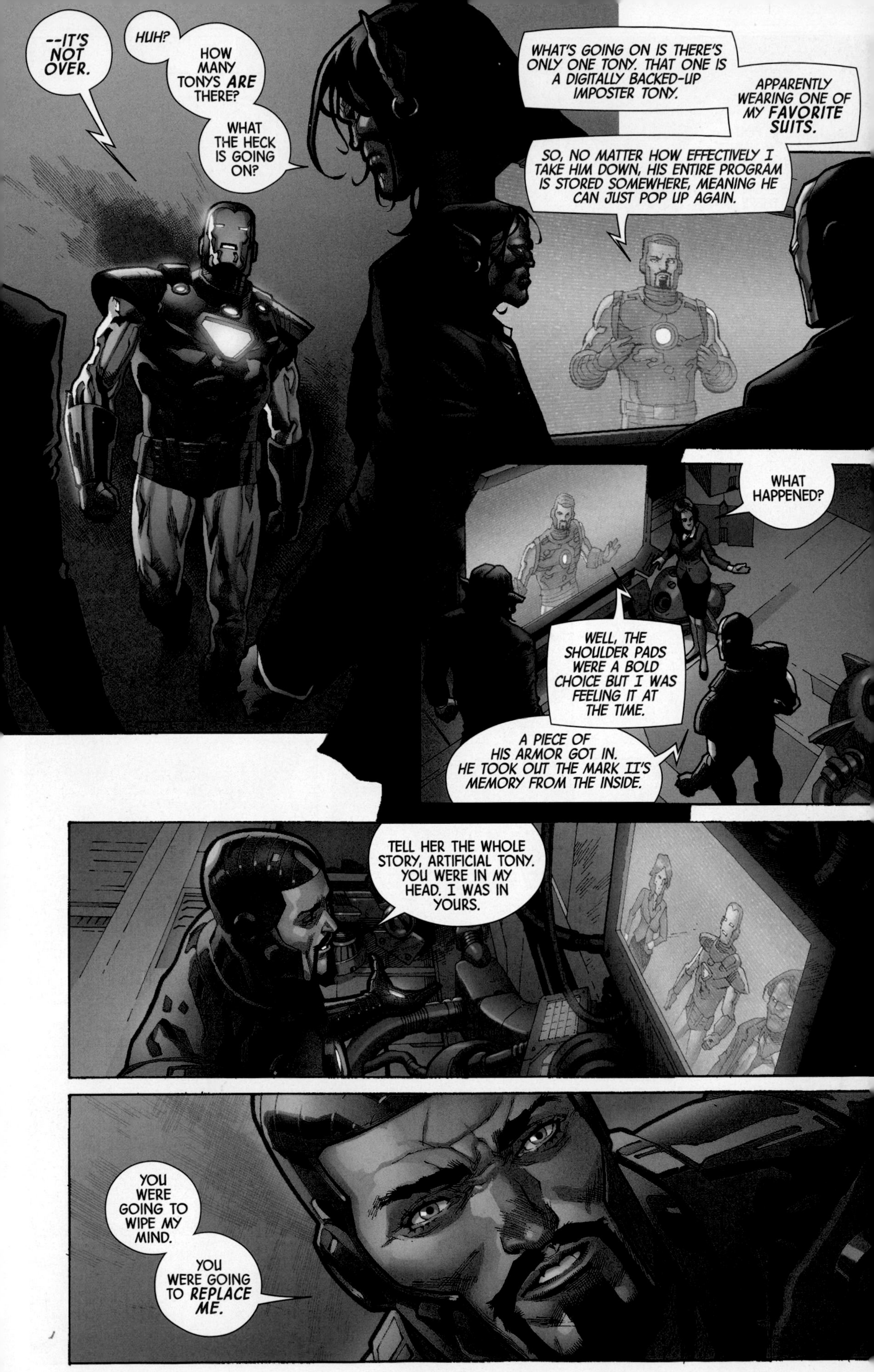
--IT'S NOT OVER.
HUH?
HOW MANY TONYS ARE THERE?
WHAT THE HECK IS GOING ON?
WHAT'S GOING ON IS THERE'S ONLY ONE TONY. THAT ONE IS A DIGITALLY BACKED-UP IMPOSTER TONY.
APPARENTLY WEARING ONE OF MY FAVORITE SUITS.
SO, NO MATTER HOW EFFECTIVELY I TAKE HIM DOWN, HIS ENTIRE PROGRAM IS STORED SOMEWHERE, MEANING HE CAN JUST POP UP AGAIN.
WHAT HAPPENED?
WELL, THE SHOULDER PADS WERE A BOLD CHOICE BUT I WAS FEELING IT AT THE TIME.
A PIECE OF HIS ARMOR GOT IN. HE TOOK OUT THE MARK II'S MEMORY FROM THE INSIDE.
TELL HER THE WHOLE STORY, ARTIFICIAL TONY. YOU WERE IN MY HEAD. I WAS IN YOURS.
YOU WERE GOING TO WIPE MY MIND.
YOU WERE GOING TO REPLACE ME.

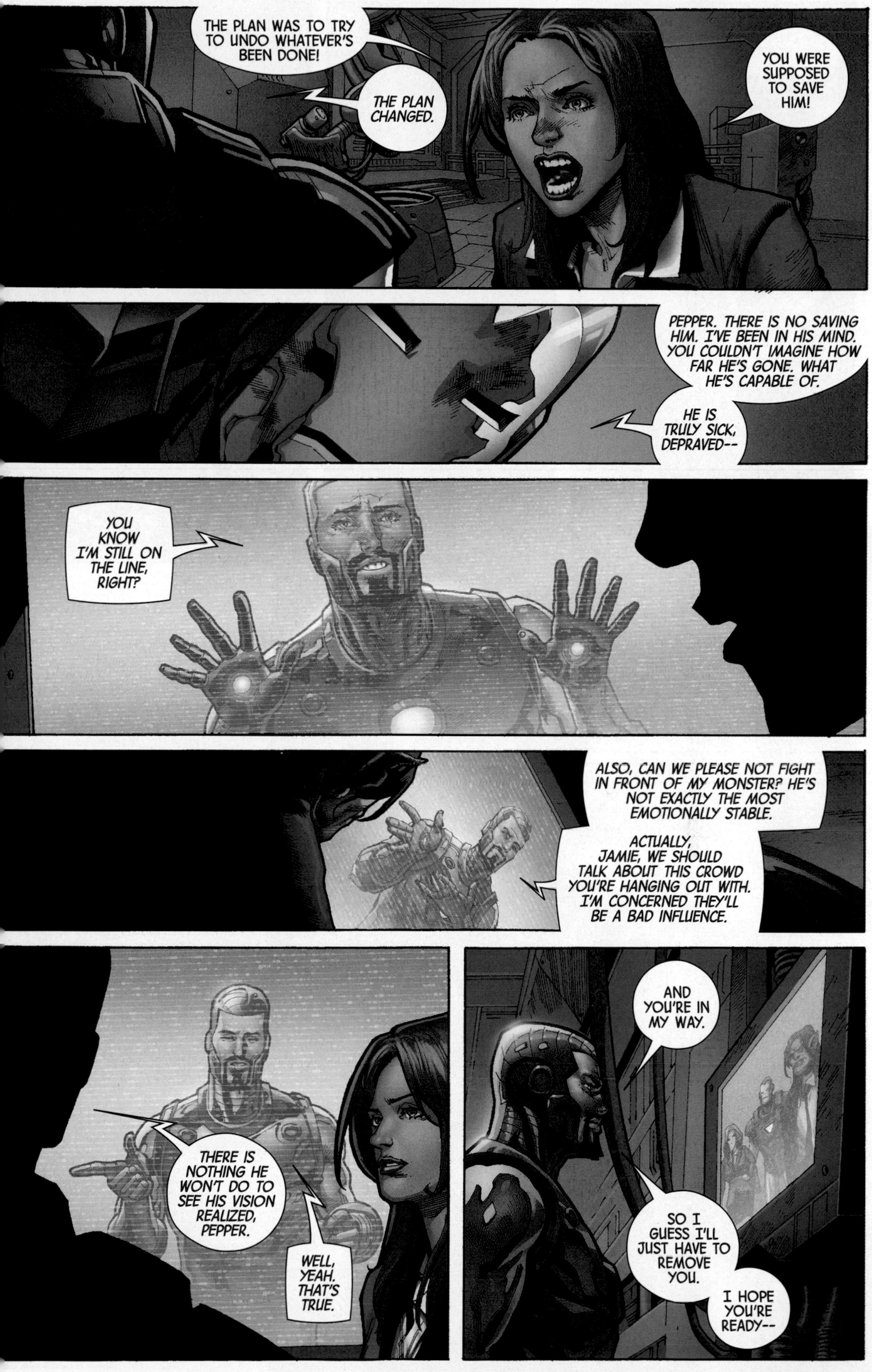
THE PLAN WAS TO TRY TO UNDO WHATEVER'S BEEN DONE!
THE PLAN CHANGED.
YOU WERE SUPPOSED TO SAVE HIM!
PEPPER. THERE IS NO SAVING HIM. I'VE BEEN IN HIS MIND. YOU COULDN'T IMAGINE HOW FAR HE'S GONE. WHAT HE'S CAPABLE OF.
HE IS TRULY SICK, DEPRAVED--
YOU KNOW I'M STILL ON THE LINE, RIGHT?
ALSO, CAN WE PLEASE NOT FIGHT IN FRONT OF MY MONSTER? HE'S NOT EXACTLY THE MOST EMOTIONALLY STABLE.
ACTUALLY, JAMIE, WE SHOULD TALK ABOUT THIS CROWD YOU'RE HANGING OUT WITH. I'M CONCERNED THEY'LL BE A BAD INFLUENCE.
THERE IS NOTHING HE WON'T DO TO SEE HIS VISION REALIZED, PEPPER.
WELL, YEAH. THAT'S TRUE.
AND YOU'RE IN MY WAY.
SO I GUESS I'LL JUST HAVE TO REMOVE YOU.
I HOPE YOU'RE READY--

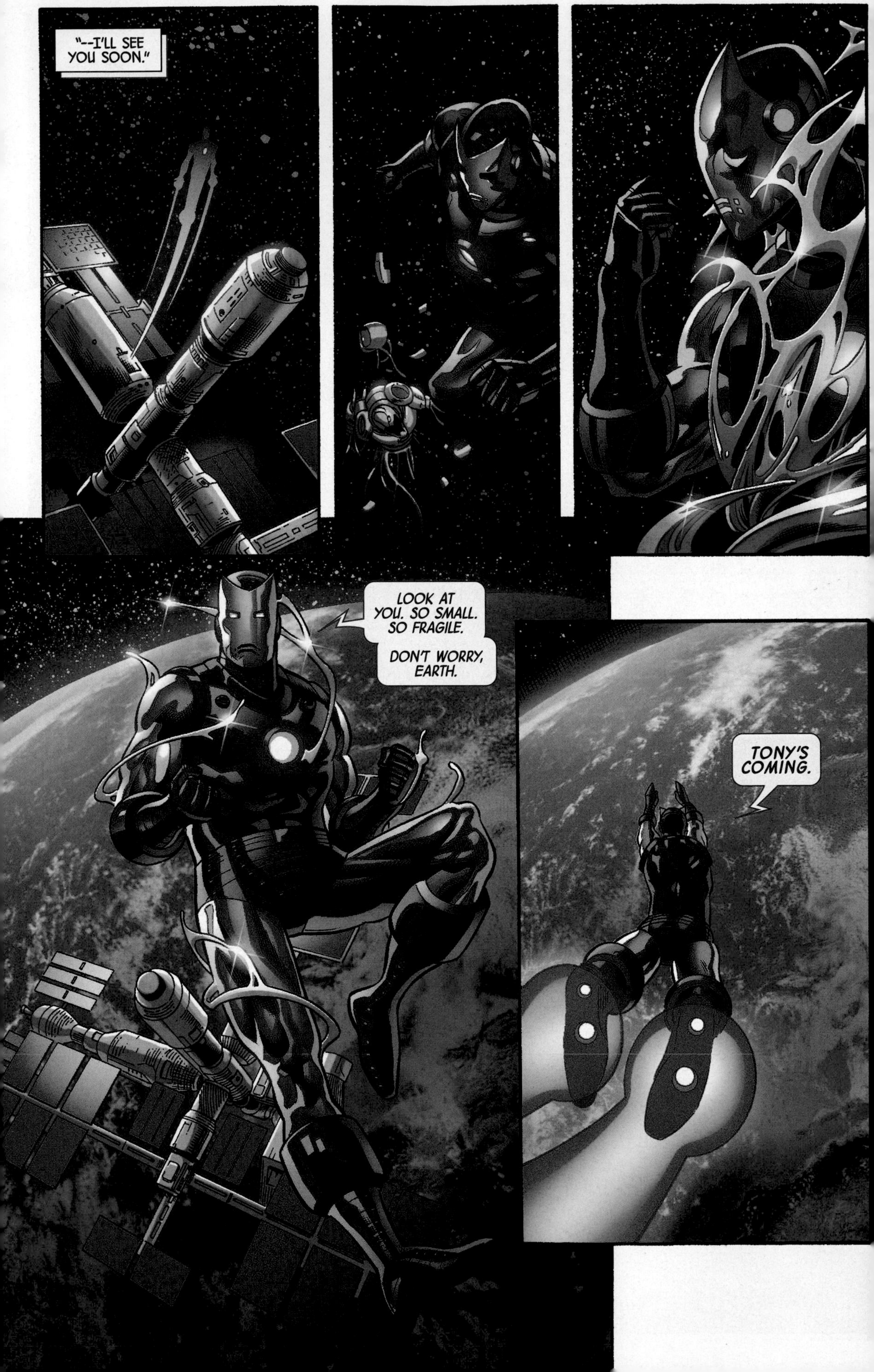
"--I'LL SEE YOU SOON."
LOOK AT YOU. SO SMALL. SO FRAGILE.
DON'T WORRY, EARTH.
TONY'S COMING.

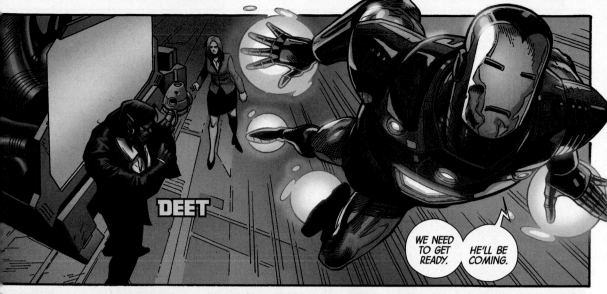

DEET

WE NEED TO GET READY.

HE'LL BE COMING.

YEAH... I DON'T THINK HE'S COMING.

WHAT IS IT?

IT'S THE EXTREMIS APP... HE JUST SENT A MESSAGE OVER IT.

San Francisco,

I've had a bad day and I require people to wear very little clothing and drink all of my booze with me.

Meet at Stark Island.

Love, Tony.

DID HE...?

YES. HE JUST SENT A BOOTY CALL OUT TO AN ENTIRE CITY.

HE ALSO JUST SURROUNDED HIMSELF WITH INNOCENT BYSTANDERS.

WHAT DO WE DO?

NOTHING. FOR NOW.

DO YOU REALLY THINK IT'S A GOOD IDEA TO GIVE HIM TIME TO PREPARE?

IT GIVES ME TIME TO PREPARE, TOO.

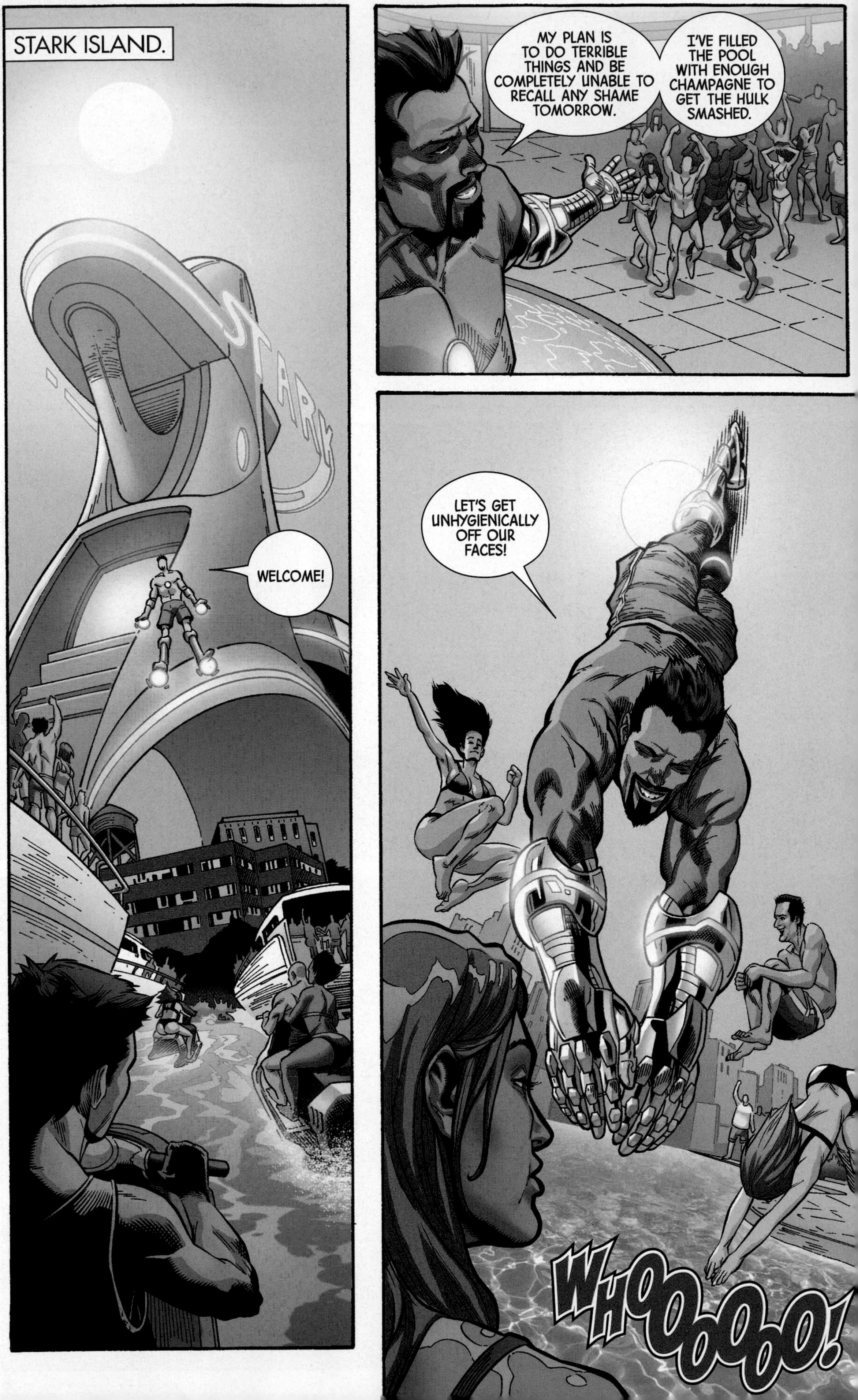
STARK ISLAND.
WELCOME!
MY PLAN IS TO DO TERRIBLE THINGS AND BE COMPLETELY UNABLE TO RECALL ANY SHAME TOMORROW.
I'VE FILLED THE POOL WITH ENOUGH CHAMPAGNE TO GET THE HULK SMASHED.
LET'S GET UNHYGIENICALLY OFF OUR FACES!
WHOOOOOOO!

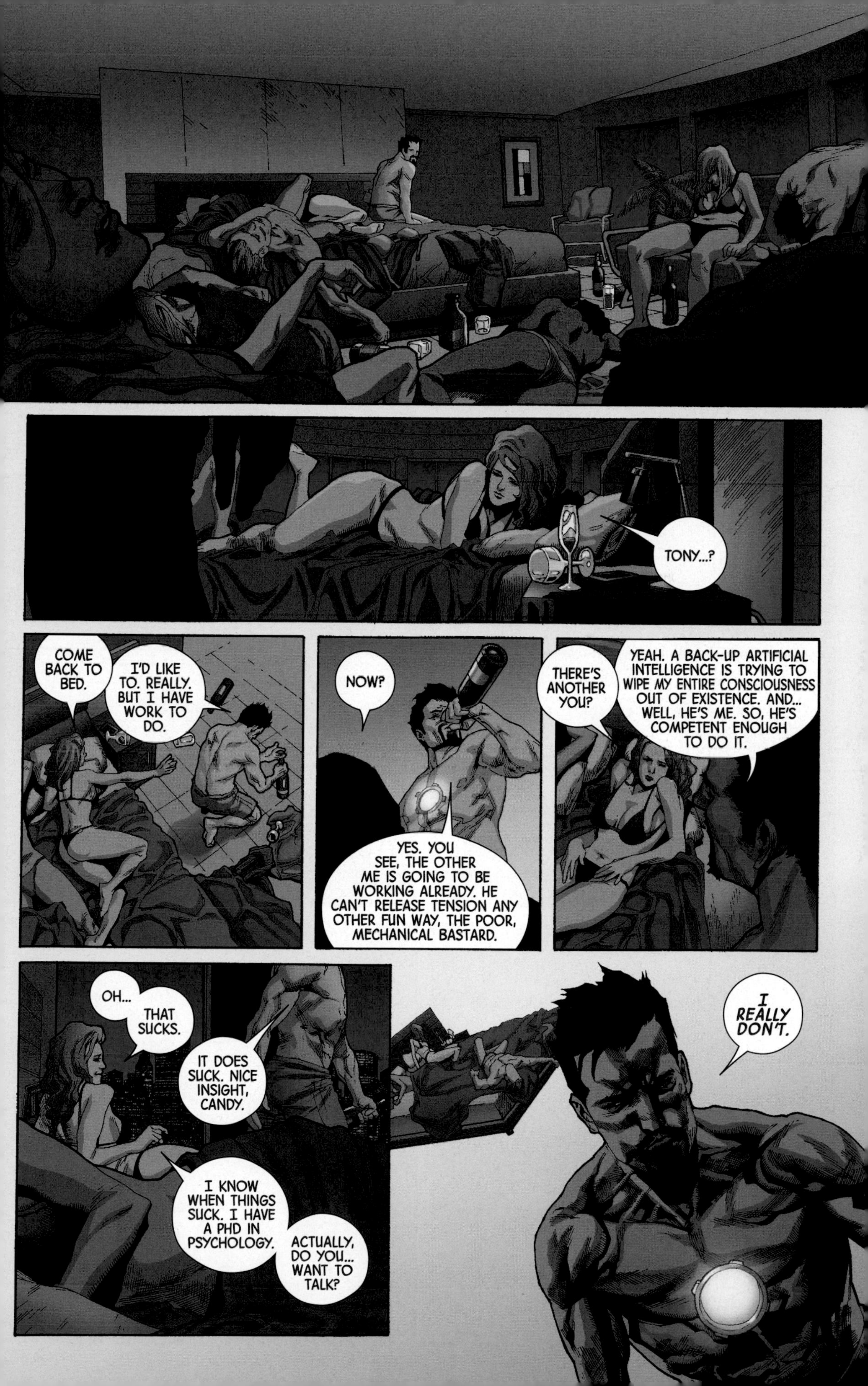
TONY...?
COME BACK TO BED.
I'D LIKE TO. REALLY. BUT I HAVE WORK TO DO.
NOW?
YES. YOU SEE, THE OTHER ME IS GOING TO BE WORKING ALREADY. HE CAN'T RELEASE TENSION ANY OTHER FUN WAY, THE POOR, MECHANICAL BASTARD.
THERE'S ANOTHER YOU?
YEAH. A BACK-UP ARTIFICIAL INTELLIGENCE IS TRYING TO WIPE MY ENTIRE CONSCIOUSNESS OUT OF EXISTENCE. AND... WELL, HE'S ME. SO, HE'S COMPETENT ENOUGH TO DO IT.
OH... THAT SUCKS.
IT DOES SUCK. NICE INSIGHT, CANDY.
I KNOW WHEN THINGS SUCK. I HAVE A PHD IN PSYCHOLOGY.
ACTUALLY, DO YOU... WANT TO TALK?
I REALLY DON'T.

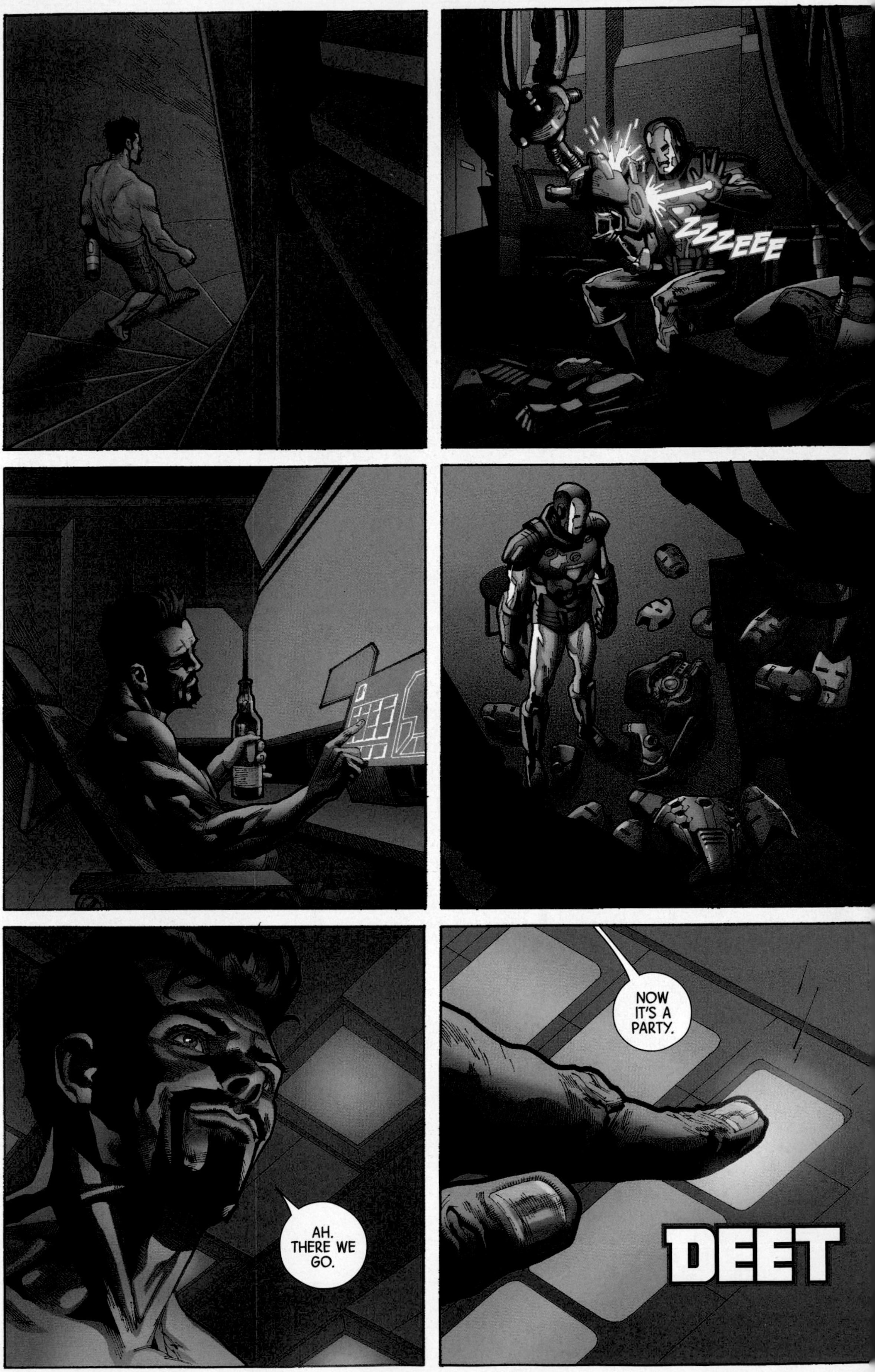
ZZZEEE
AH. THERE WE GO.
NOW IT'S A PARTY.
DEET

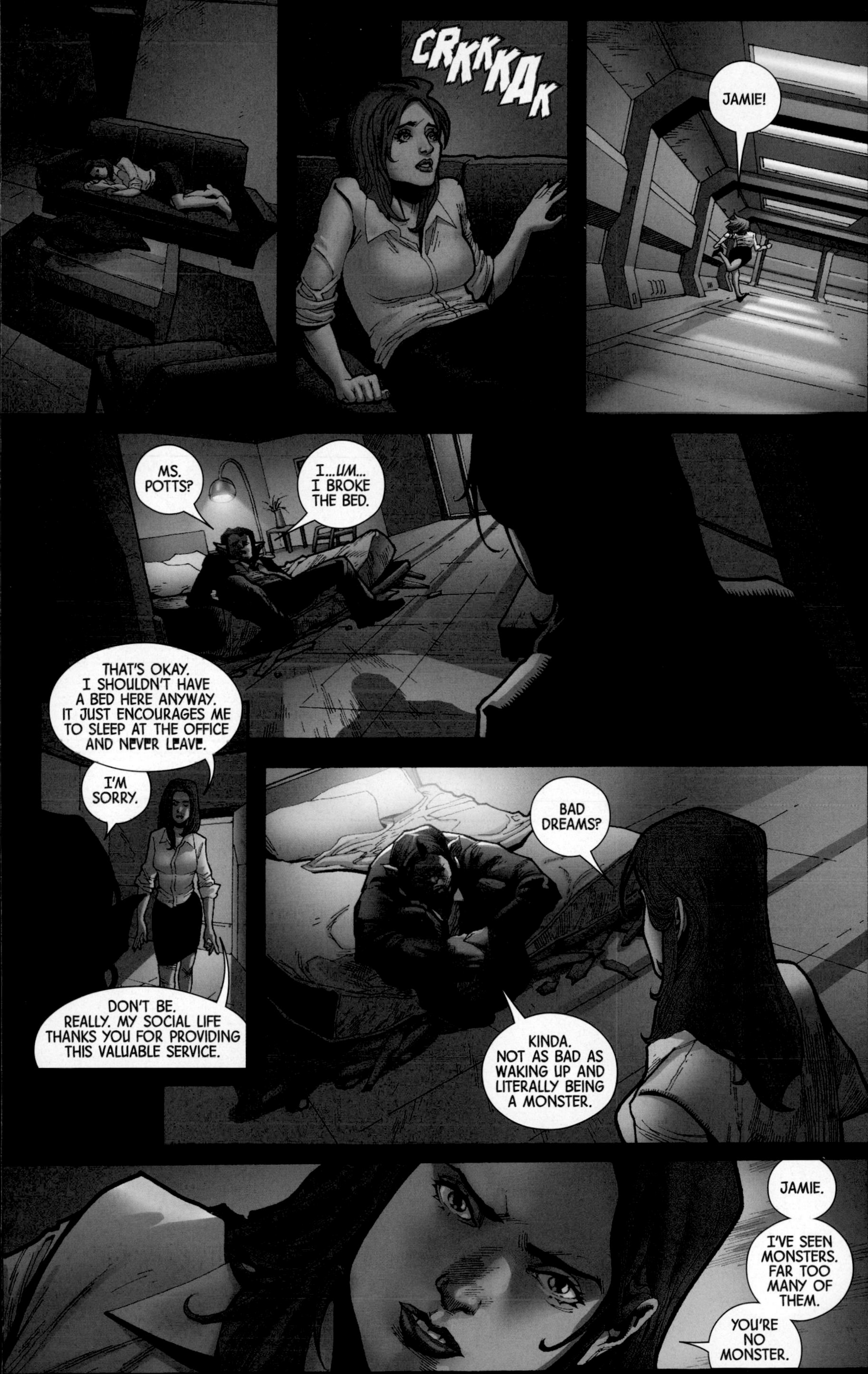
CRKKKAK
JAMIE!
MS. POTTS?
I...UM... I BROKE THE BED.
THAT'S OKAY. I SHOULDN'T HAVE A BED HERE ANYWAY. IT JUST ENCOURAGES ME TO SLEEP AT THE OFFICE AND NEVER LEAVE.
I'M SORRY.
DON'T BE. REALLY. MY SOCIAL LIFE THANKS YOU FOR PROVIDING THIS VALUABLE SERVICE.
BAD DREAMS?
KINDA. NOT AS BAD AS WAKING UP AND LITERALLY BEING A MONSTER.
JAMIE.
I'VE SEEN MONSTERS. FAR TOO MANY OF THEM.
YOU'RE NO MONSTER.

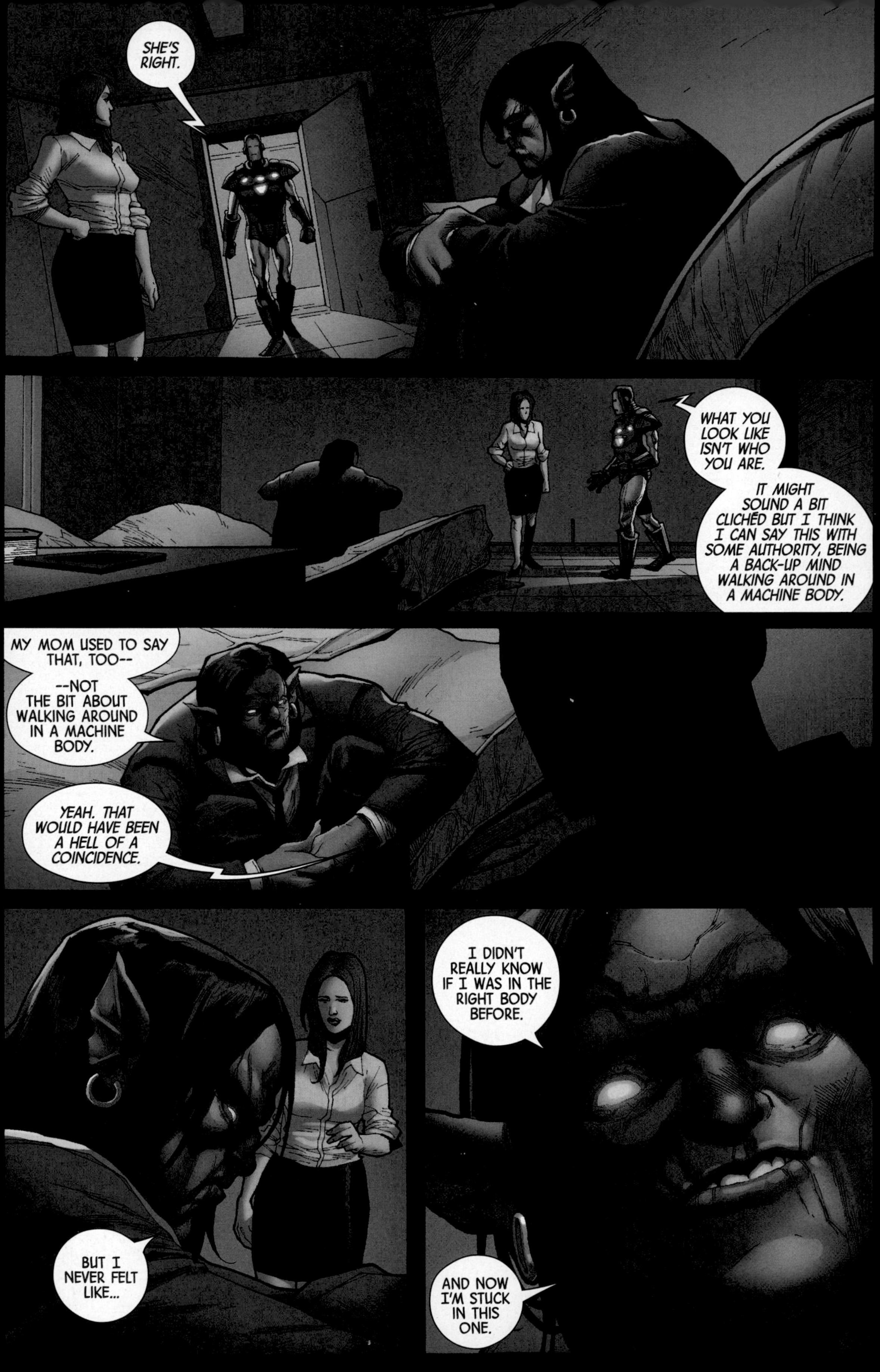
SHE'S RIGHT.
WHAT YOU LOOK LIKE ISN'T WHO YOU ARE.
IT MIGHT SOUND A BIT CLICHÉD BUT I THINK I CAN SAY THIS WITH SOME AUTHORITY, BEING A BACK-UP MIND WALKING AROUND IN A MACHINE BODY.
MY MOM USED TO SAY THAT, TOO--
--NOT THE BIT ABOUT WALKING AROUND IN A MACHINE BODY.
YEAH. THAT WOULD HAVE BEEN A HELL OF A COINCIDENCE.
BUT I NEVER FELT LIKE...
I DIDN'T REALLY KNOW IF I WAS IN THE RIGHT BODY BEFORE.
AND NOW I'M STUCK IN THIS ONE.

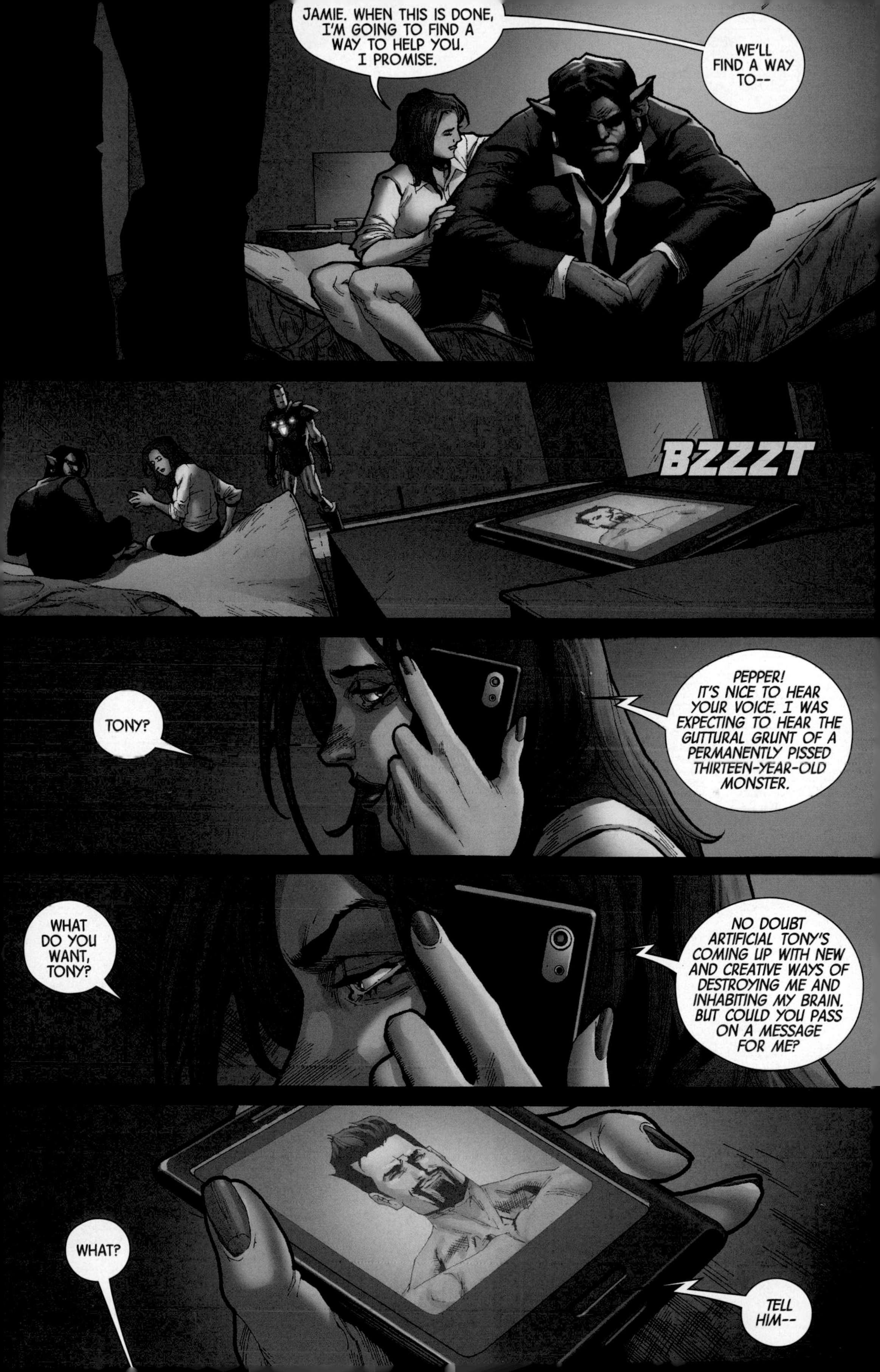
JAMIE. WHEN THIS IS DONE, I'M GOING TO FIND A WAY TO HELP YOU. I PROMISE.
WE'LL FIND A WAY TO--
BZZZT
TONY?
PEPPER! IT'S NICE TO HEAR YOUR VOICE. I WAS EXPECTING TO HEAR THE GUTTURAL GRUNT OF A PERMANENTLY PISSED THIRTEEN-YEAR-OLD MONSTER.
WHAT DO YOU WANT, TONY?
NO DOUBT ARTIFICIAL TONY'S COMING UP WITH NEW AND CREATIVE WAYS OF DESTROYING ME AND INHABITING MY BRAIN. BUT COULD YOU PASS ON A MESSAGE FOR ME?
WHAT?
TELL HIM--

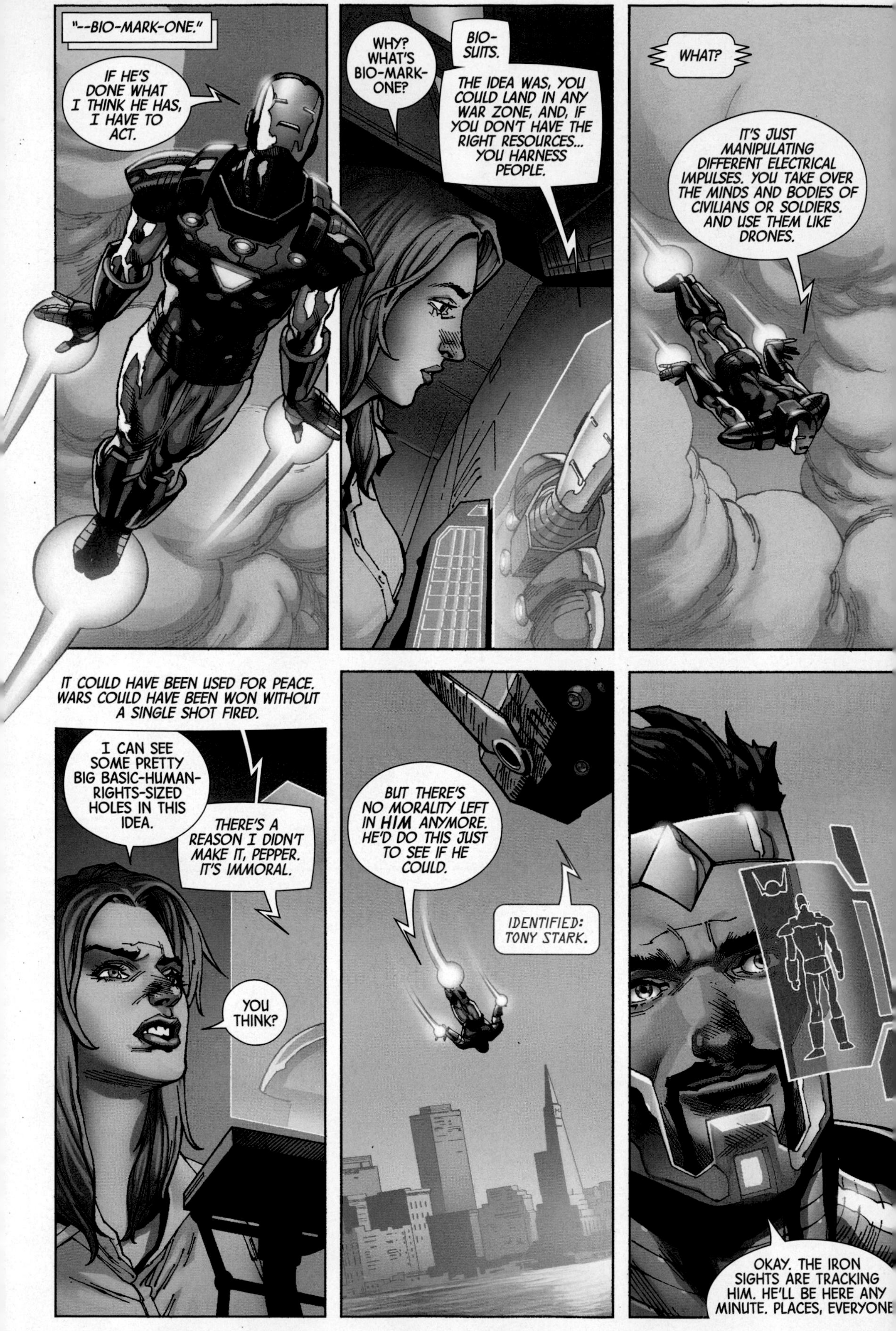
"--BIO-MARK-ONE."
IF HE'S DONE WHAT I THINK HE HAS, I HAVE TO ACT.
WHY? WHAT'S BIO-MARK-ONE?
BIO-SUITS.
THE IDEA WAS, YOU COULD LAND IN ANY WAR ZONE, AND, IF YOU DON'T HAVE THE RIGHT RESOURCES... YOU HARNESS PEOPLE.
WHAT?
IT'S JUST MANIPULATING DIFFERENT ELECTRICAL IMPULSES. YOU TAKE OVER THE MINDS AND BODIES OF CIVILIANS OR SOLDIERS. AND USE THEM LIKE DRONES.
IT COULD HAVE BEEN USED FOR PEACE. WARS COULD HAVE BEEN WON WITHOUT A SINGLE SHOT FIRED.
I CAN SEE SOME PRETTY BIG BASIC-HUMAN-RIGHTS-SIZED HOLES IN THIS IDEA.
THERE'S A REASON I DIDN'T MAKE IT, PEPPER. IT'S IMMORAL.
YOU THINK?
BUT THERE'S NO MORALITY LEFT IN HIM ANYMORE. HE'D DO THIS JUST TO SEE IF HE COULD.
IDENTIFIED: TONY STARK.
OKAY. THE IRON SIGHTS ARE TRACKING HIM. HE'LL BE HERE ANY MINUTE. PLACES, EVERYONE

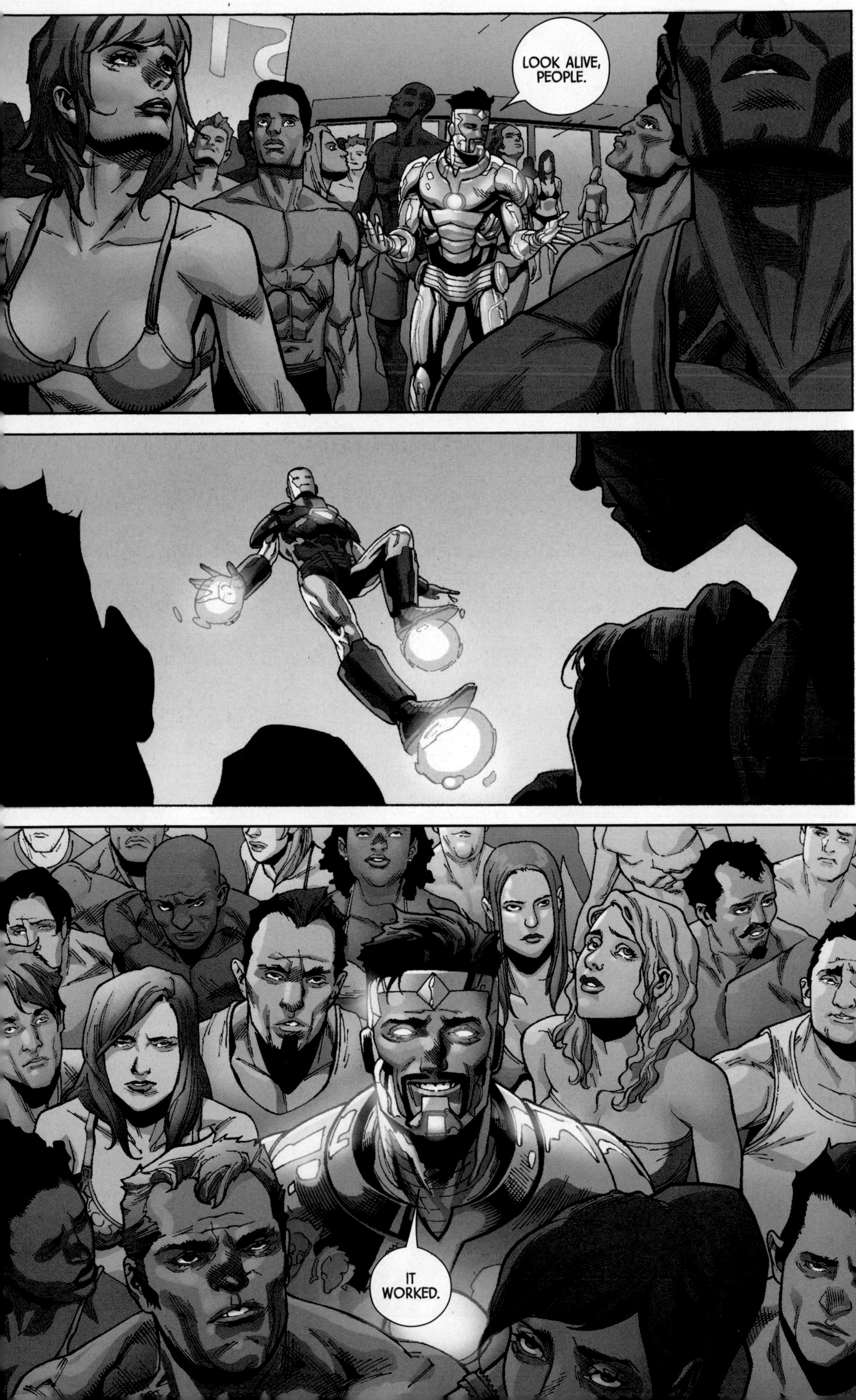
LOOK ALIVE, PEOPLE.
IT WORKED.

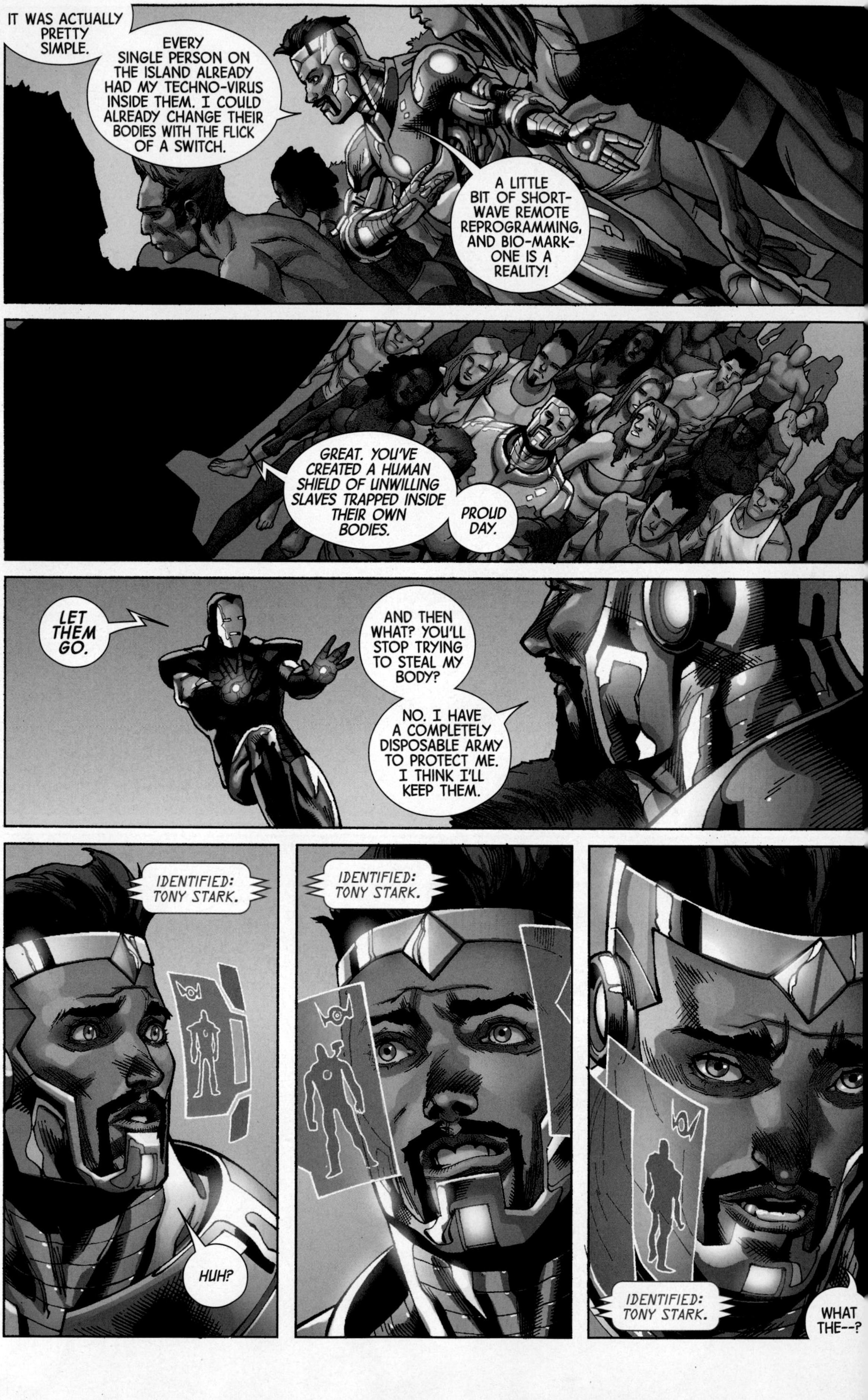
IT WAS ACTUALLY PRETTY SIMPLE.
EVERY SINGLE PERSON ON THE ISLAND ALREADY HAD MY TECHNO-VIRUS INSIDE THEM. I COULD ALREADY CHANGE THEIR BODIES WITH THE FLICK OF A SWITCH.
A LITTLE BIT OF SHORT-WAVE REMOTE REPROGRAMMING, AND BIO-MARK-ONE IS A REALITY!
GREAT. YOU'VE CREATED A HUMAN SHIELD OF UNWILLING SLAVES TRAPPED INSIDE THEIR OWN BODIES.
PROUD DAY.
LET THEM GO.
AND THEN WHAT? YOU'LL STOP TRYING TO STEAL MY BODY?
NO. I HAVE A COMPLETELY DISPOSABLE ARMY TO PROTECT ME. I THINK I'LL KEEP THEM.
IDENTIFIED: TONY STARK.
HUH?
IDENTIFIED: TONY STARK.
IDENTIFIED: TONY STARK.
WHAT THE--?

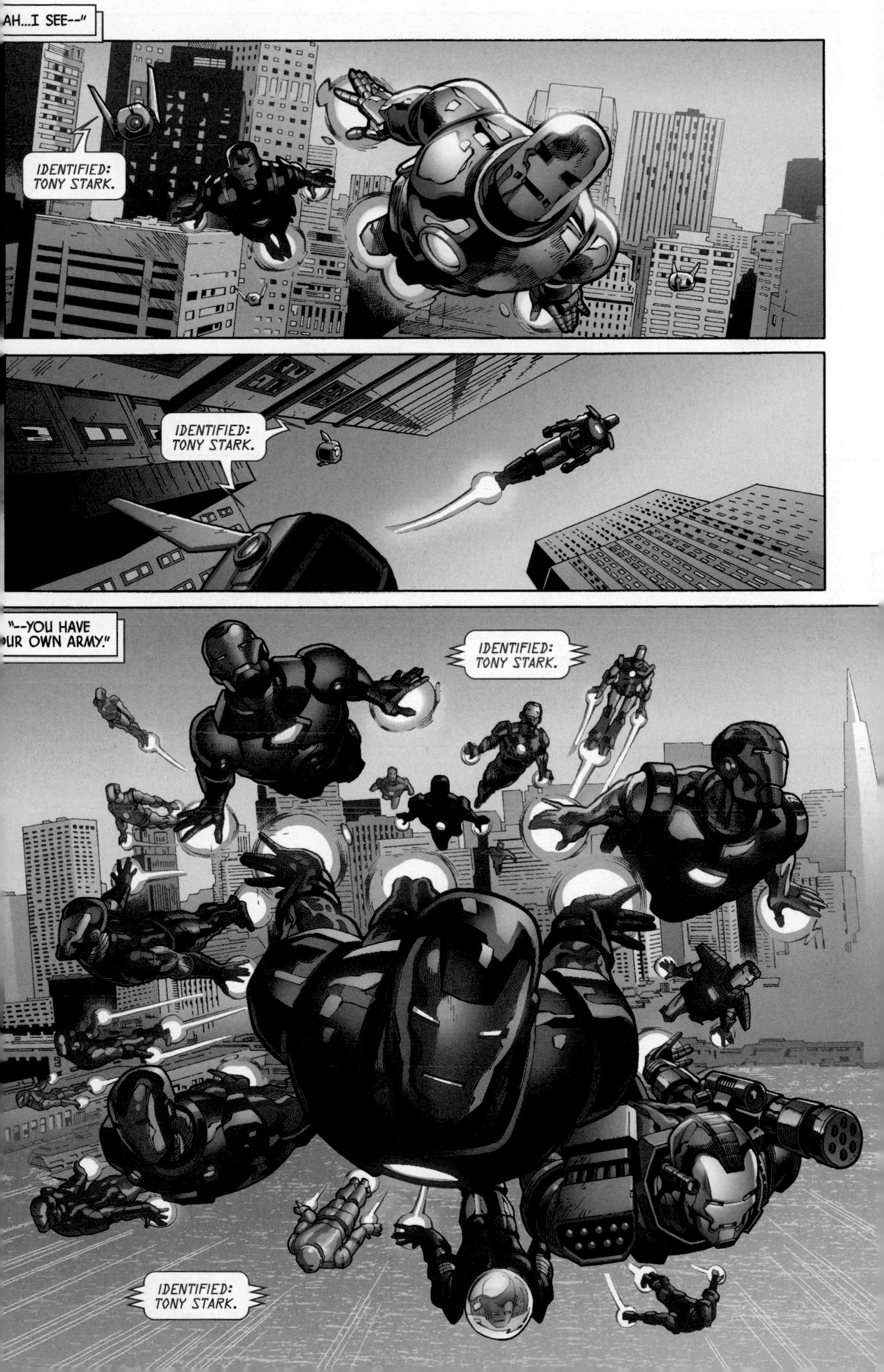
AH...I SEE--"
IDENTIFIED: TONY STARK.
IDENTIFIED: TONY STARK.
"--YOU HAVE
UR OWN ARMY."
IDENTIFIED: TONY STARK.
IDENTIFIED: TONY STARK.

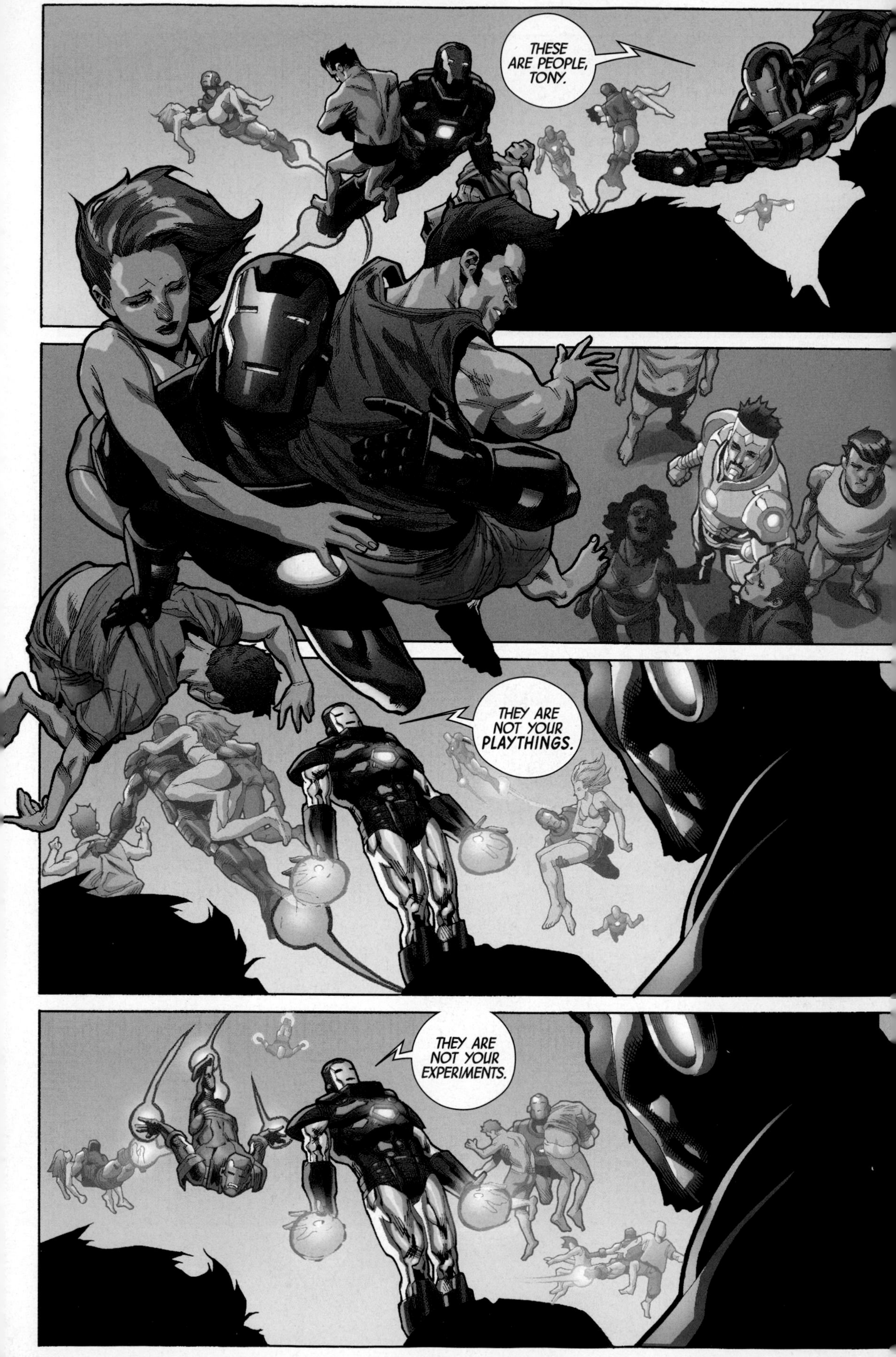
THESE ARE PEOPLE, TONY.
THEY ARE NOT YOUR PLAYTHINGS.
THEY ARE NOT YOUR EXPERIMENTS.

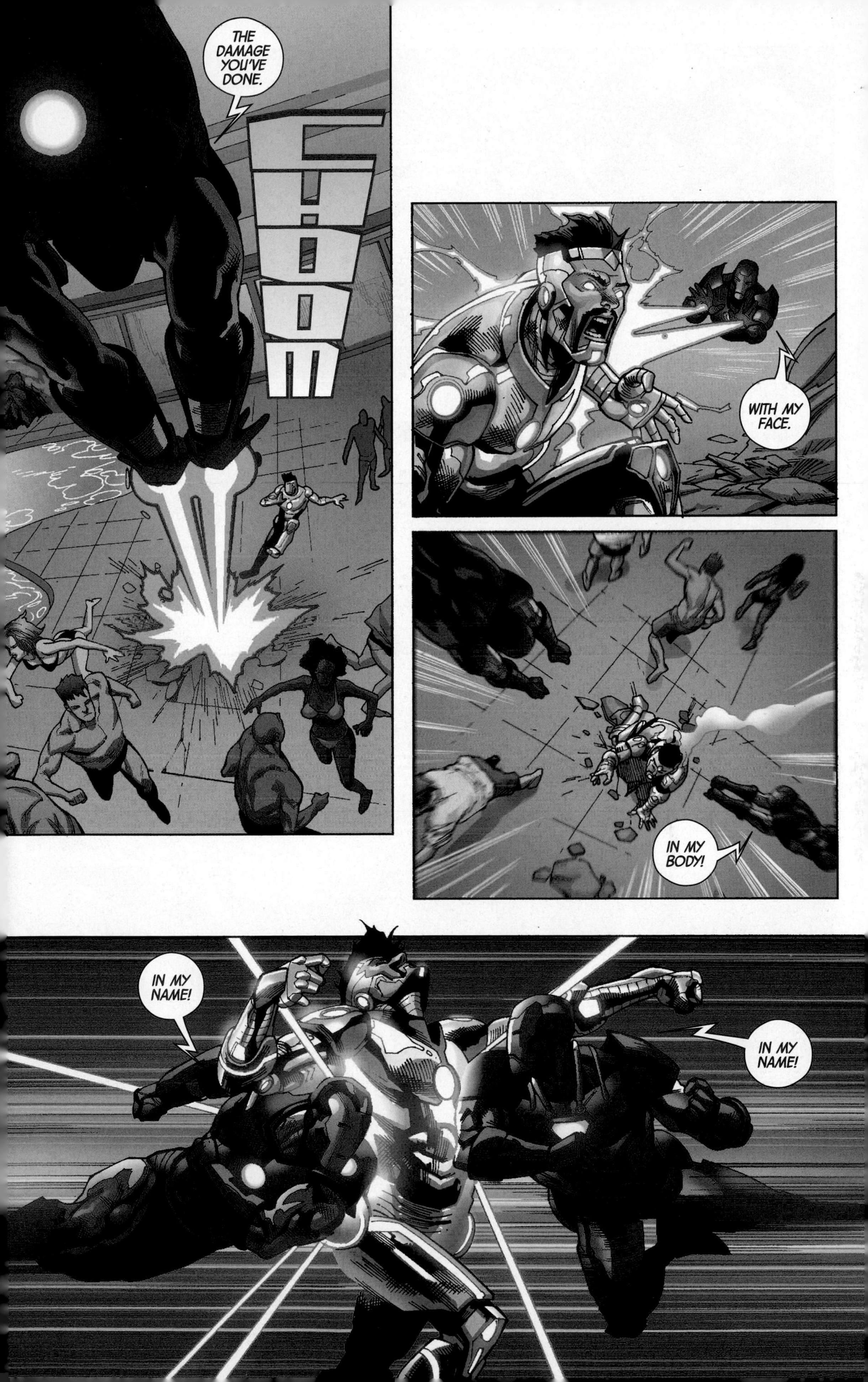
THE DAMAGE YOU'VE DONE.
CHOOM
WITH MY FACE.
IN MY BODY!
IN MY NAME!
IN MY NAME!

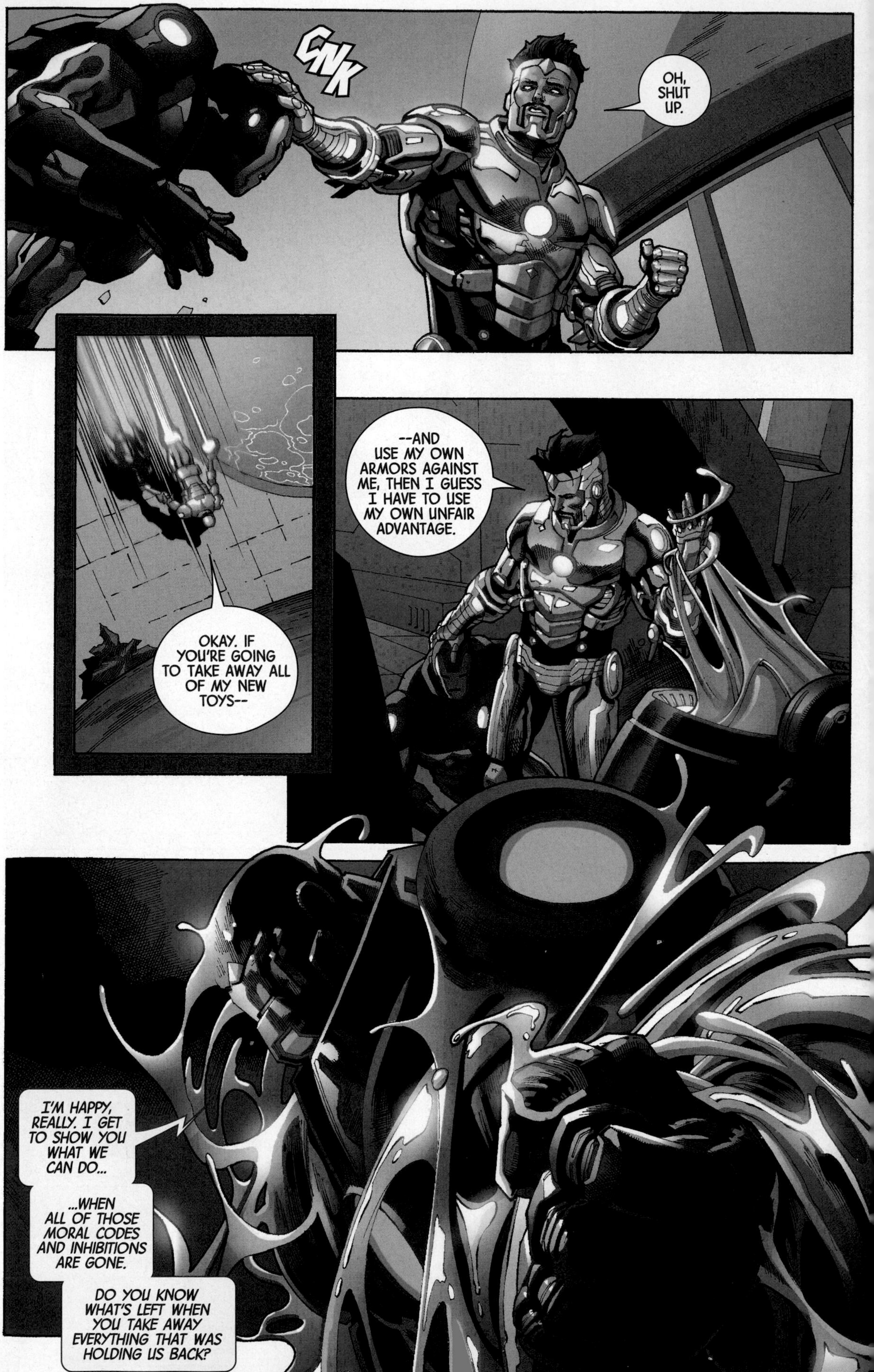
CNK
OH, SHUT UP.
OKAY. IF YOU'RE GOING TO TAKE AWAY ALL OF MY NEW TOYS--
--AND USE MY OWN ARMORS AGAINST ME, THEN I GUESS I HAVE TO USE MY OWN UNFAIR ADVANTAGE.
I'M HAPPY, REALLY. I GET TO SHOW YOU WHAT WE CAN DO...
...WHEN ALL OF THOSE MORAL CODES AND INHIBITIONS ARE GONE.
DO YOU KNOW WHAT'S LEFT WHEN YOU TAKE AWAY EVERYTHING THAT WAS HOLDING US BACK?

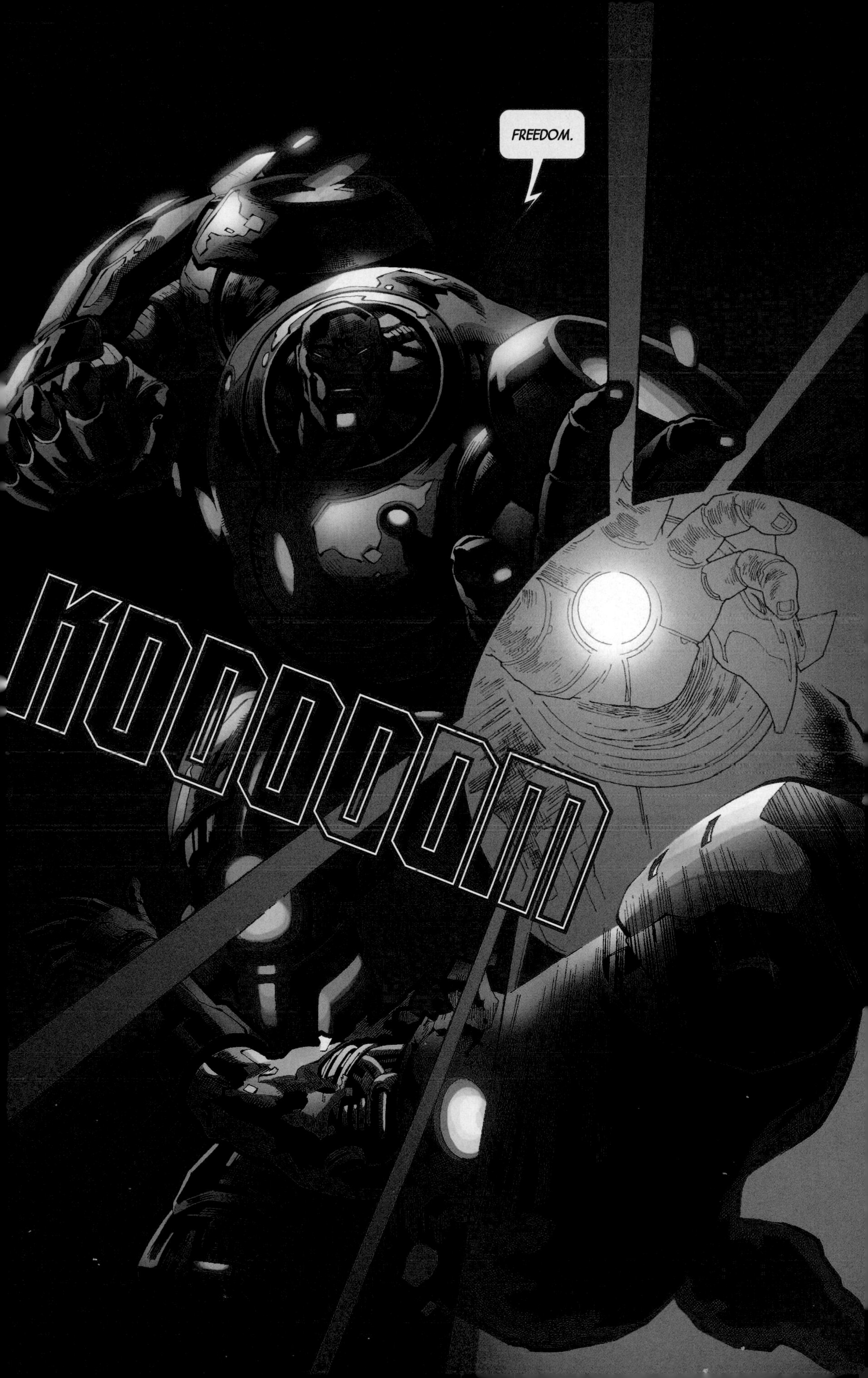
FREEDOM.
KDOOOOM

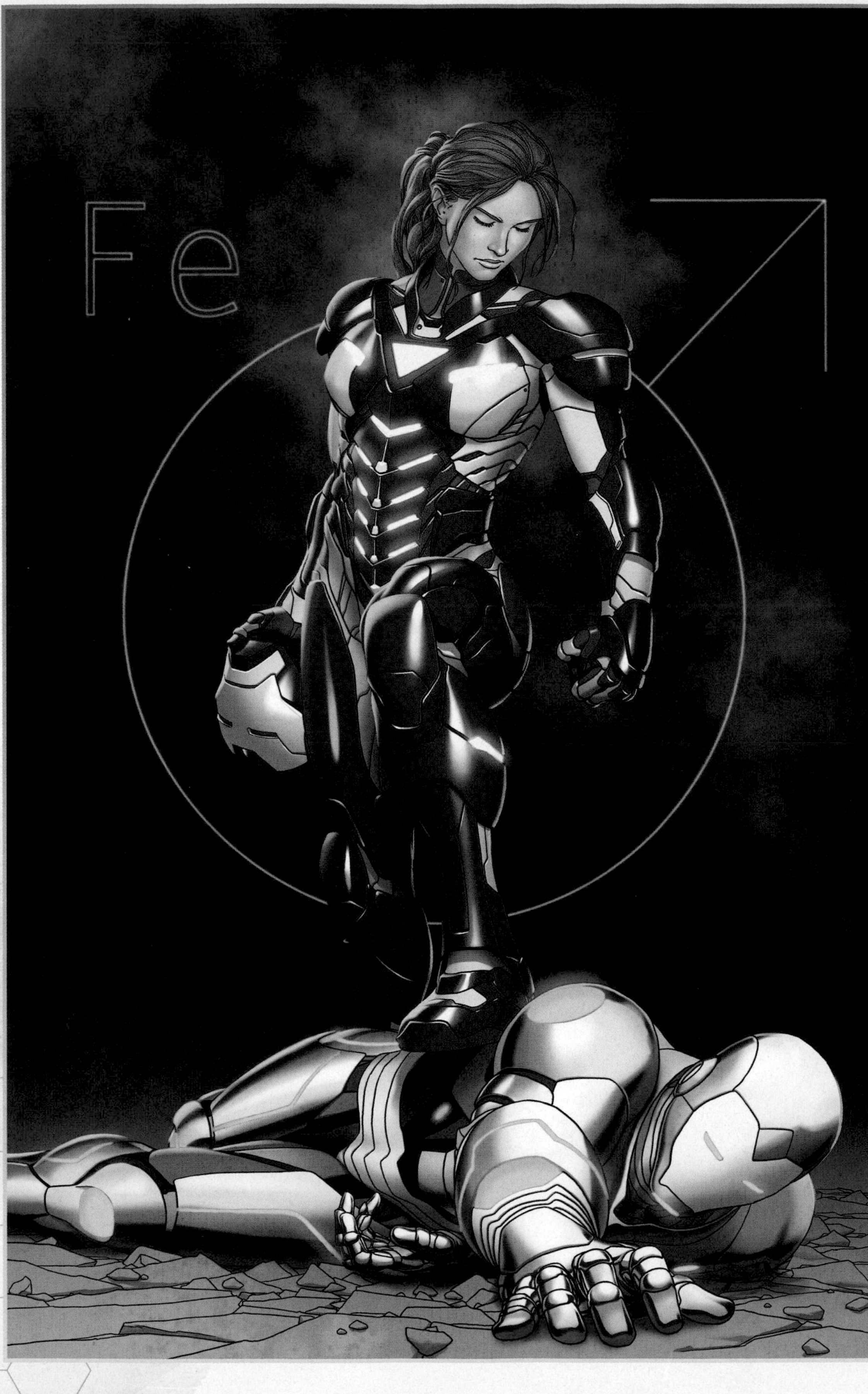
Fe

# 9: FREEDOM

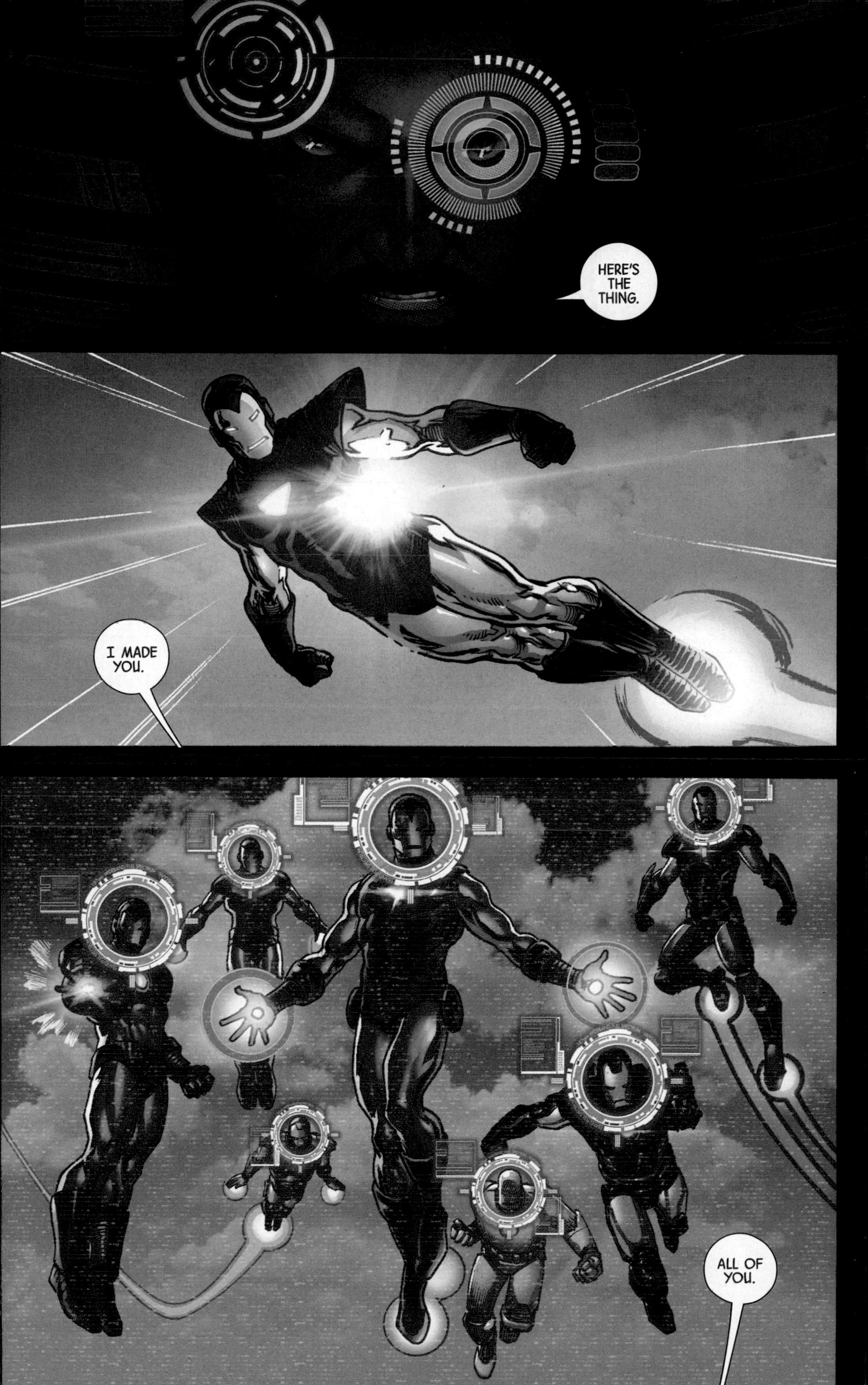
HERE'S THE THING.
I MADE YOU.
ALL OF YOU.

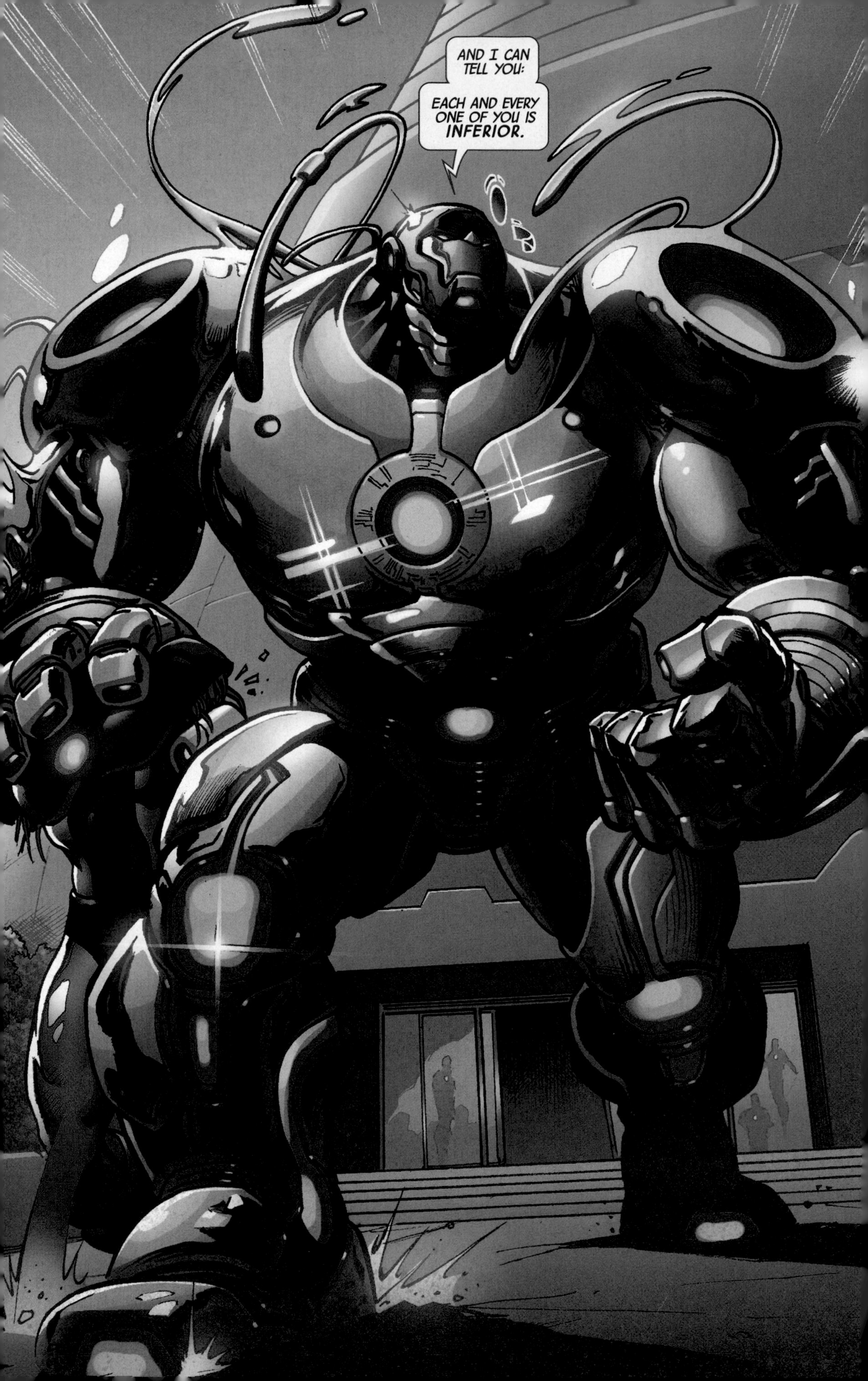
AND I CAN TELL YOU:
EACH AND EVERY ONE OF YOU IS **INFERIOR.**

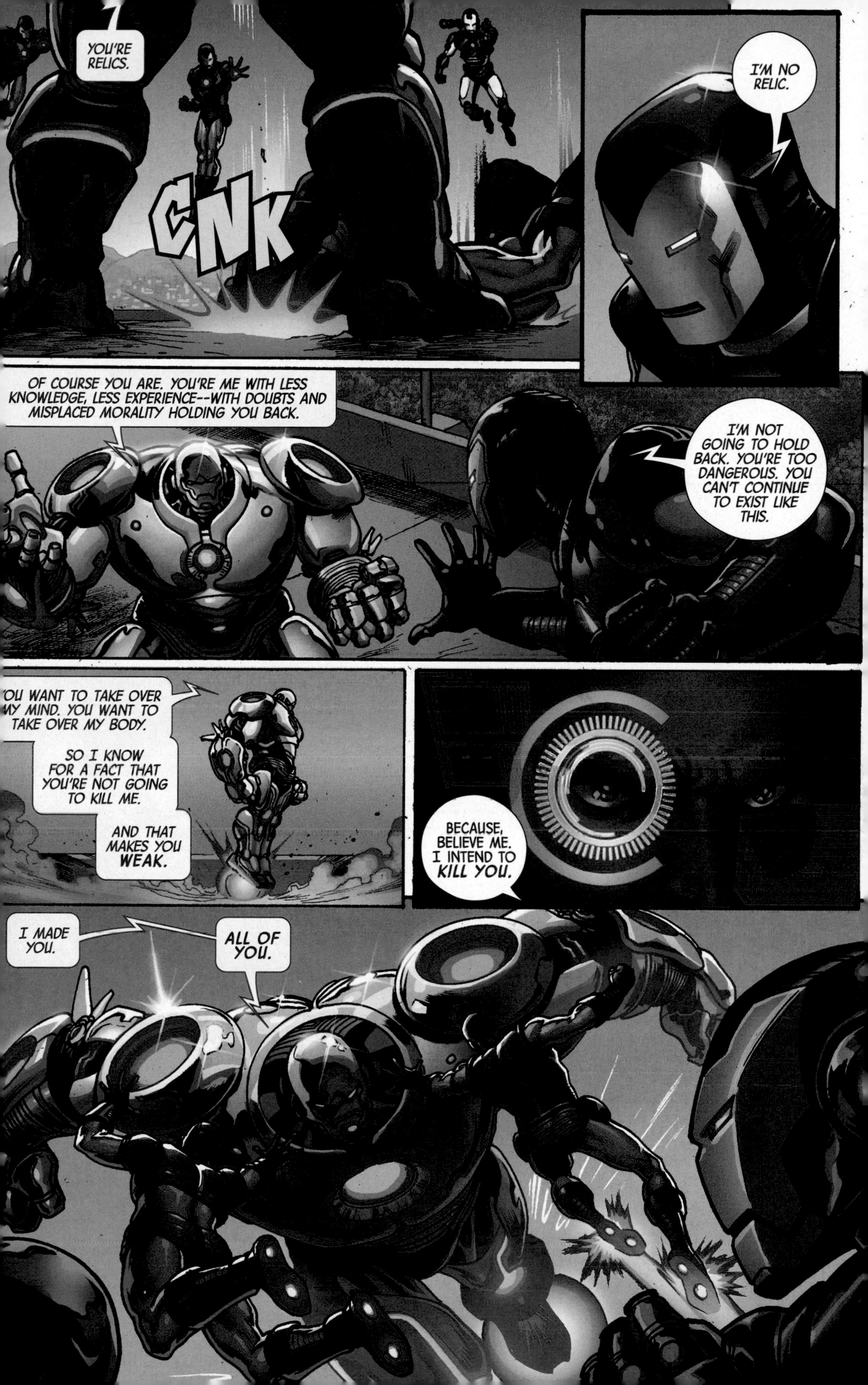
YOU'RE RELICS.
CNK
I'M NO RELIC.
OF COURSE YOU ARE. YOU'RE ME WITH LESS KNOWLEDGE, LESS EXPERIENCE--WITH DOUBTS AND MISPLACED MORALITY HOLDING YOU BACK.
I'M NOT GOING TO HOLD BACK. YOU'RE TOO DANGEROUS. YOU CAN'T CONTINUE TO EXIST LIKE THIS.
YOU WANT TO TAKE OVER MY MIND. YOU WANT TO TAKE OVER MY BODY.
SO I KNOW FOR A FACT THAT YOU'RE NOT GOING TO KILL ME.
AND THAT MAKES YOU WEAK.
BECAUSE, BELIEVE ME. I INTEND TO KILL YOU.
I MADE YOU.
ALL OF YOU.

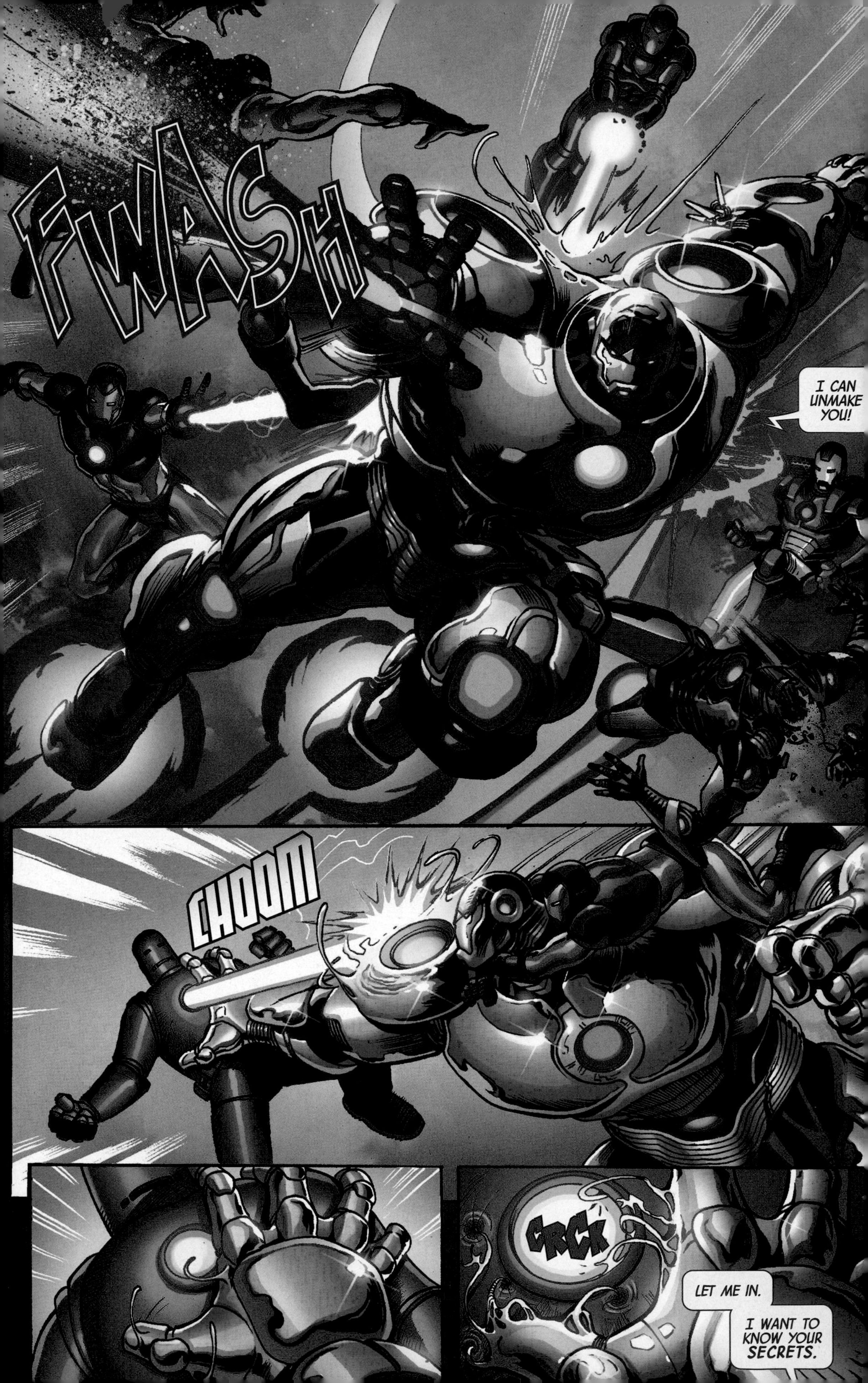
FWASH
I CAN UNMAKE YOU!
CHOOM
CRCK
LET ME IN.
I WANT TO KNOW YOUR SECRETS.

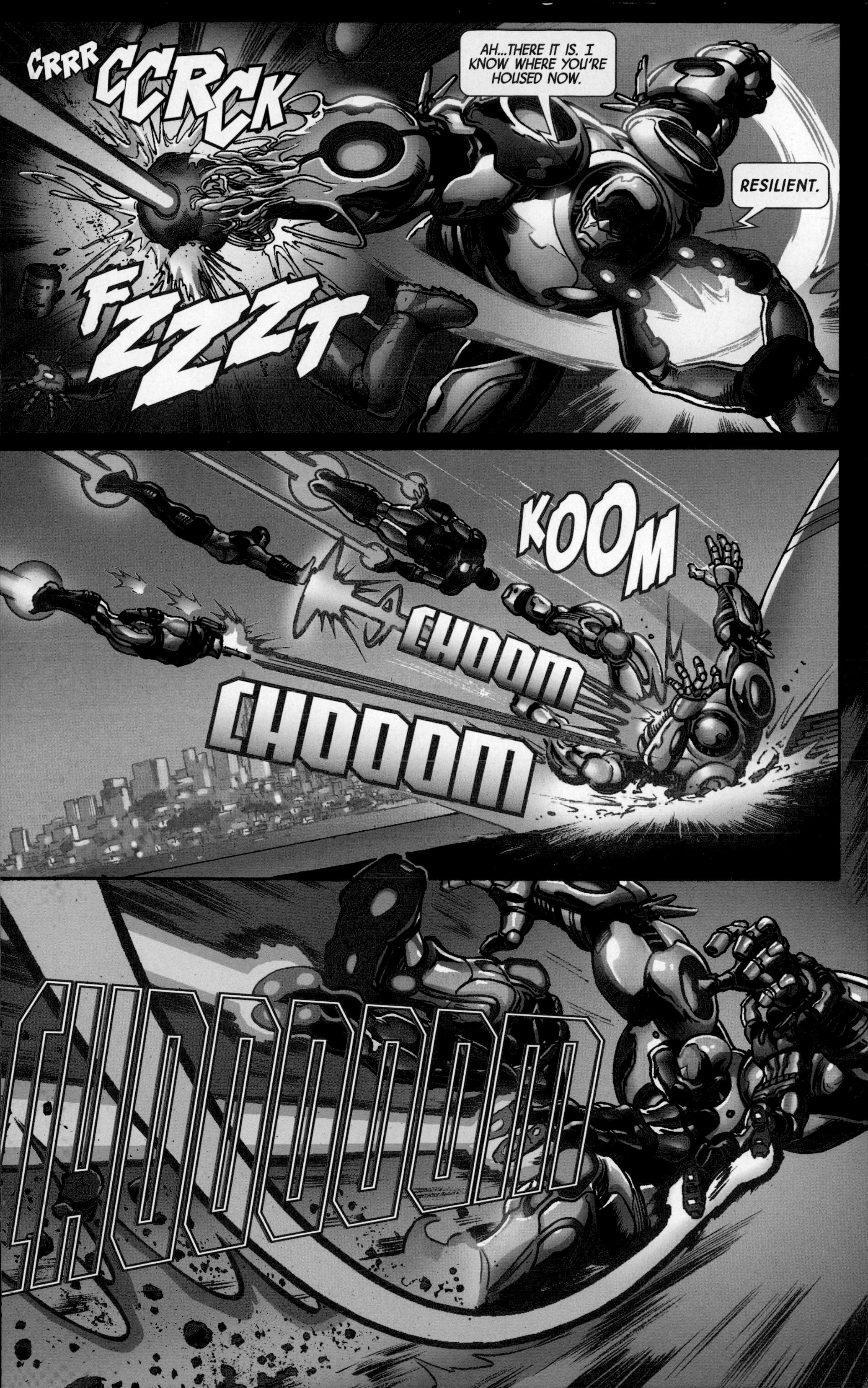
CRRR CCRCK
AH...THERE IT IS. I KNOW WHERE YOU'RE HOUSED NOW.
RESILIENT.
FZZZT
KOOM
CHOOM
CHOOOM
CHOOOOOM

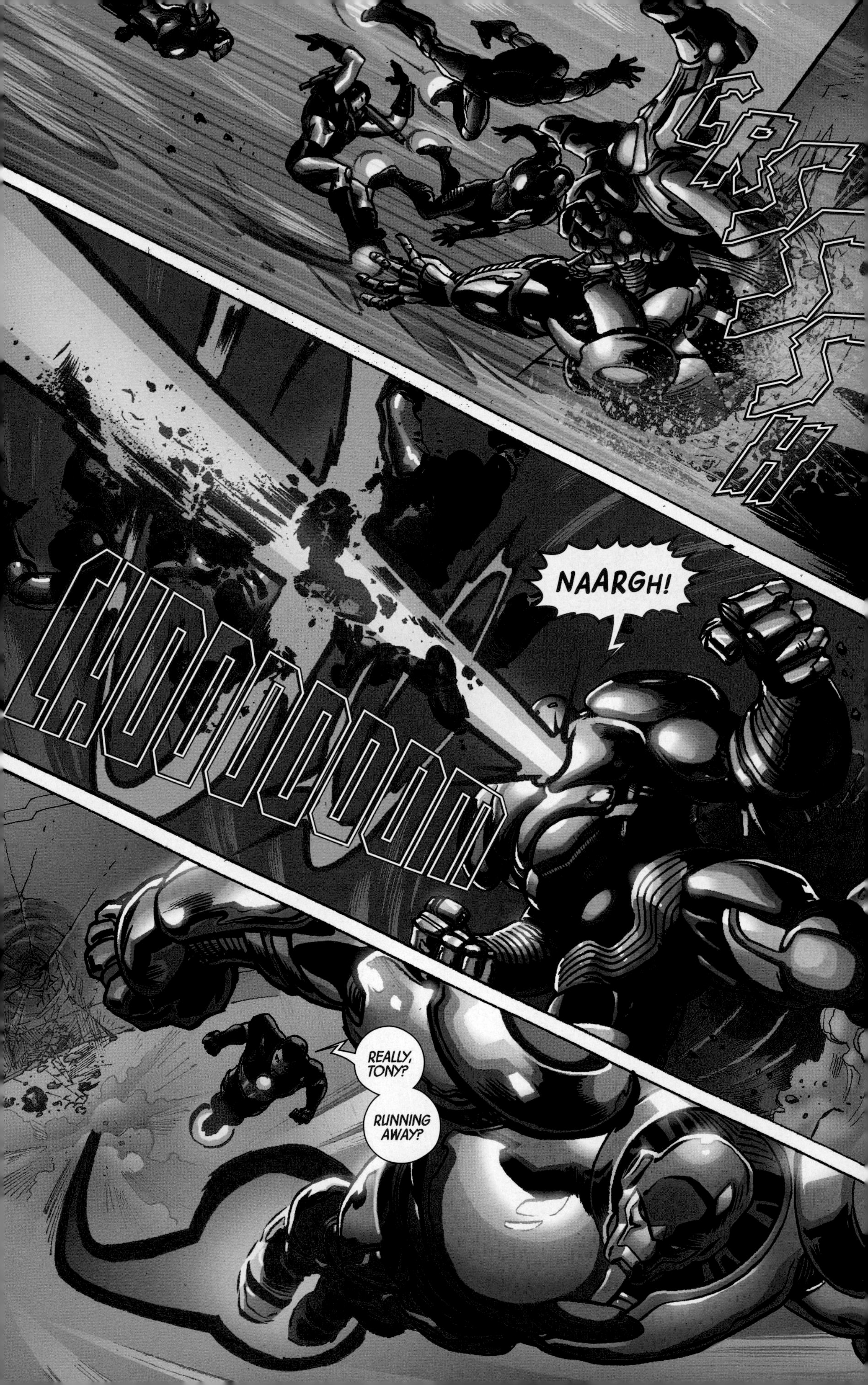
NAARGH!
REALLY, TONY?
RUNNING AWAY?

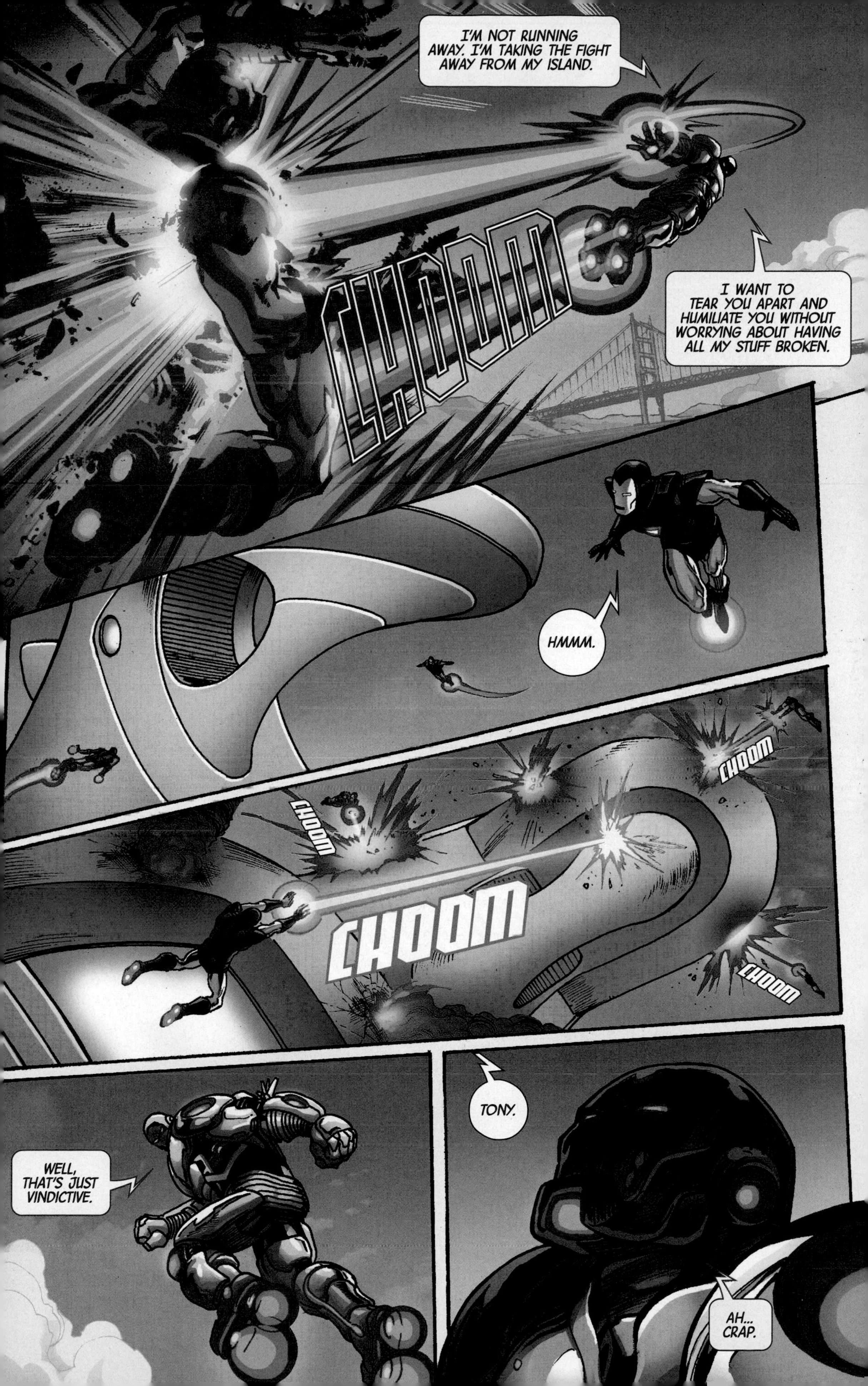
I'M NOT RUNNING AWAY. I'M TAKING THE FIGHT AWAY FROM MY ISLAND.
CHOOM
I WANT TO TEAR YOU APART AND HUMILIATE YOU WITHOUT WORRYING ABOUT HAVING ALL MY STUFF BROKEN.
HMMM.
CHOOM
CHOOM
CHOOM
CHOOM
TONY.
WELL, THAT'S JUST VINDICTIVE.
AH... CRAP.

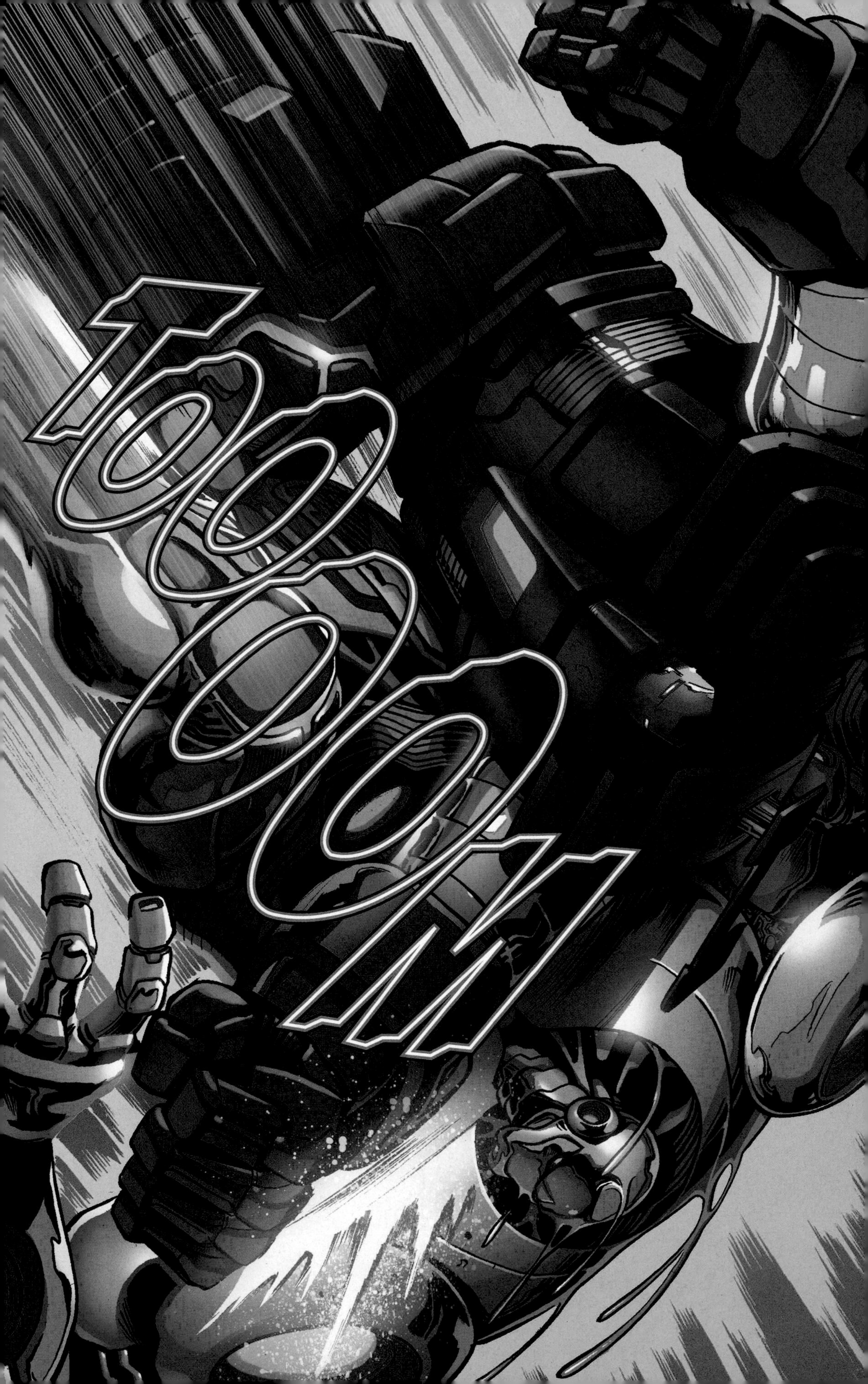
TOOOOM

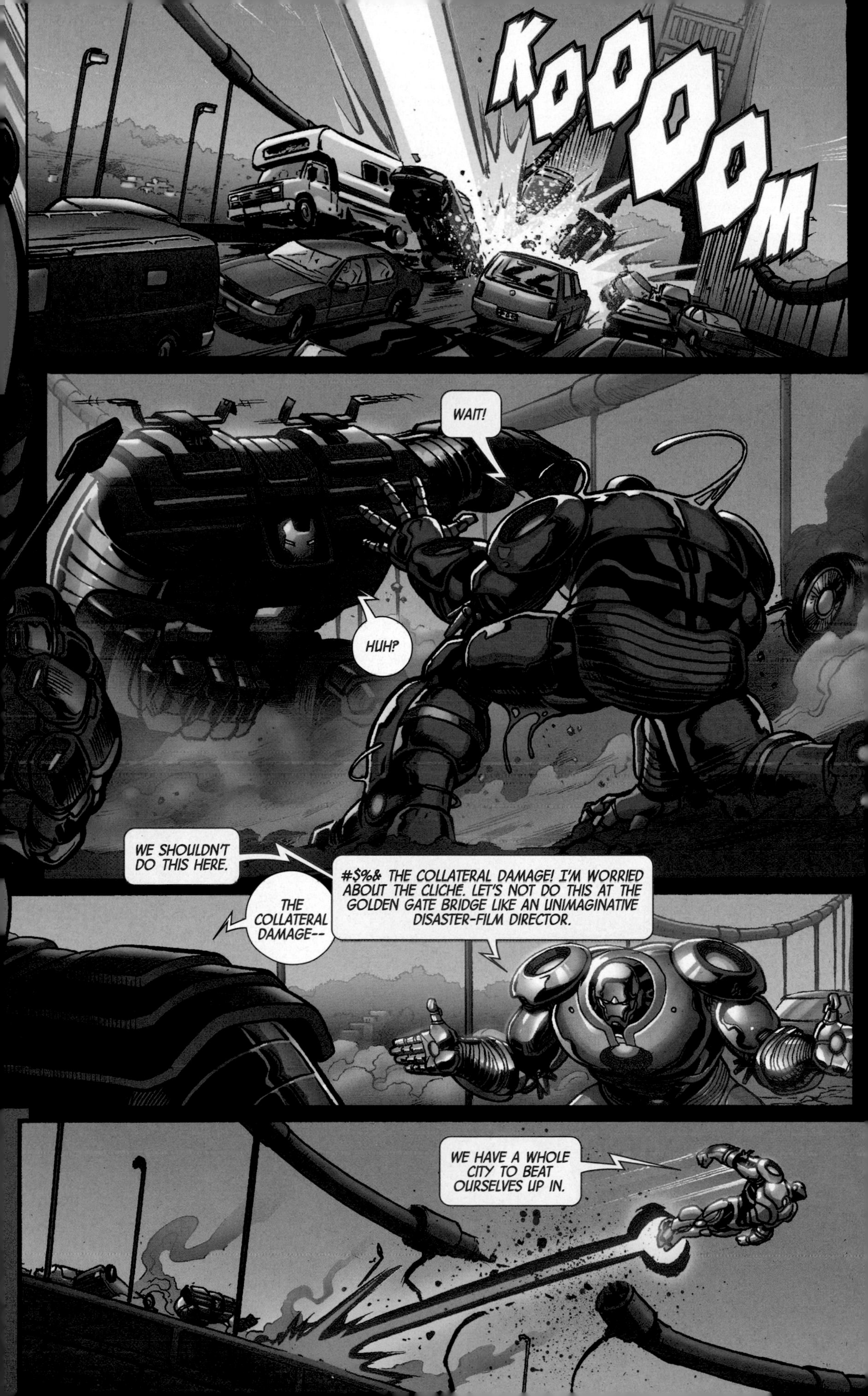
KOOOOOM
WAIT!
HUH?
WE SHOULDN'T DO THIS HERE.
THE COLLATERAL DAMAGE--
#$%& THE COLLATERAL DAMAGE! I'M WORRIED ABOUT THE CLICHE. LET'S NOT DO THIS AT THE GOLDEN GATE BRIDGE LIKE AN UNIMAGINATIVE DISASTER-FILM DIRECTOR.
WE HAVE A WHOLE CITY TO BEAT OURSELVES UP IN.

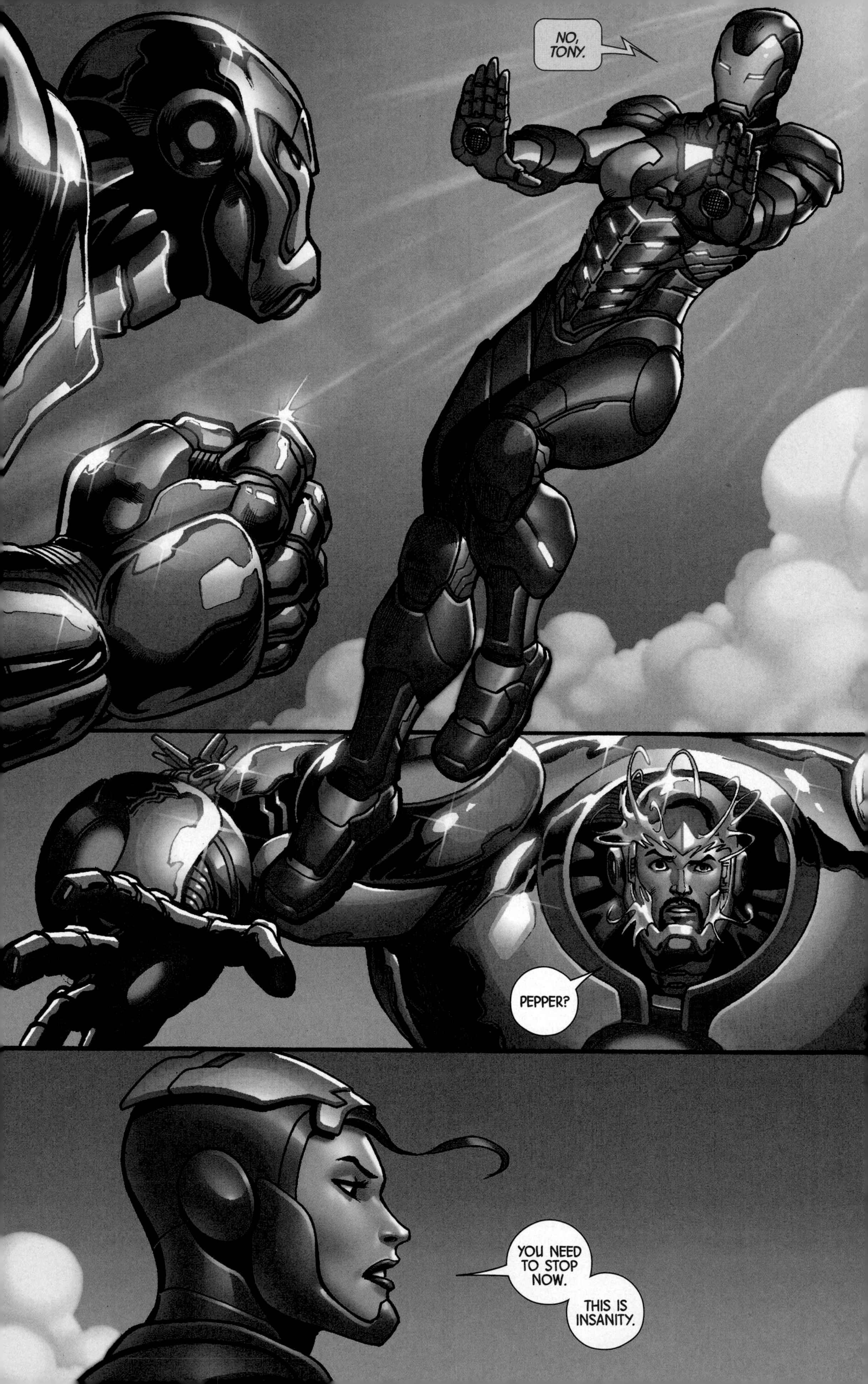
NO, TONY.
PEPPER?
YOU NEED TO STOP NOW.
THIS IS INSANITY.

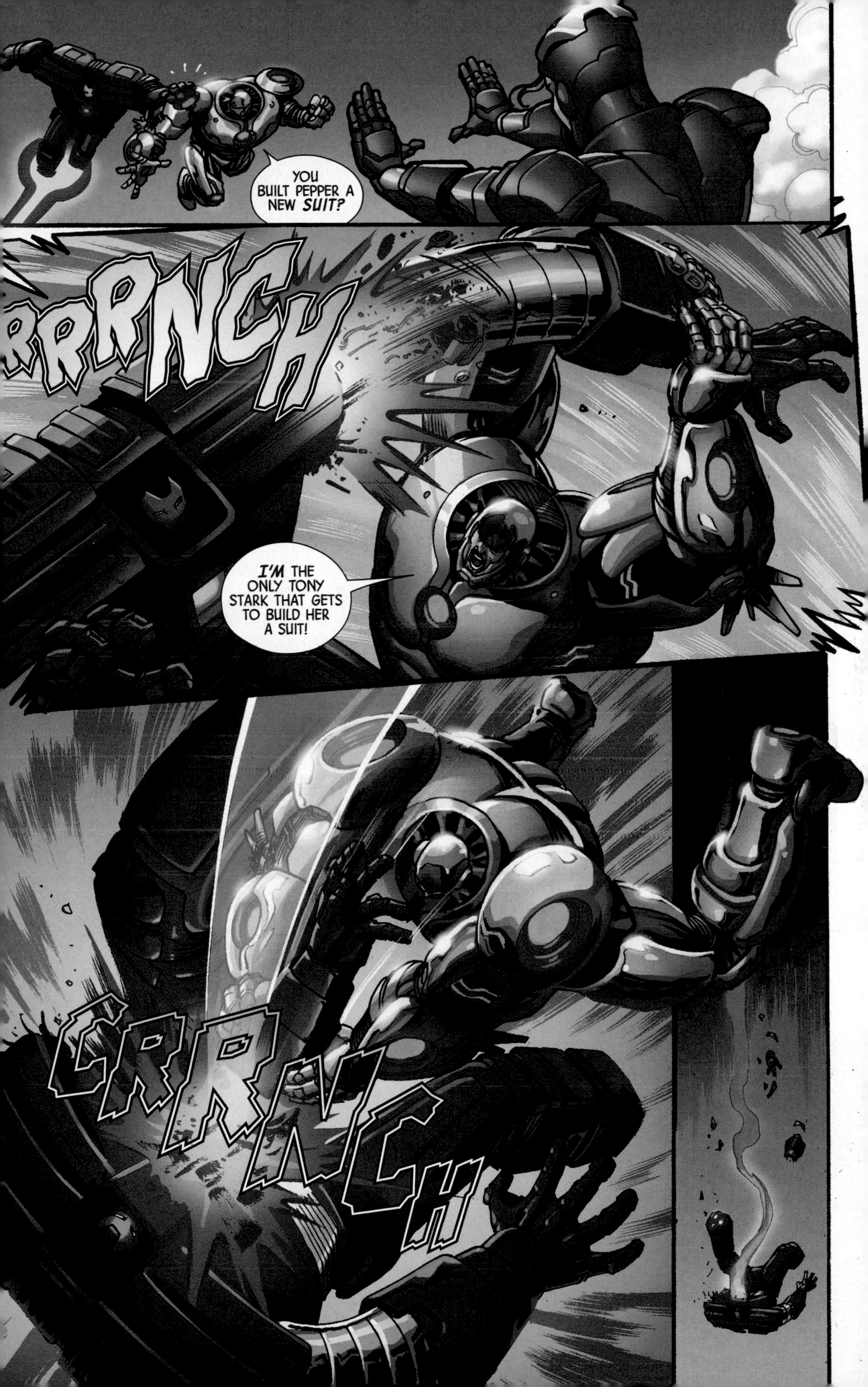
YOU BUILT PEPPER A NEW *SUIT?*
RRRNCH
*I'M* THE ONLY TONY STARK THAT GETS TO BUILD HER A SUIT!
CRRNCH

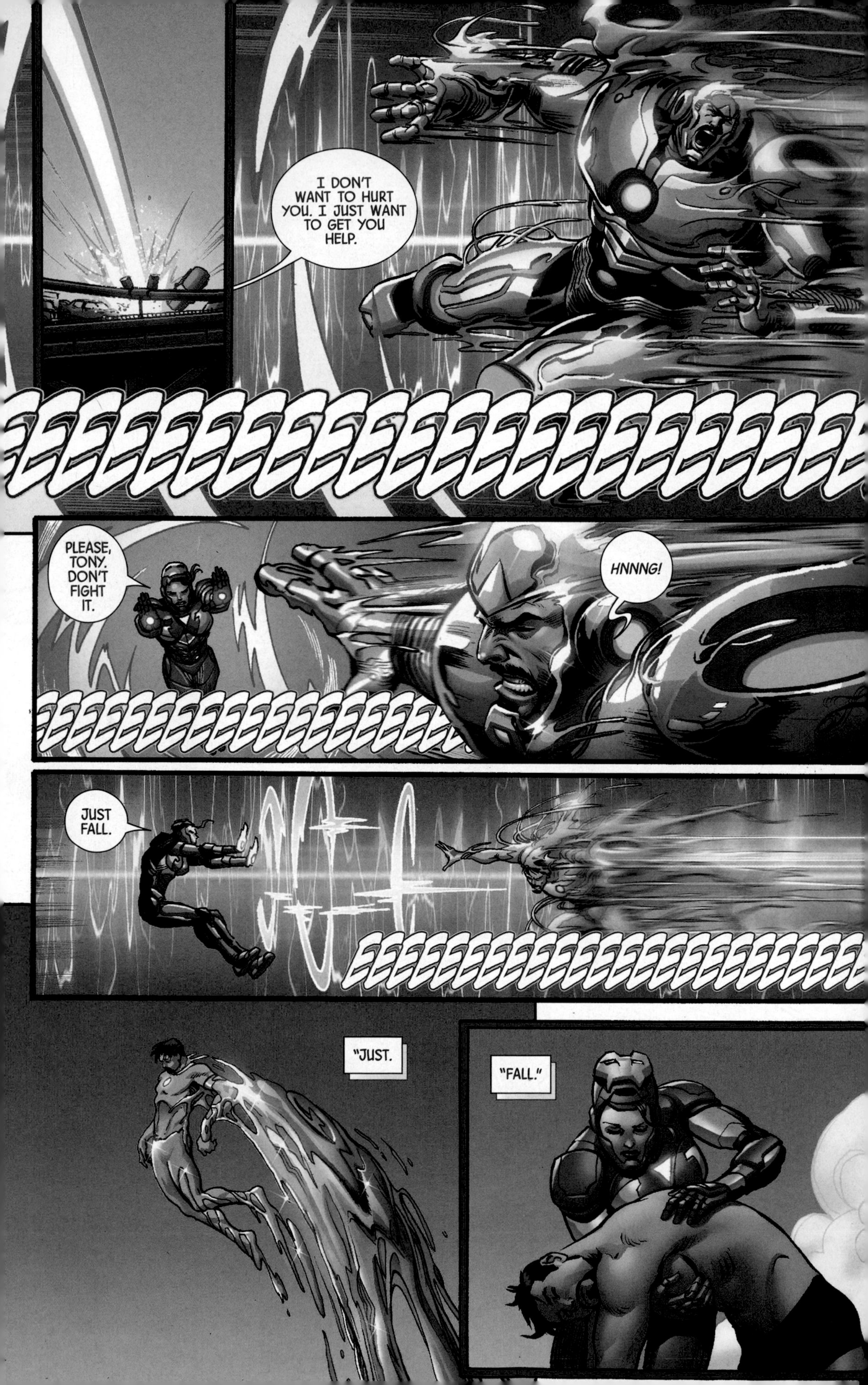

I DON'T WANT TO HURT YOU. I JUST WANT TO GET YOU HELP.
EEEEEEEEEEEEEEEEEEEEEEEEEEEE
PLEASE, TONY. DON'T FIGHT IT.
HNNNG!
EEEEEEEEEEEEEEEEEEEEEEE
JUST FALL.
EEEEEEEEEEEEEEEEEEEEEEEEEEEEEE
"JUST.
"FALL."

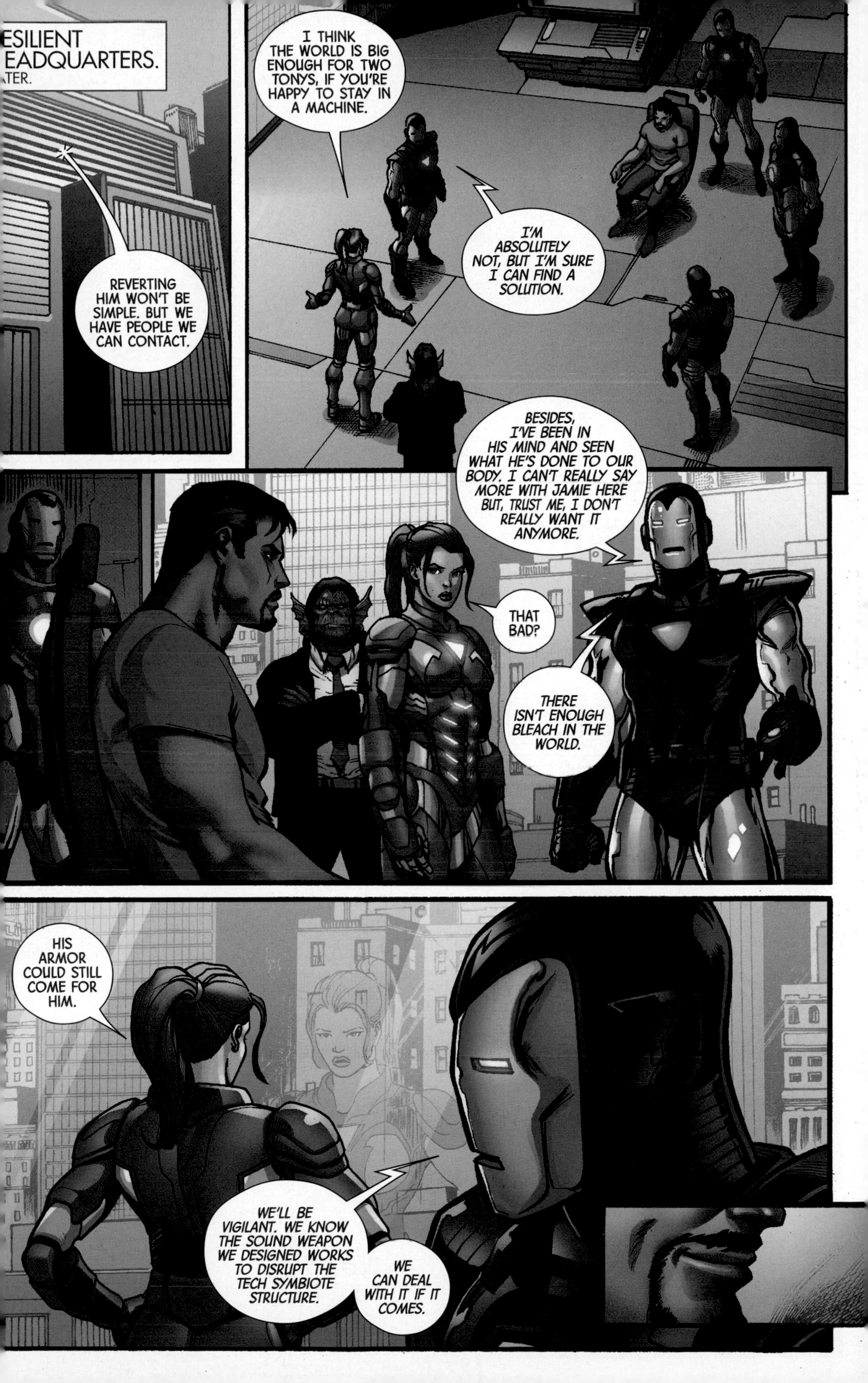
ESILIENT
EADQUARTERS.
ATER.
REVERTING HIM WON'T BE SIMPLE. BUT WE HAVE PEOPLE WE CAN CONTACT.
I THINK THE WORLD IS BIG ENOUGH FOR TWO TONYS, IF YOU'RE HAPPY TO STAY IN A MACHINE.
I'M ABSOLUTELY NOT, BUT I'M SURE I CAN FIND A SOLUTION.
BESIDES, I'VE BEEN IN HIS MIND AND SEEN WHAT HE'S DONE TO OUR BODY. I CAN'T REALLY SAY MORE WITH JAMIE HERE BUT, TRUST ME, I DON'T REALLY WANT IT ANYMORE.
THAT BAD?
THERE ISN'T ENOUGH BLEACH IN THE WORLD.
HIS ARMOR COULD STILL COME FOR HIM.
WE'LL BE VIGILANT. WE KNOW THE SOUND WEAPON WE DESIGNED WORKS TO DISRUPT THE TECH SYMBIOTE STRUCTURE.
WE CAN DEAL WITH IT IF IT COMES.

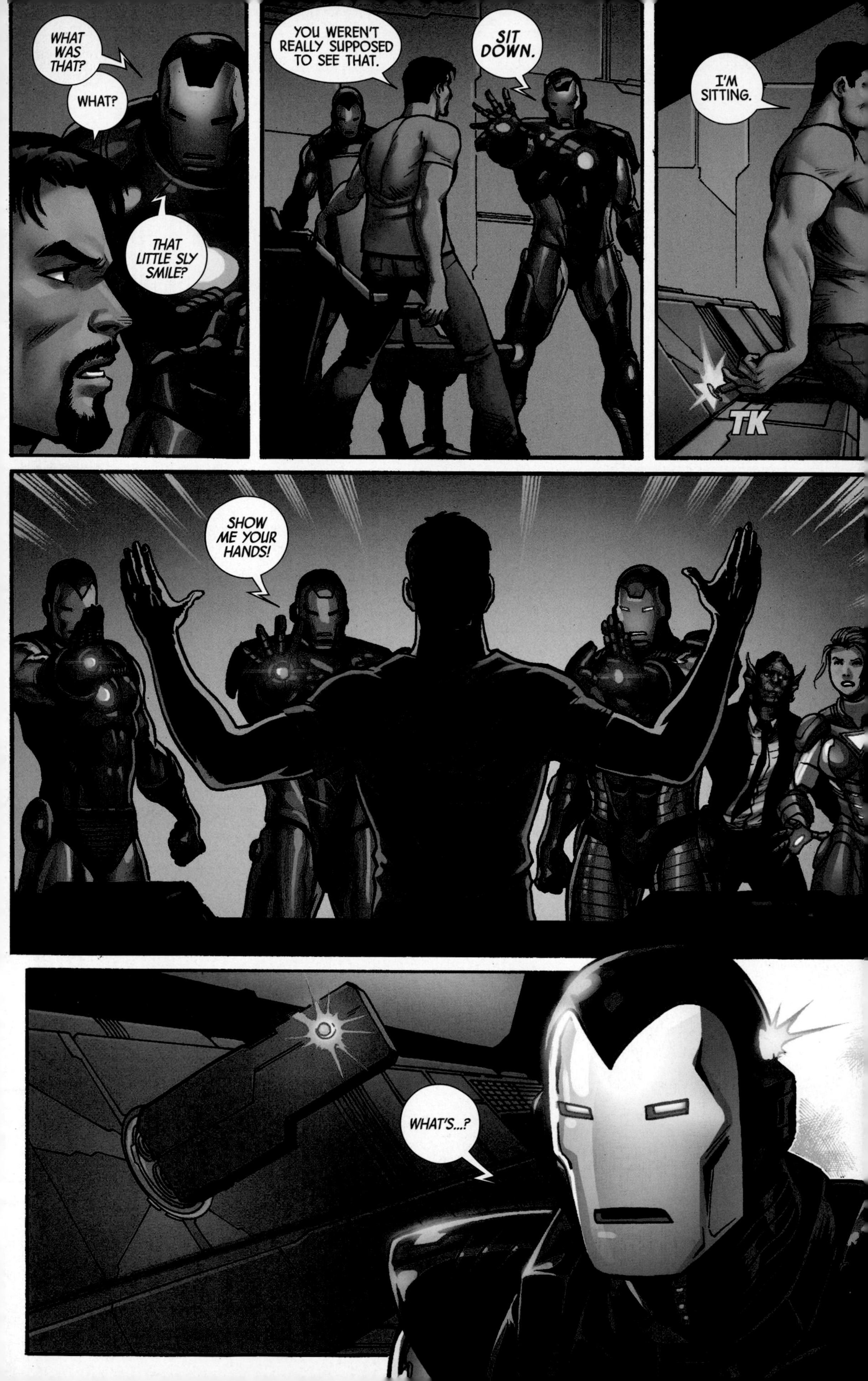
WHAT WAS THAT?
WHAT?
THAT LITTLE SLY SMILE?
YOU WEREN'T REALLY SUPPOSED TO SEE THAT.
SIT DOWN.
I'M SITTING.
TK
SHOW ME YOUR HANDS!
WHAT'S...?

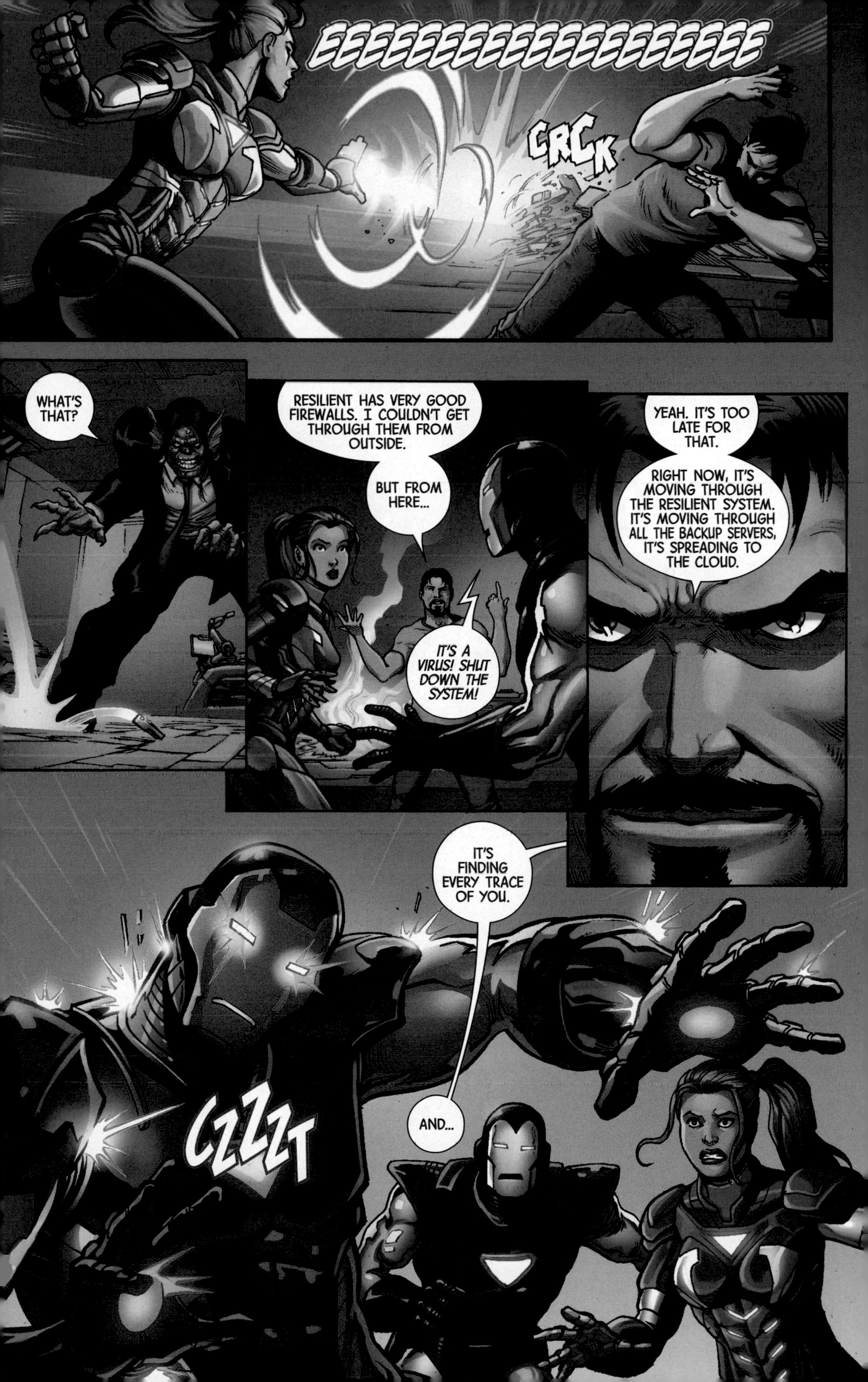
EEEEEEEEEEEEEEEEEEEEEE
CRCK
WHAT'S THAT?
RESILIENT HAS VERY GOOD FIREWALLS. I COULDN'T GET THROUGH THEM FROM OUTSIDE.
BUT FROM HERE...
IT'S A VIRUS! SHUT DOWN THE SYSTEM!
YEAH. IT'S TOO LATE FOR THAT.
RIGHT NOW, IT'S MOVING THROUGH THE RESILIENT SYSTEM. IT'S MOVING THROUGH ALL THE BACKUP SERVERS, IT'S SPREADING TO THE CLOUD.
IT'S FINDING EVERY TRACE OF YOU.
AND...
CZZZT

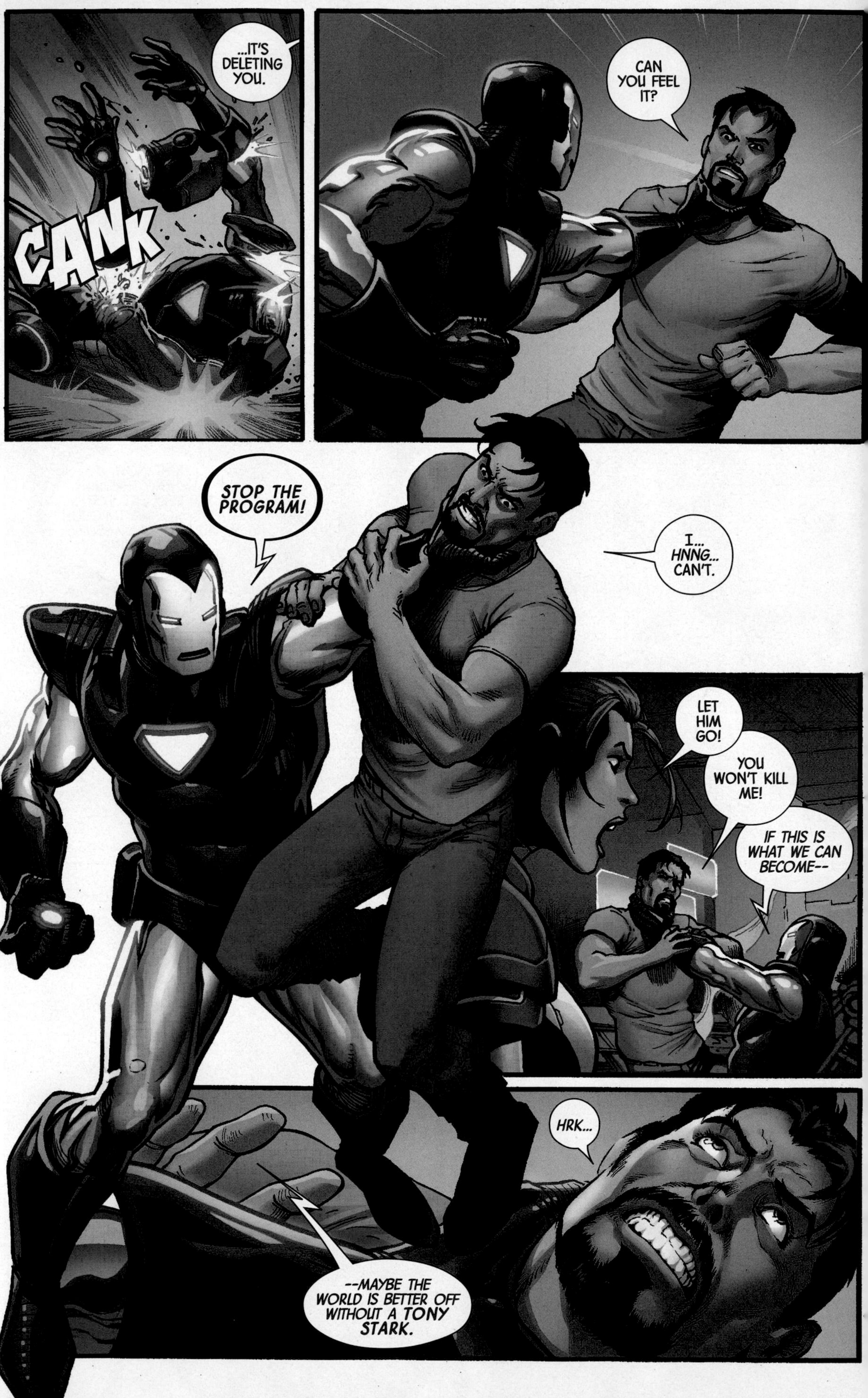
...IT'S DELETING YOU.
CANK
CAN YOU FEEL IT?
STOP THE PROGRAM!
I... HNNG... CAN'T.
LET HIM GO!
YOU WON'T KILL ME!
IF THIS IS WHAT WE CAN BECOME--
HRK...
--MAYBE THE WORLD IS BETTER OFF WITHOUT A TONY STARK.

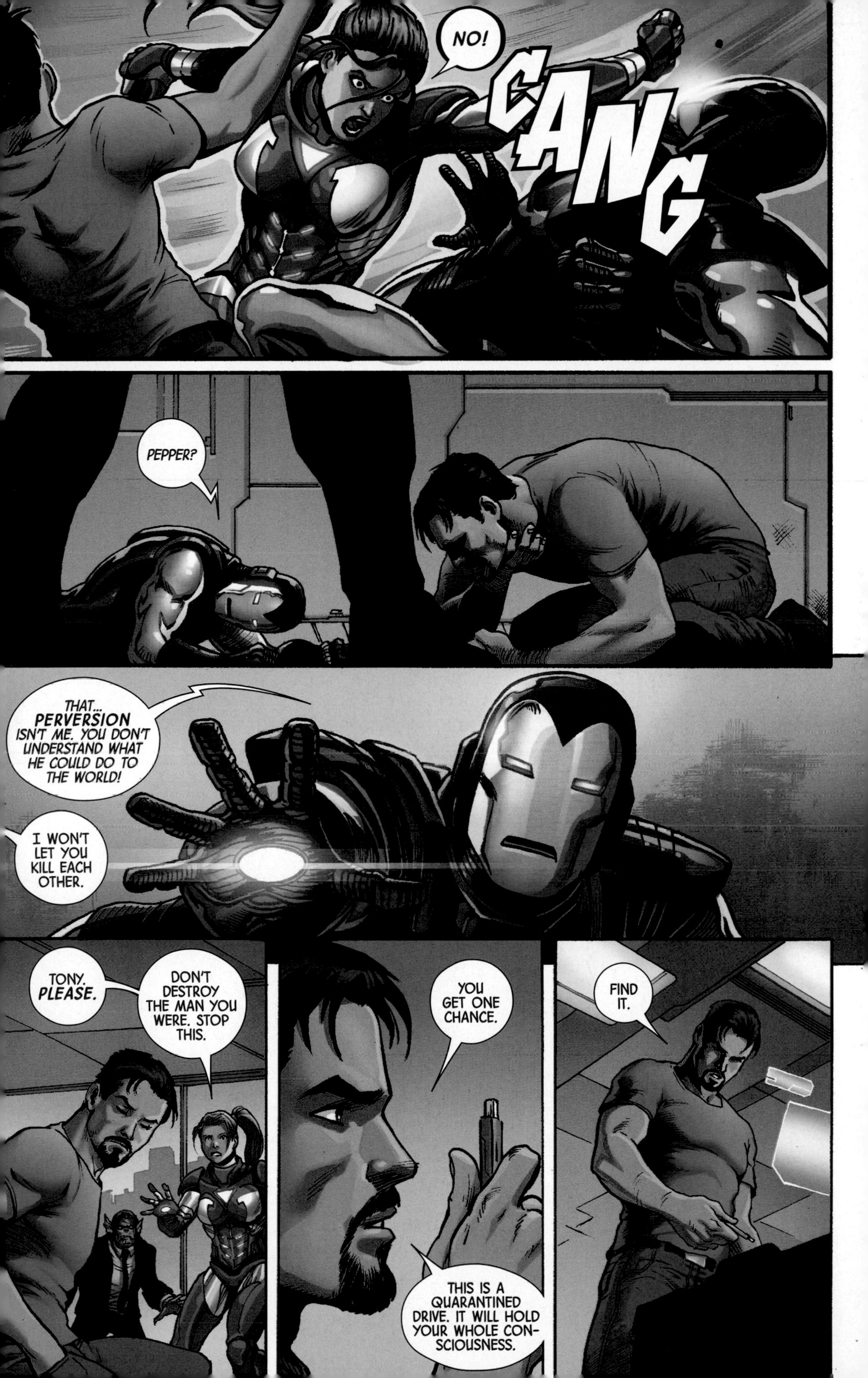
NO!
CANG
PEPPER?
THAT... PERVERSION ISN'T ME. YOU DON'T UNDERSTAND WHAT HE COULD DO TO THE WORLD!
I WON'T LET YOU KILL EACH OTHER.
TONY. PLEASE.
DON'T DESTROY THE MAN YOU WERE. STOP THIS.
YOU GET ONE CHANCE.
THIS IS A QUARANTINED DRIVE. IT WILL HOLD YOUR WHOLE CONSCIOUSNESS.
FIND IT.

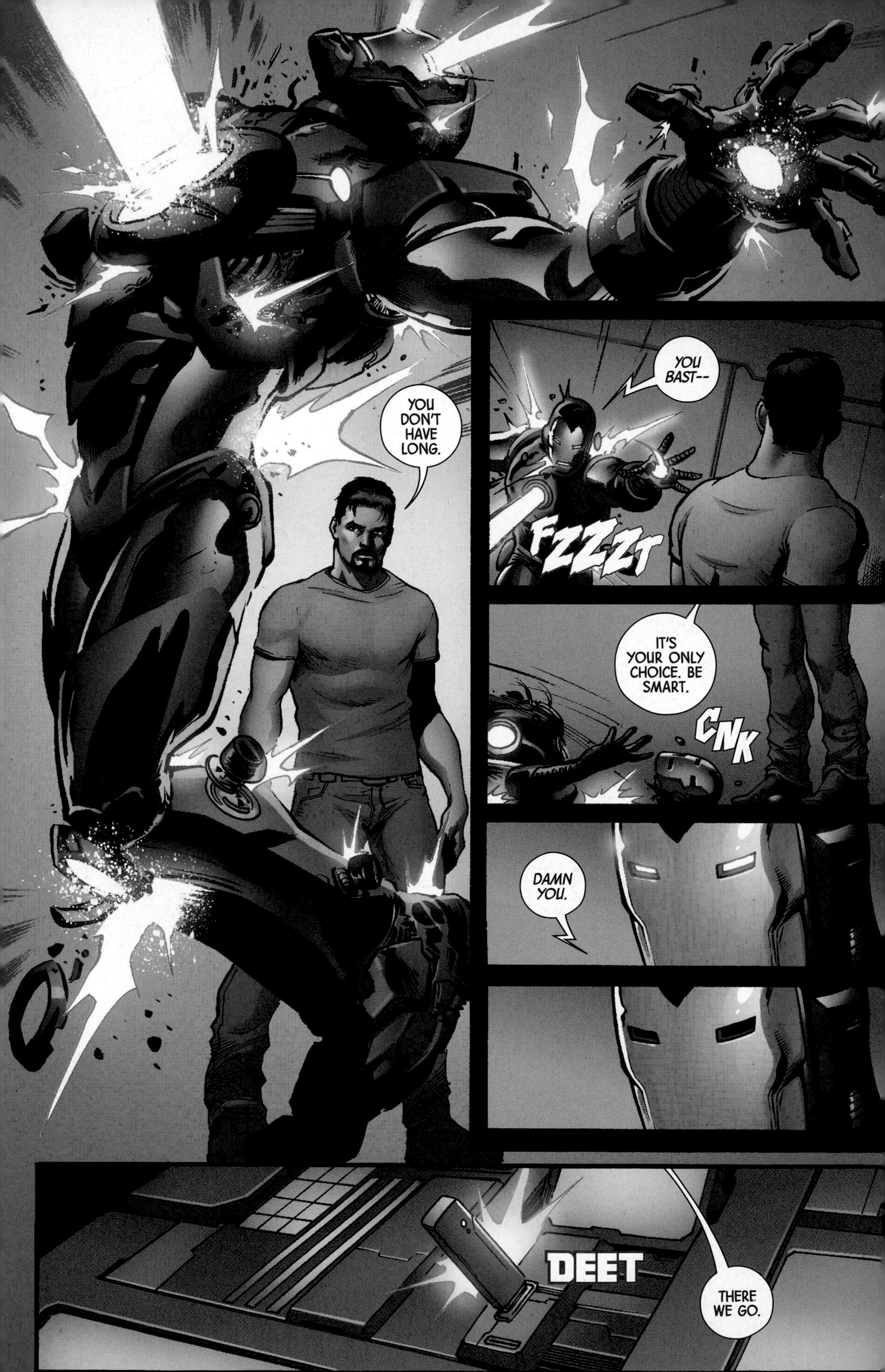
YOU DON'T HAVE LONG.
YOU BAST--
FZZZZT
IT'S YOUR ONLY CHOICE. BE SMART.
CNK
DAMN YOU.
DEET
THERE WE GO.

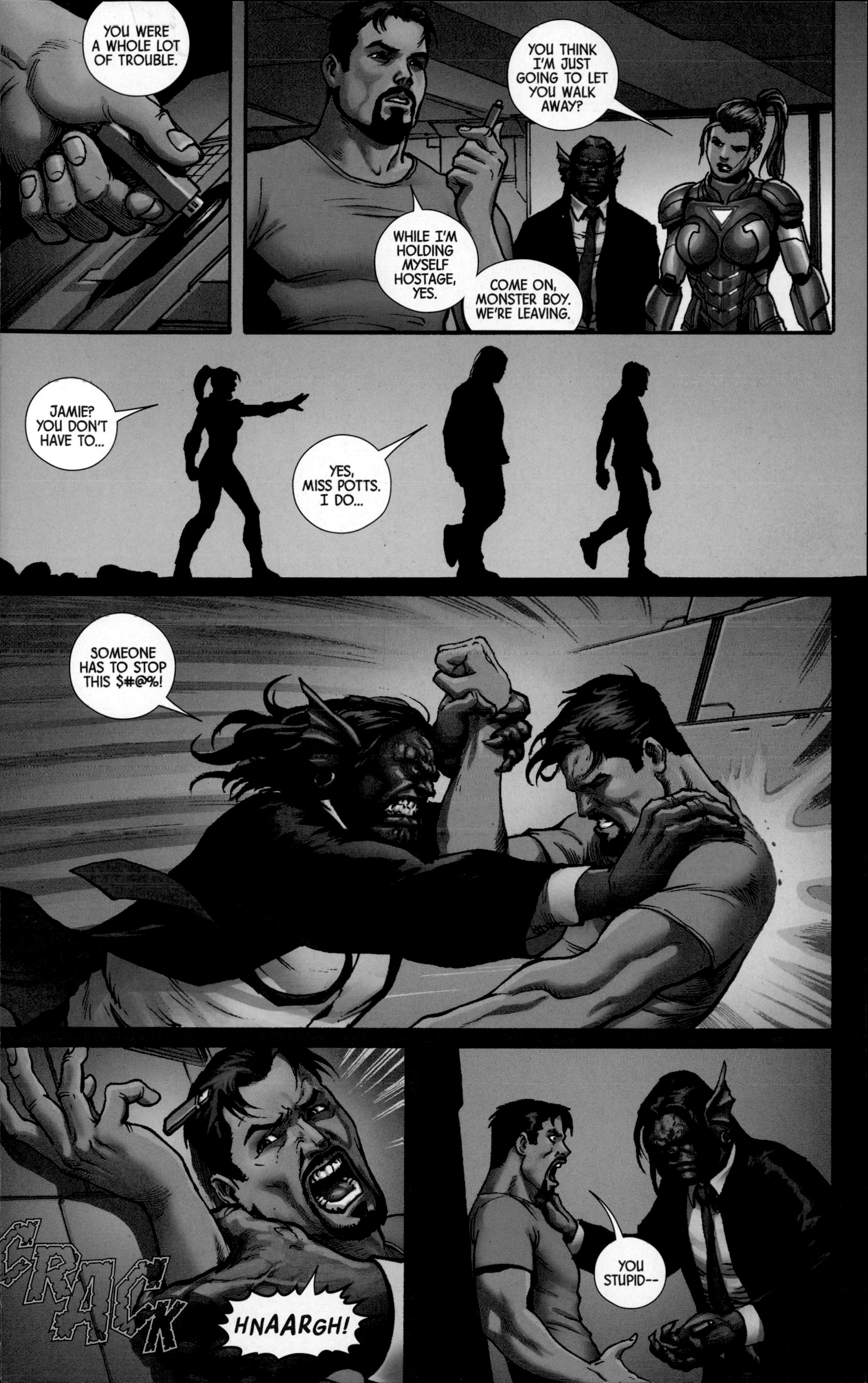
YOU WERE A WHOLE LOT OF TROUBLE.
YOU THINK I'M JUST GOING TO LET YOU WALK AWAY?
WHILE I'M HOLDING MYSELF HOSTAGE, YES.
COME ON, MONSTER BOY. WE'RE LEAVING.
JAMIE? YOU DON'T HAVE TO...
YES, MISS POTTS. I DO...
SOMEONE HAS TO STOP THIS $#@%!
CRACK
HNAARGH!
YOU STUPID--

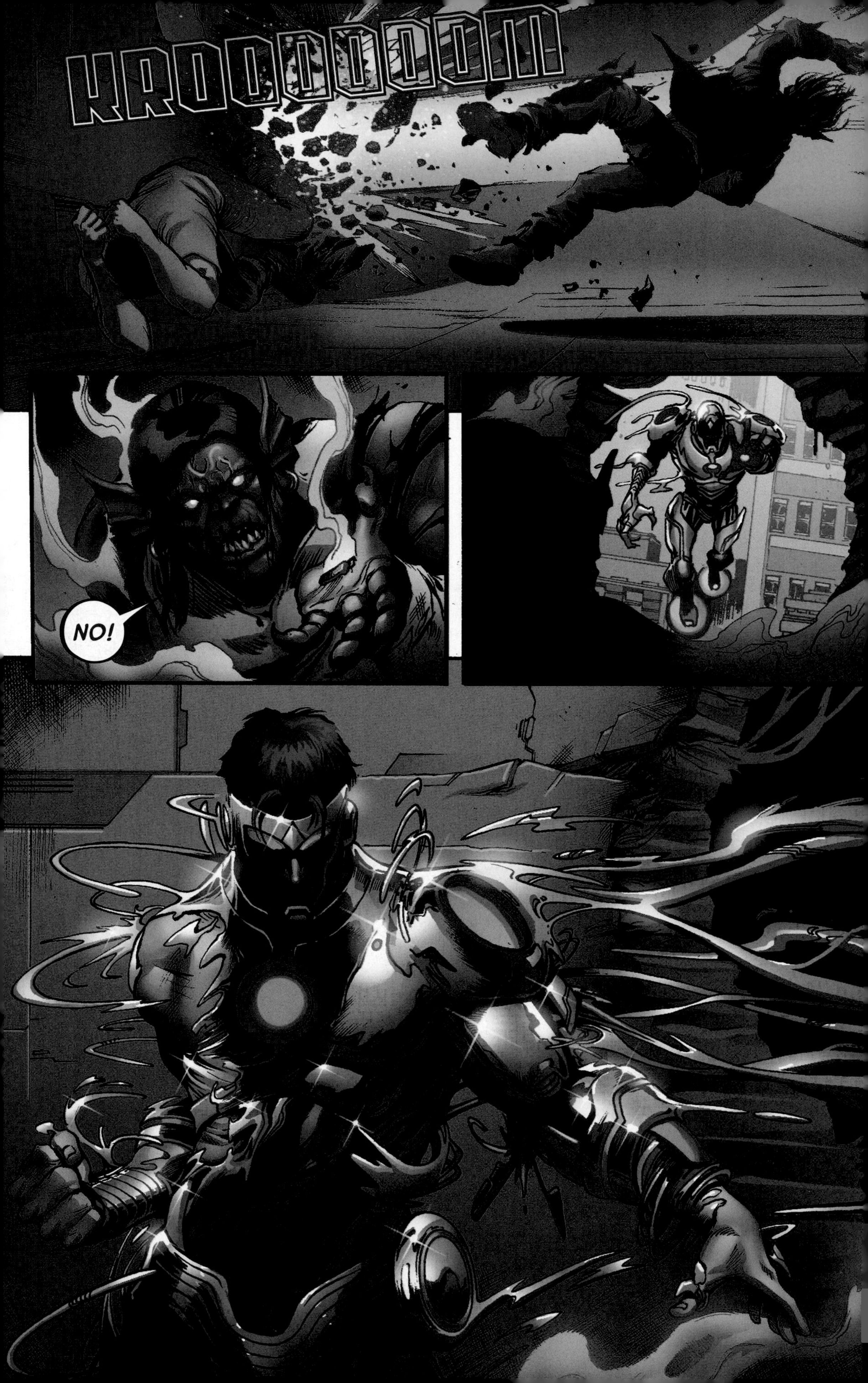
KROOOOOOM
NO!

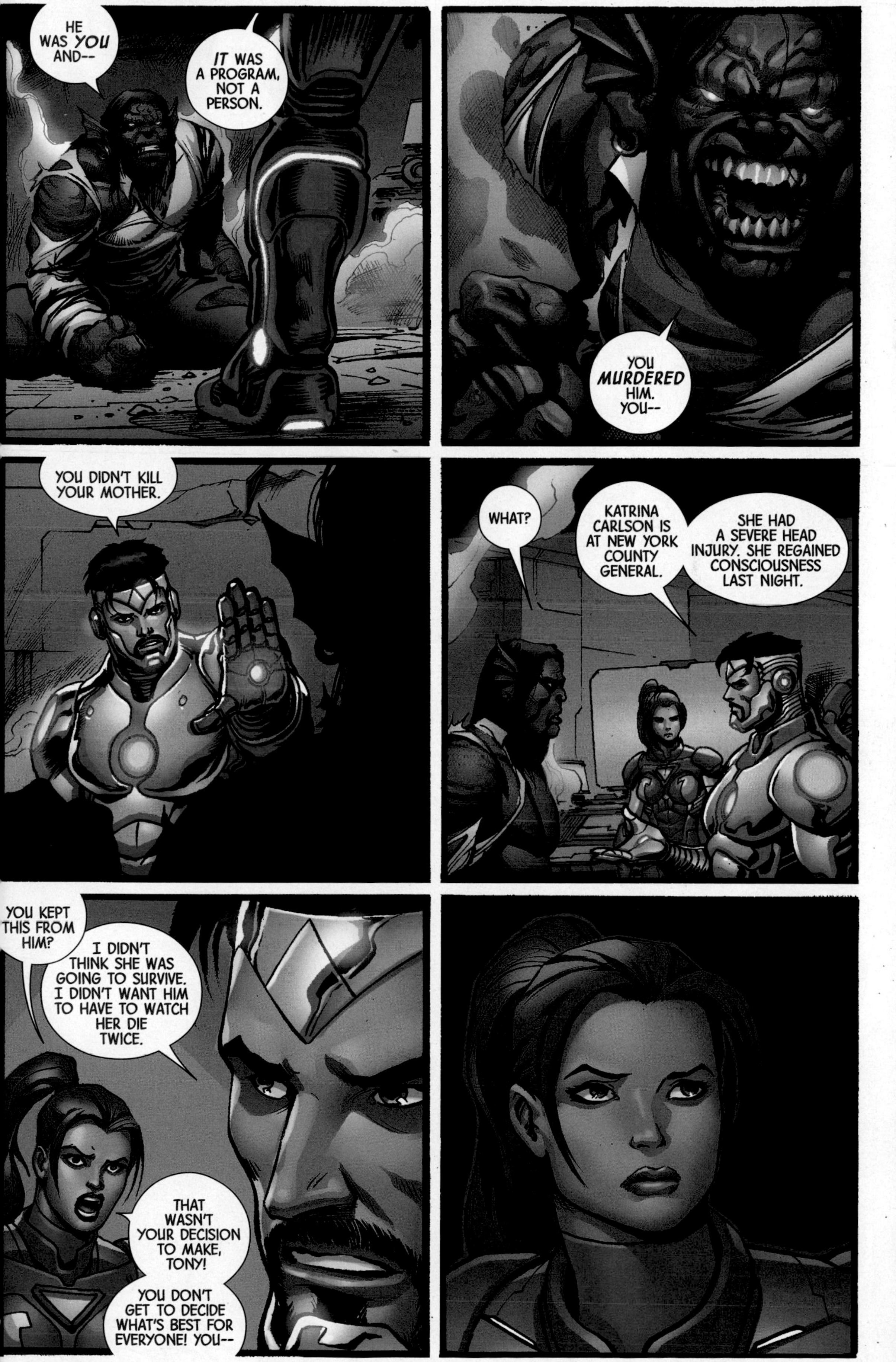
HE WAS YOU AND--
IT WAS A PROGRAM, NOT A PERSON.
YOU MURDERED HIM. YOU--
YOU DIDN'T KILL YOUR MOTHER.
WHAT?
KATRINA CARLSON IS AT NEW YORK COUNTY GENERAL.
SHE HAD A SEVERE HEAD INJURY. SHE REGAINED CONSCIOUSNESS LAST NIGHT.
YOU KEPT THIS FROM HIM?
I DIDN'T THINK SHE WAS GOING TO SURVIVE. I DIDN'T WANT HIM TO HAVE TO WATCH HER DIE TWICE.
THAT WASN'T YOUR DECISION TO MAKE, TONY!
YOU DON'T GET TO DECIDE WHAT'S BEST FOR EVERYONE! YOU--

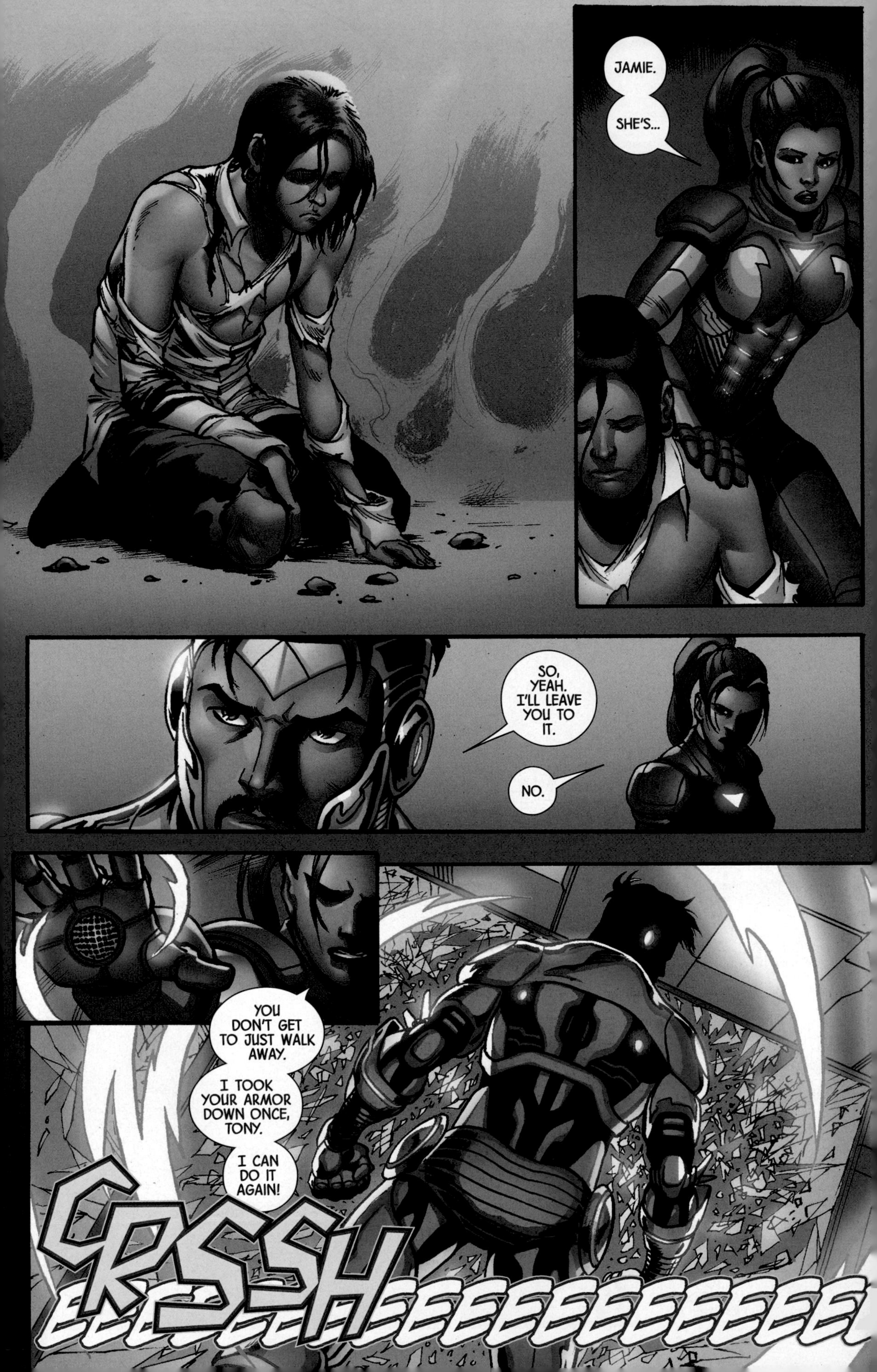
JAMIE.
SHE'S...
SO, YEAH. I'LL LEAVE YOU TO IT.
NO.
YOU DON'T GET TO JUST WALK AWAY.
I TOOK YOUR ARMOR DOWN ONCE, TONY.
I CAN DO IT AGAIN!
CRSSHEEEEEEEEEEEEEEEEEEEE

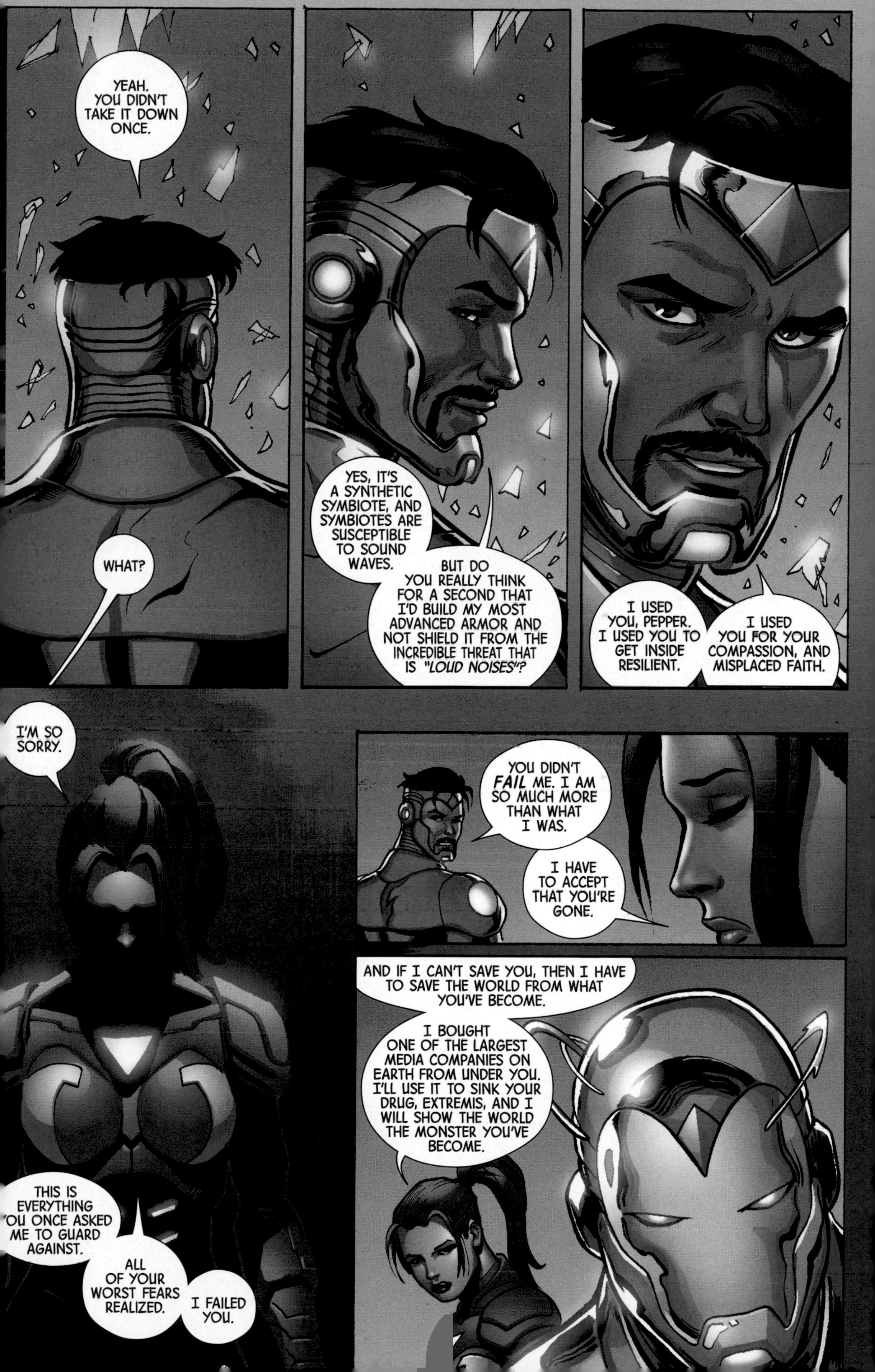
YEAH. YOU DIDN'T TAKE IT DOWN ONCE.
WHAT?
YES, IT'S A SYNTHETIC SYMBIOTE, AND SYMBIOTES ARE SUSCEPTIBLE TO SOUND WAVES.
BUT DO YOU REALLY THINK FOR A SECOND THAT I'D BUILD MY MOST ADVANCED ARMOR AND NOT SHIELD IT FROM THE INCREDIBLE THREAT THAT IS "LOUD NOISES"?
I USED YOU, PEPPER. I USED YOU TO GET INSIDE RESILIENT.
I USED YOU FOR YOUR COMPASSION, AND MISPLACED FAITH.
I'M SO SORRY.
THIS IS EVERYTHING YOU ONCE ASKED ME TO GUARD AGAINST.
ALL OF YOUR WORST FEARS REALIZED.
I FAILED YOU.
YOU DIDN'T FAIL ME. I AM SO MUCH MORE THAN WHAT I WAS.
I HAVE TO ACCEPT THAT YOU'RE GONE.
AND IF I CAN'T SAVE YOU, THEN I HAVE TO SAVE THE WORLD FROM WHAT YOU'VE BECOME.
I BOUGHT ONE OF THE LARGEST MEDIA COMPANIES ON EARTH FROM UNDER YOU. I'LL USE IT TO SINK YOUR DRUG, EXTREMIS, AND I WILL SHOW THE WORLD THE MONSTER YOU'VE BECOME.

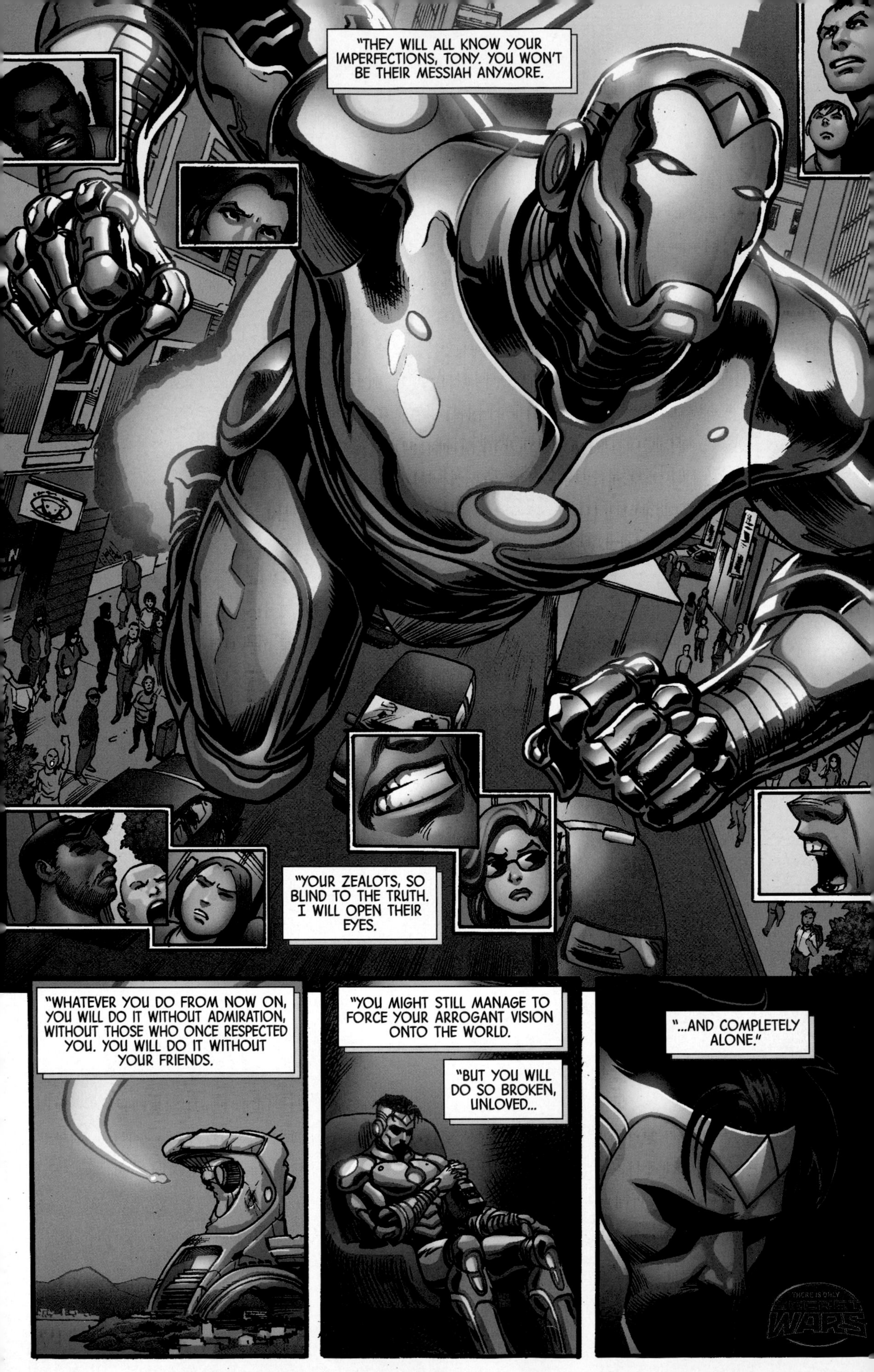
"THEY WILL ALL KNOW YOUR IMPERFECTIONS, TONY. YOU WON'T BE THEIR MESSIAH ANYMORE.
"YOUR ZEALOTS, SO BLIND TO THE TRUTH. I WILL OPEN THEIR EYES.
"WHATEVER YOU DO FROM NOW ON, YOU WILL DO IT WITHOUT ADMIRATION, WITHOUT THOSE WHO ONCE RESPECTED YOU. YOU WILL DO IT WITHOUT YOUR FRIENDS.
"YOU MIGHT STILL MANAGE TO FORCE YOUR ARROGANT VISION ONTO THE WORLD.
"BUT YOU WILL DO SO BROKEN, UNLOVED...
"...AND COMPLETELY ALONE."

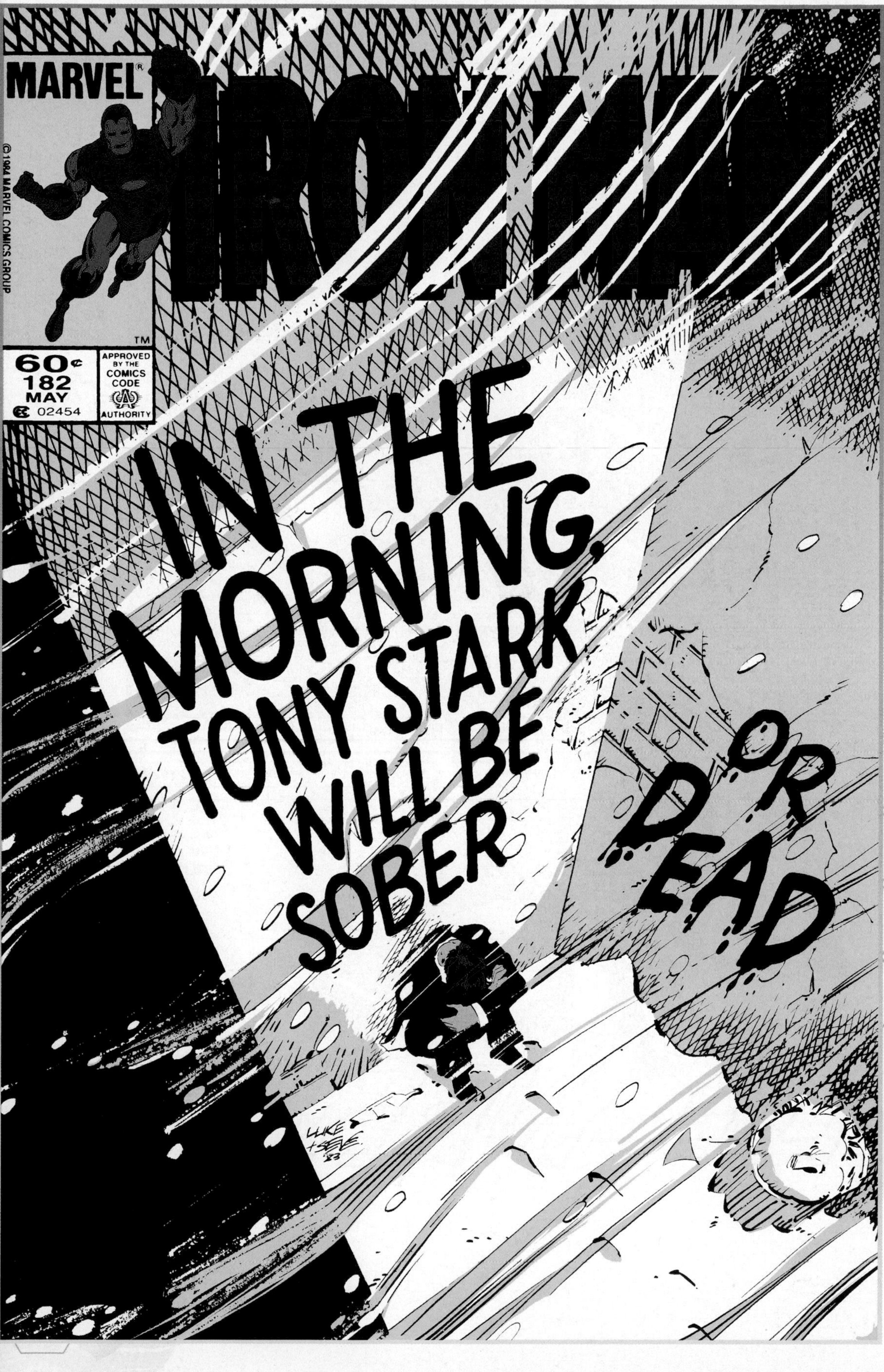
MARVEL
IRON MAN
© 1984 MARVEL COMICS GROUP
60¢
182
MAY
02454
APPROVED BY THE COMICS CODE AUTHORITY
IN THE MORNING, TONY STARK WILL BE SOBER
OR DEAD

Stan Lee PRESENTS: THE ALL NEW IRON MAN®

DENNY O'NEIL WRITER
LUKE McDONNELL PENCILER
STEVE MITCHELL INKER
RICK PARKER LETTERER
BOB SHAREN COLORIST
MARK GRUENWALD EDITOR
JIM SHOOTER EDITOR IN CHIEF

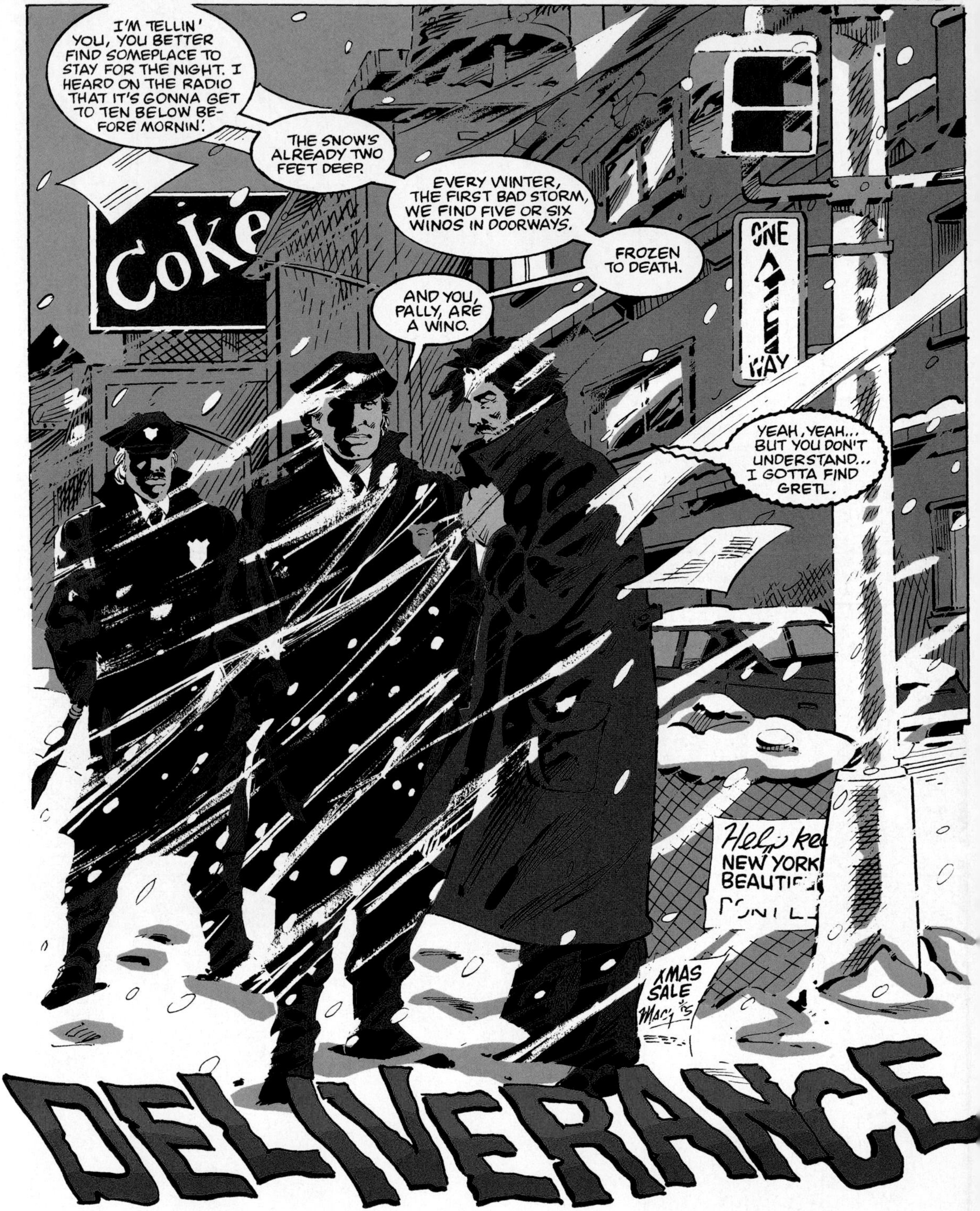

I'M TELLIN' YOU, YOU BETTER FIND SOMEPLACE TO STAY FOR THE NIGHT. I HEARD ON THE RADIO THAT IT'S GONNA GET TO TEN BELOW BEFORE MORNIN'.
THE SNOW'S ALREADY TWO FEET DEEP.
EVERY WINTER, THE FIRST BAD STORM, WE FIND FIVE OR SIX WINOS IN DOORWAYS.
FROZEN TO DEATH.
AND YOU, PALLY, ARE A WINO.
YEAH, YEAH... BUT YOU DON'T UNDERSTAND... I GOTTA FIND GRETL.
Coke
ONE WAY
NEW YORK
XMAS SALE
DELIVERANCE

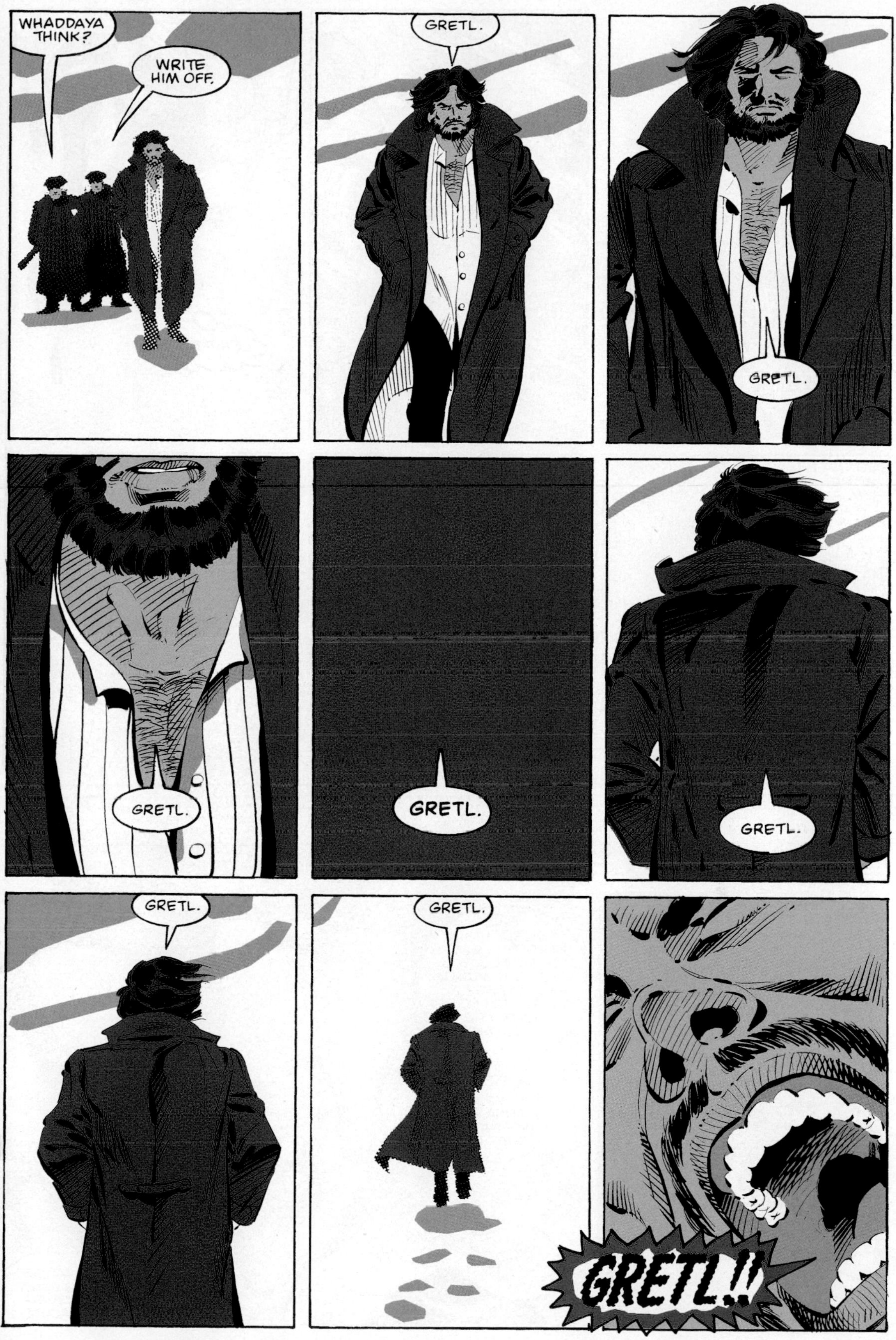
WHADDAYA THINK?
WRITE HIM OFF.
GRETL.
GRETL.
GRETL.
GRETL.
GRETL.
GRETL.
GRETL.
GRETL!!

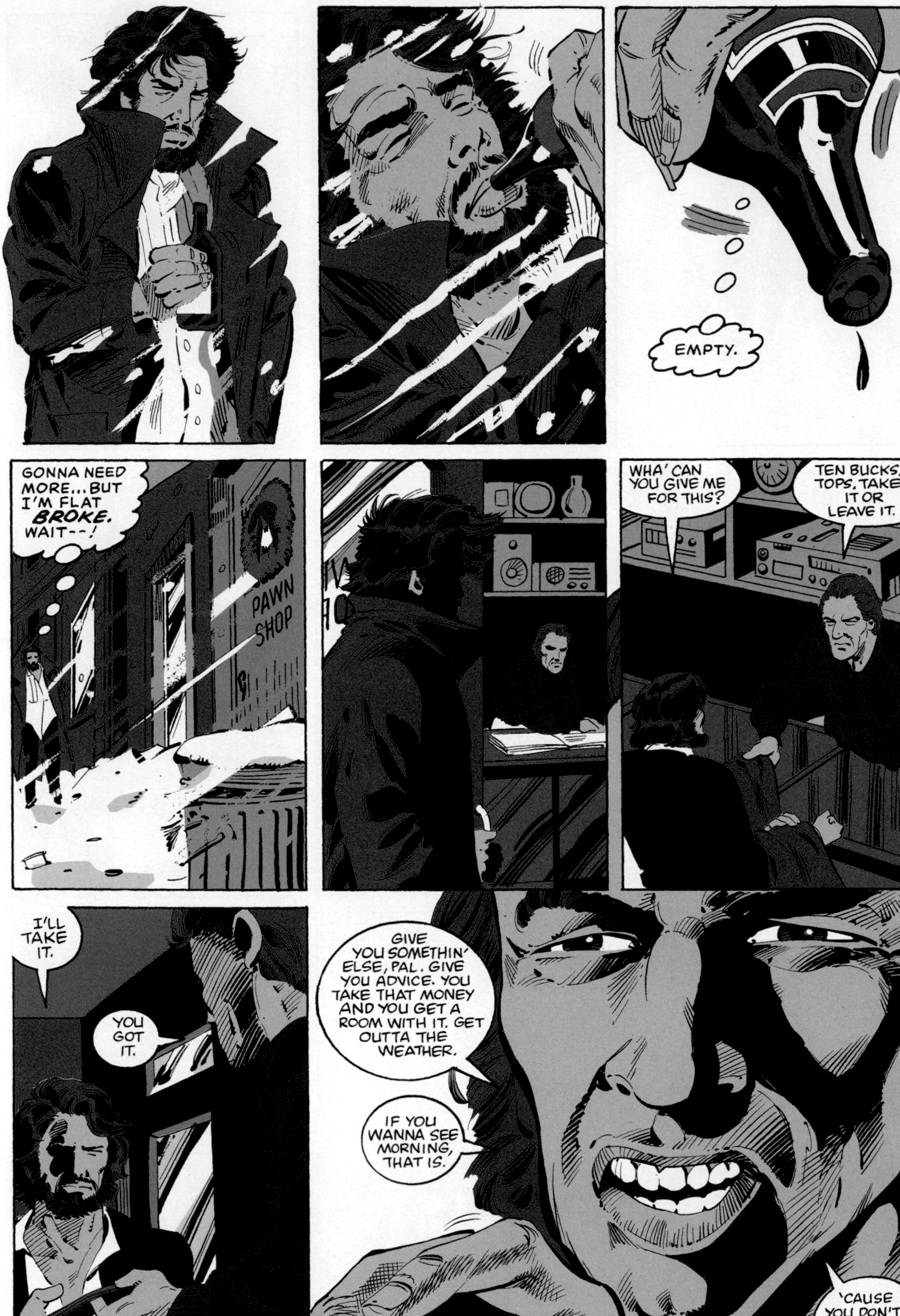
EMPTY.
GONNA NEED MORE... BUT I'M FLAT BROKE. WAIT--!
PAWN SHOP
WHA' CAN YOU GIVE ME FOR THIS?
TEN BUCKS. TOPS. TAKE IT OR LEAVE IT.
I'LL TAKE IT.
YOU GOT IT.
GIVE YOU SOMETHIN' ELSE, PAL. GIVE YOU ADVICE. YOU TAKE THAT MONEY AND YOU GET A ROOM WITH IT. GET OUTTA THE WEATHER.
IF YOU WANNA SEE MORNING, THAT IS.
'CAUSE YOU DON'T LOOK SO HEALTHY.

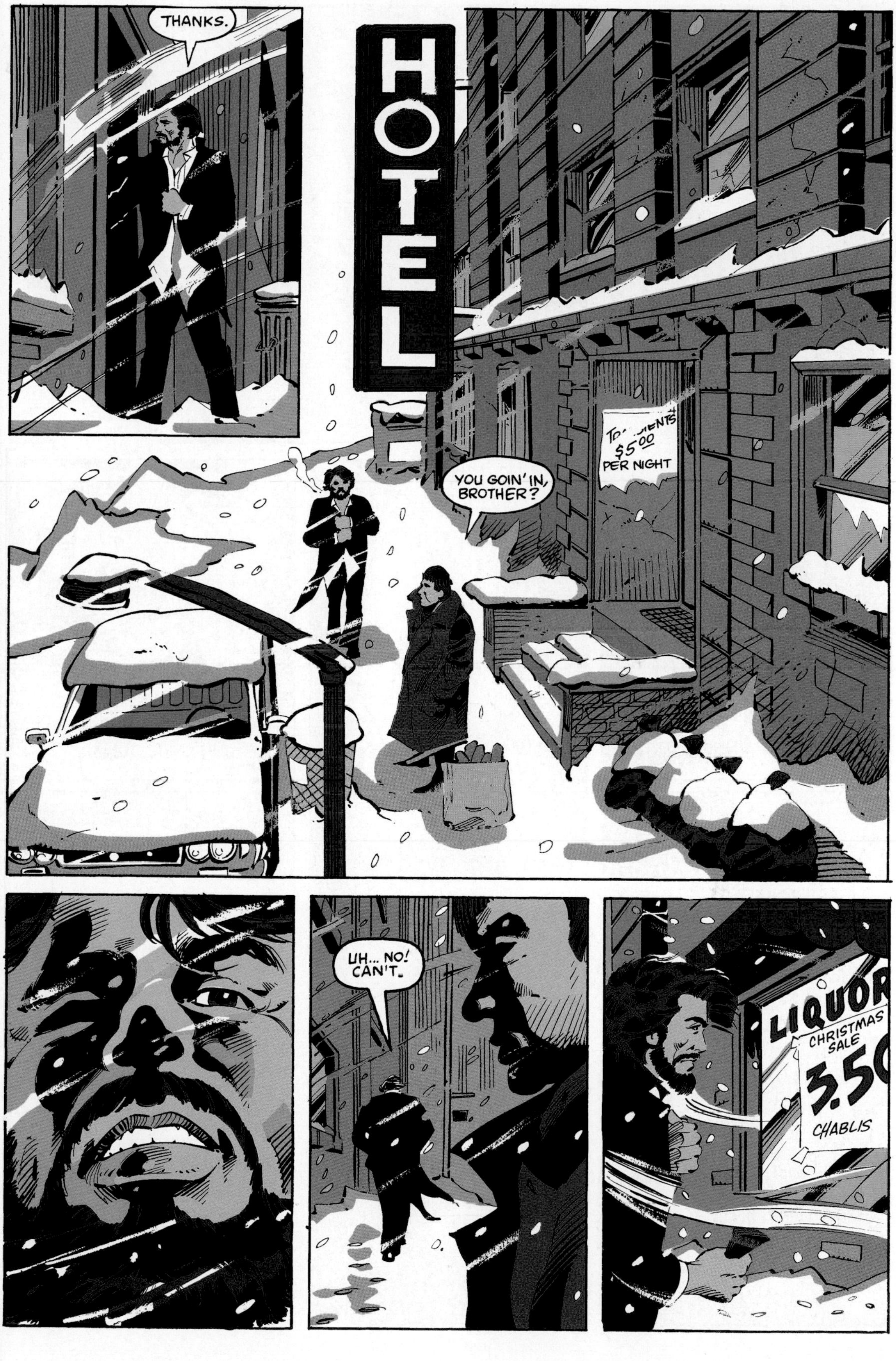
THANKS.
HOTEL
$5.00
PER NIGHT
YOU GOIN' IN, BROTHER?
UH... NO! CAN'T.
LIQUOR
CHRISTMAS SALE
3.5
CHABLIS

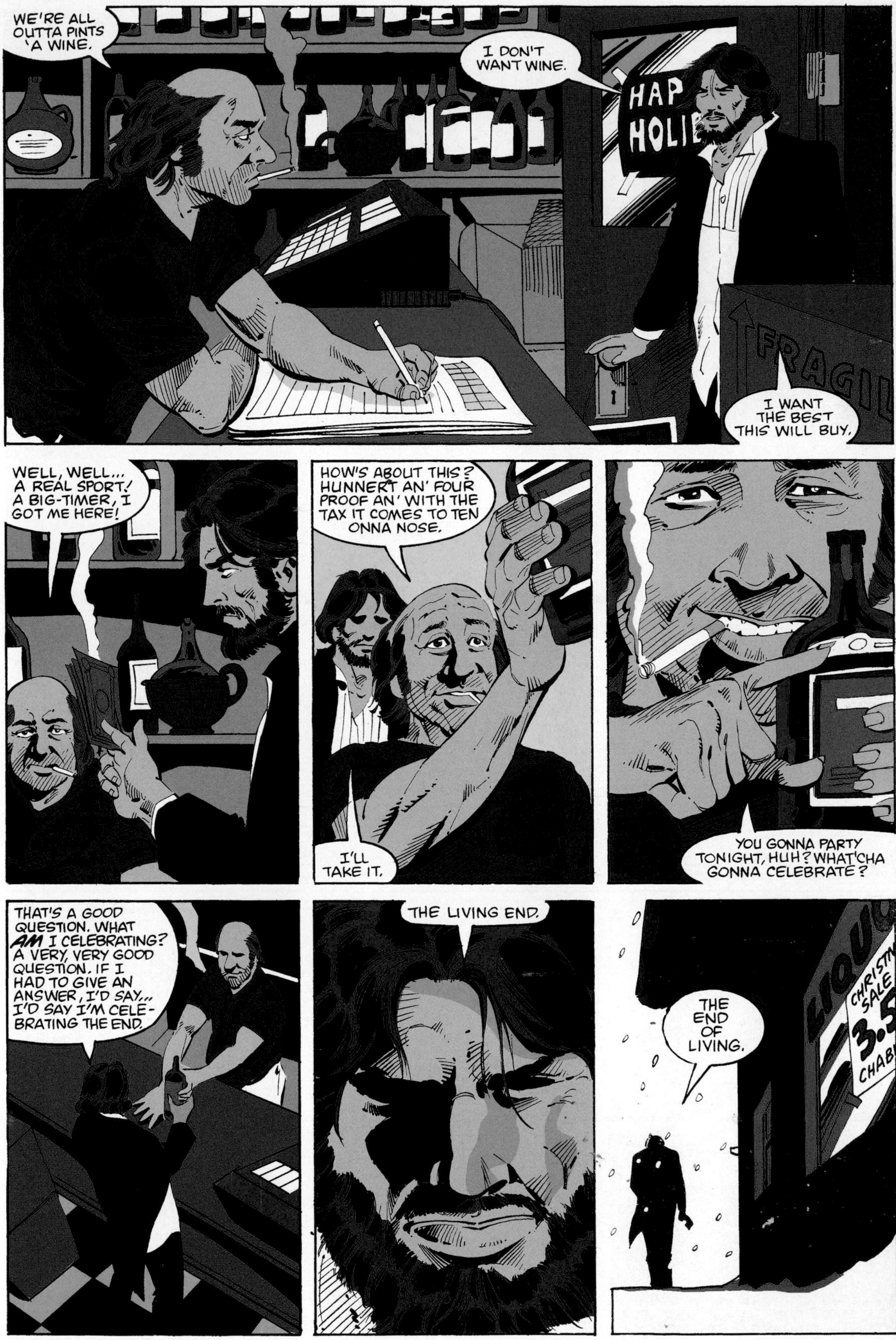
WE'RE ALL OUTTA PINTS 'A WINE.
I DON'T WANT WINE.
HAP HOLI
I WANT THE BEST THIS WILL BUY.
FRAGIL
WELL, WELL... A REAL SPORT! A BIG-TIMER, I GOT ME HERE!
HOW'S ABOUT THIS? HUNNERT AN' FOUR PROOF AN' WITH THE TAX IT COMES TO TEN ONNA NOSE.
I'LL TAKE IT.
YOU GONNA PARTY TONIGHT, HUH? WHAT'CHA GONNA CELEBRATE?
THAT'S A GOOD QUESTION. WHAT AM I CELEBRATING? A VERY, VERY GOOD QUESTION. IF I HAD TO GIVE AN ANSWER, I'D SAY... I'D SAY I'M CELEBRATING THE END.
THE LIVING END.
THE END OF LIVING.
LIQUO
CHRISTM SALE
3.5
CHAB

FEELIN' NO PAIN, HUH, PALLY?

FEELING NO PAIN...

HIS LAUGHTER IS SOFTER THAN THE SNOWFLAKES--

--AND THE WORDS THAT FOLLOW ARE SOFTER STILL...

HAD IT ALL, DIDN'T I? MILLIONAIRE, INDUSTRIALIST PLAYBOY, INVENTOR--

--HERO, EVEN, I CAN'T FORGET HERO, CAN I? ADMIRED BY MEN, LOVED BY WOMEN AND NONE OF IT MEANT AS MUCH TO ME--

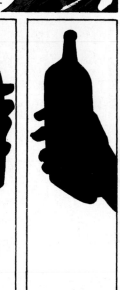

--AS THIS!

BUT I DIDN'T REALIZE THAT UNTIL IT WAS TOO LATE. SO I'M STUMBLING AROUND IN A STORM AS LOST AS ANY MAN EVER WAS--

--WITH NO ONE TO SEARCH FOR ME... NO HOPE THAT I CAN BE FOUND.

I'M COLD.

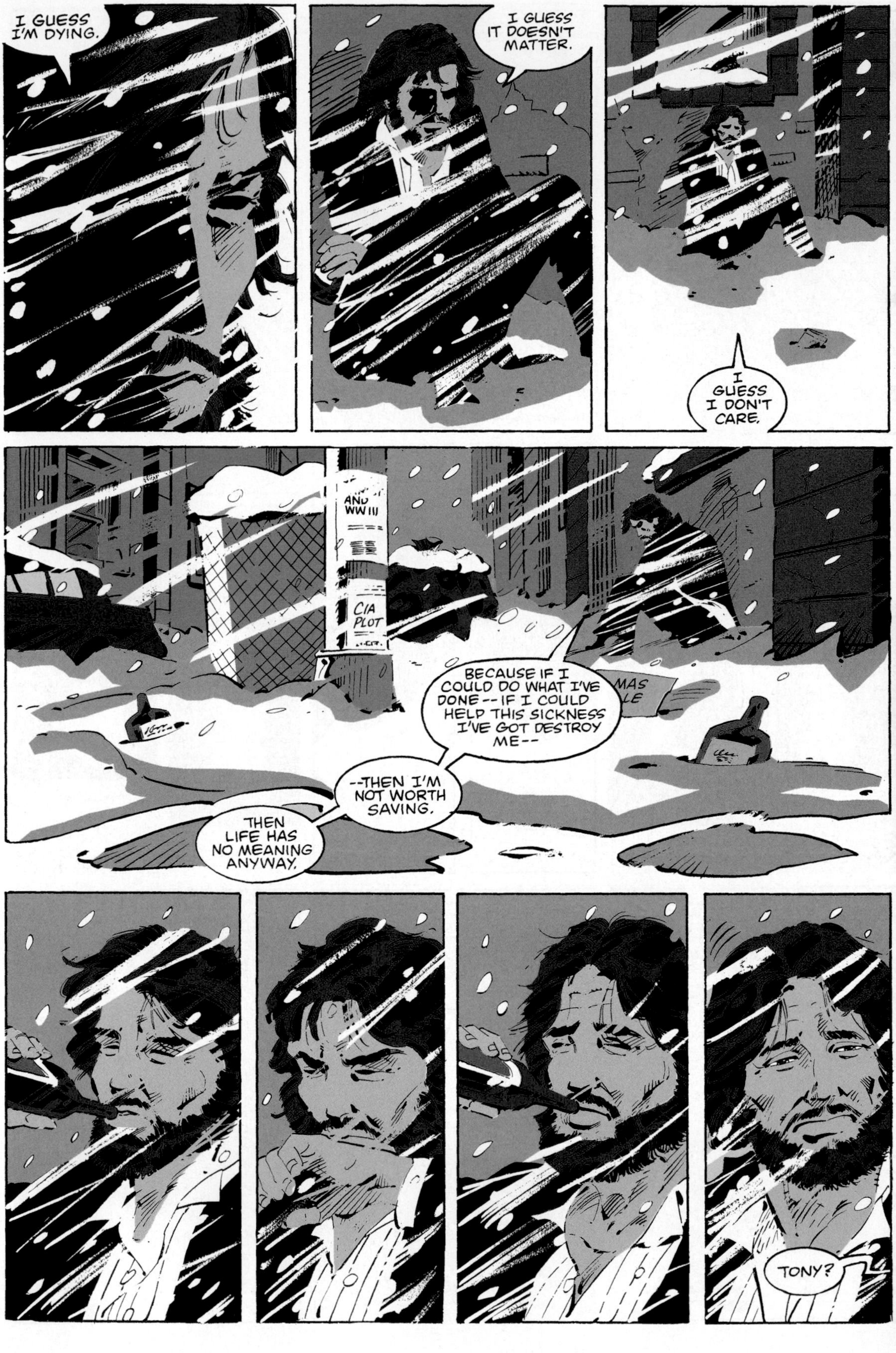
I GUESS I'M DYING.
I GUESS IT DOESN'T MATTER.
I GUESS I DON'T CARE.
AND WW III
CIA PLOT
BECAUSE IF I COULD DO WHAT I'VE DONE--IF I COULD HELP THIS SICKNESS I'VE GOT DESTROY ME--
--THEN I'M NOT WORTH SAVING.
THEN LIFE HAS NO MEANING ANYWAY.
TONY?

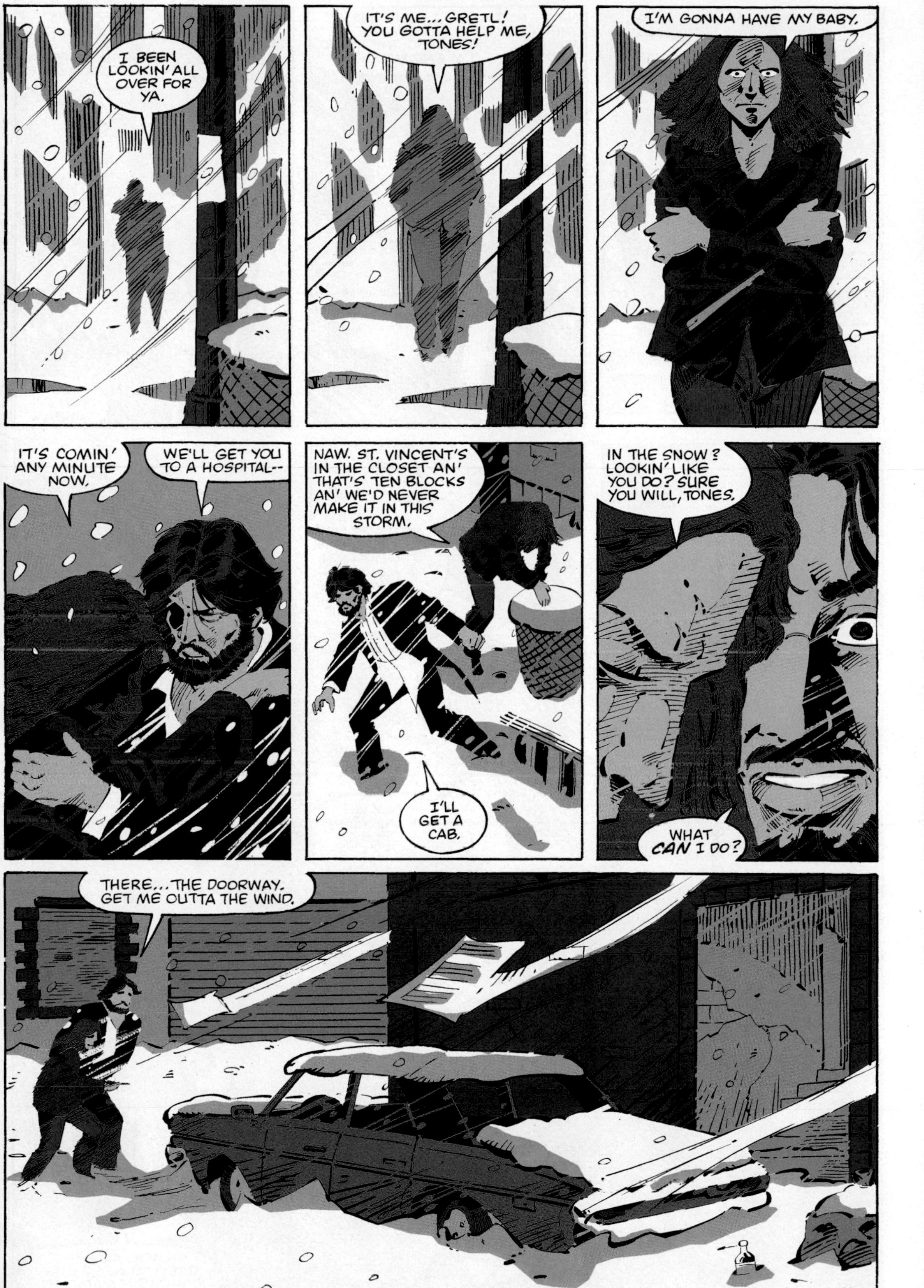
I BEEN LOOKIN' ALL OVER FOR YA.
IT'S ME... GRETL! YOU GOTTA HELP ME, TONES!
I'M GONNA HAVE MY BABY.
IT'S COMIN' ANY MINUTE NOW.
WE'LL GET YOU TO A HOSPITAL--
NAW. ST. VINCENT'S IN THE CLOSET AN' THAT'S TEN BLOCKS AN' WE'D NEVER MAKE IT IN THIS STORM.
I'LL GET A CAB.
IN THE SNOW? LOOKIN' LIKE YOU DO? SURE YOU WILL, TONES.
WHAT CAN I DO?
THERE... THE DOORWAY. GET ME OUTTA THE WIND.

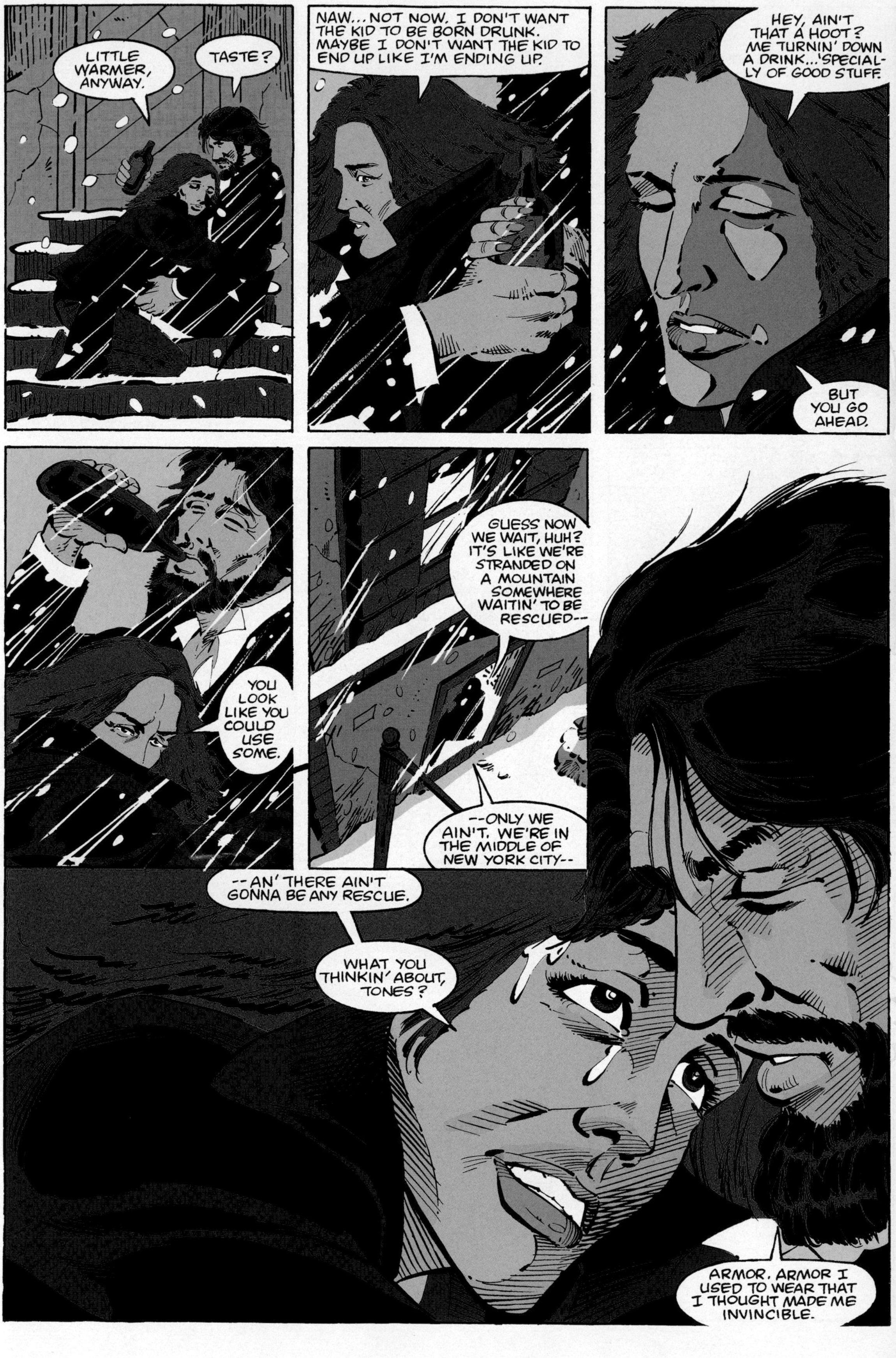
LITTLE WARMER, ANYWAY.
TASTE?
NAW... NOT NOW. I DON'T WANT THE KID TO BE BORN DRUNK. MAYBE I DON'T WANT THE KID TO END UP LIKE I'M ENDING UP.
HEY, AIN'T THAT A HOOT? ME TURNIN' DOWN A DRINK...'SPECIALLY OF GOOD STUFF.
BUT YOU GO AHEAD.
YOU LOOK LIKE YOU COULD USE SOME.
GUESS NOW WE WAIT, HUH? IT'S LIKE WE'RE STRANDED ON A MOUNTAIN SOMEWHERE WAITIN' TO BE RESCUED--
--ONLY WE AIN'T. WE'RE IN THE MIDDLE OF NEW YORK CITY--
--AN' THERE AIN'T GONNA BE ANY RESCUE.
WHAT YOU THINKIN' ABOUT, TONES?
ARMOR. ARMOR I USED TO WEAR THAT I THOUGHT MADE ME INVINCIBLE.

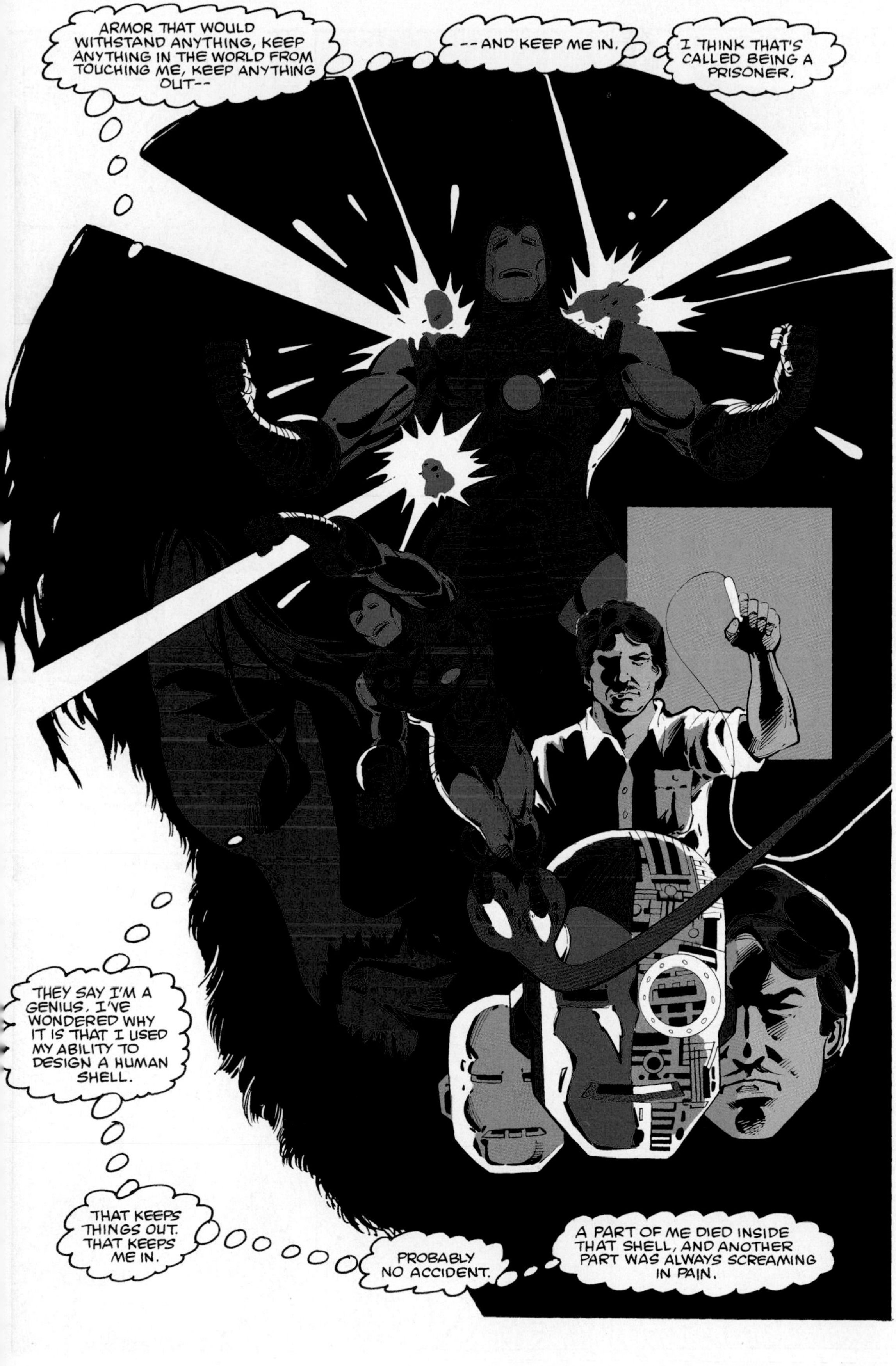
ARMOR THAT WOULD WITHSTAND ANYTHING, KEEP ANYTHING IN THE WORLD FROM TOUCHING ME, KEEP ANYTHING OUT--
--AND KEEP ME IN.
I THINK THAT'S CALLED BEING A PRISONER.
THEY SAY I'M A GENIUS. I'VE WONDERED WHY IT IS THAT I USED MY ABILITY TO DESIGN A HUMAN SHELL.
THAT KEEPS THINGS OUT. THAT KEEPS ME IN.
PROBABLY NO ACCIDENT.
A PART OF ME DIED INSIDE THAT SHELL, AND ANOTHER PART WAS ALWAYS SCREAMING IN PAIN.

THIS...THIS QUIETS THE SCREAMS, DULLS THE PAIN...

...HURRIES ALONG THE SLOW DYING...

TONES...IT'S HURTIN'!... HURTIN' A LOT...

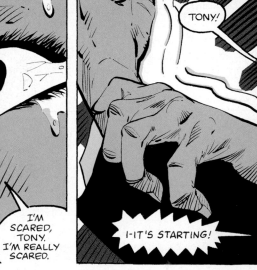

I'M SCARED, TONY. I'M REALLY SCARED.

TONY!

I-IT'S STARTING!

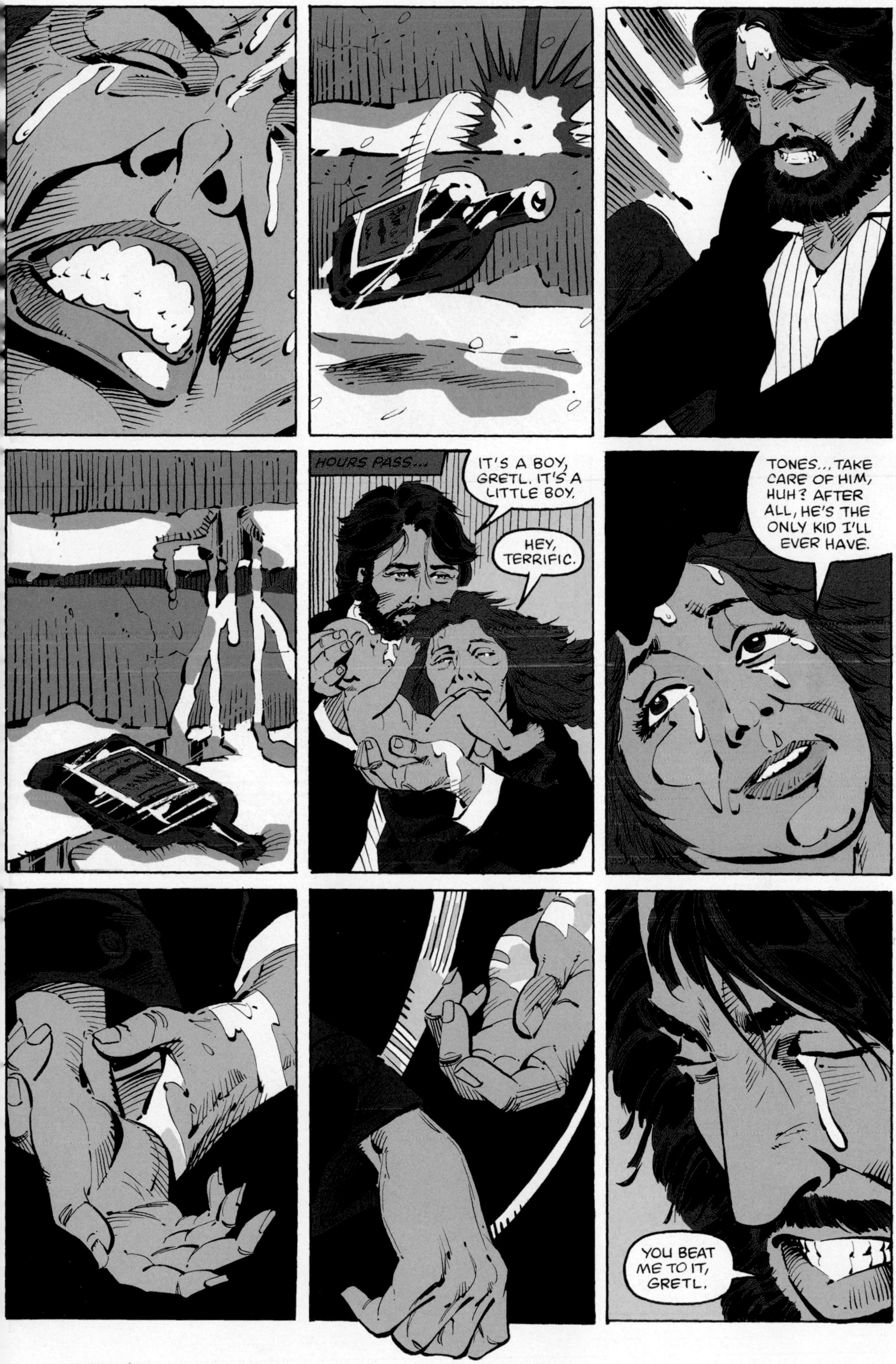
HOURS PASS...
IT'S A BOY, GRETL. IT'S A LITTLE BOY.
HEY, TERRIFIC.
TONES... TAKE CARE OF HIM, HUH? AFTER ALL, HE'S THE ONLY KID I'LL EVER HAVE.
YOU BEAT ME TO IT, GRETL.

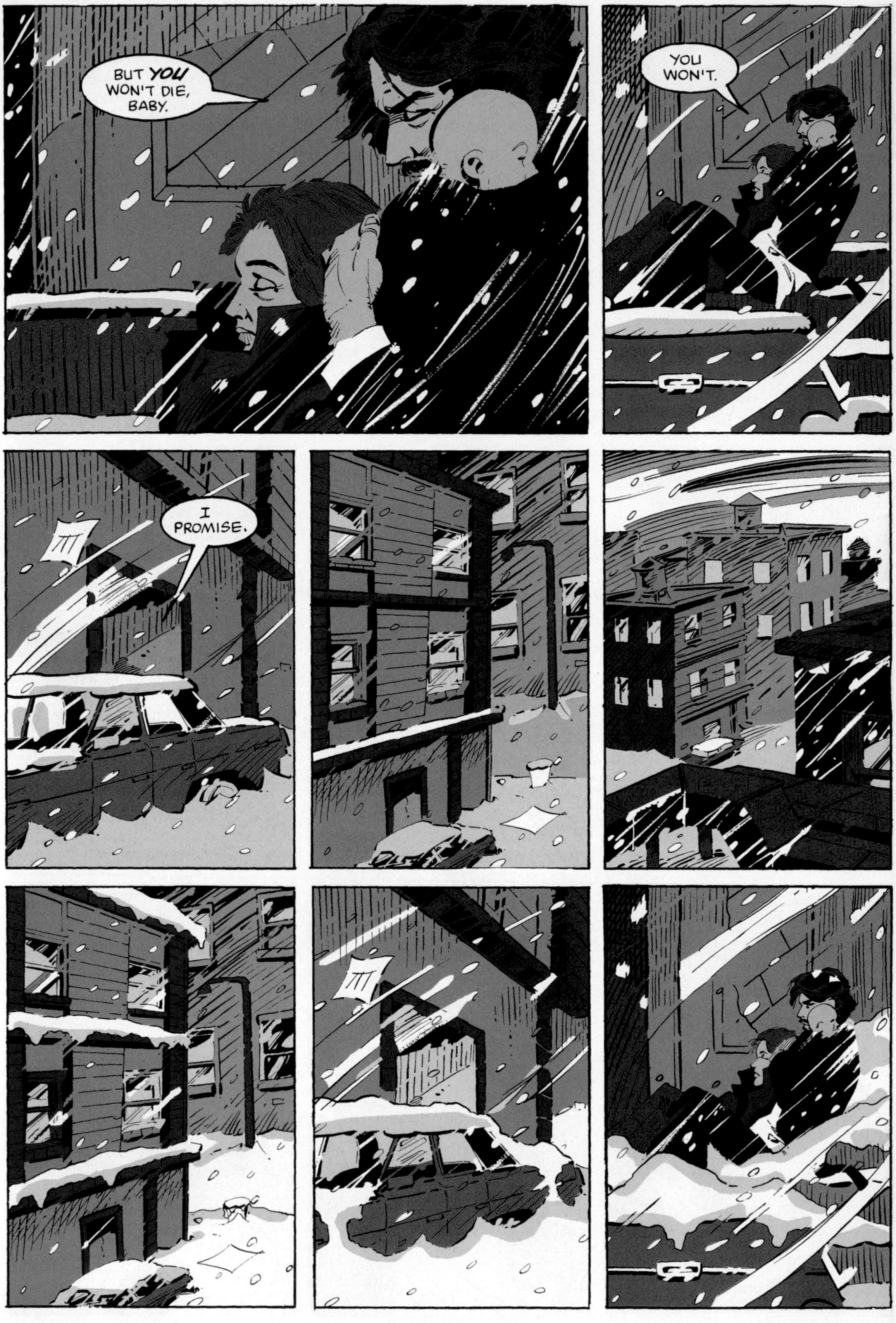
BUT YOU WON'T DIE, BABY.
YOU WON'T.
I PROMISE.

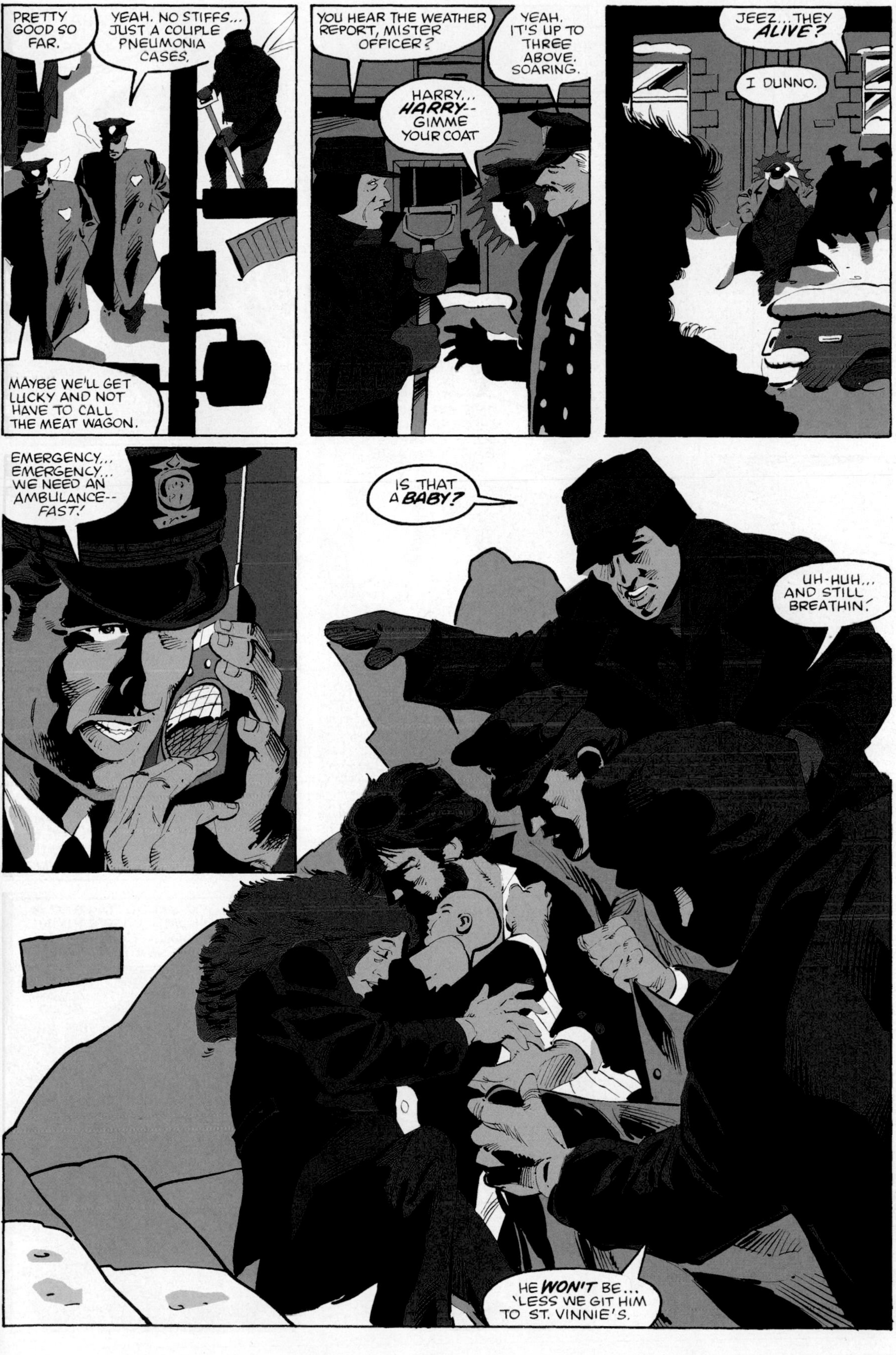
PRETTY GOOD SO FAR.
YEAH. NO STIFFS... JUST A COUPLE PNEUMONIA CASES.
MAYBE WE'LL GET LUCKY AND NOT HAVE TO CALL THE MEAT WAGON.
YOU HEAR THE WEATHER REPORT, MISTER OFFICER?
YEAH. IT'S UP TO THREE ABOVE. SOARING.
HARRY... HARRY-- GIMME YOUR COAT
JEEZ... THEY ALIVE?
I DUNNO.
EMERGENCY... EMERGENCY... WE NEED AN AMBULANCE-- FAST!
IS THAT A BABY?
UH-HUH... AND STILL BREATHIN'.
HE WON'T BE... 'LESS WE GIT HIM TO ST. VINNIE'S.

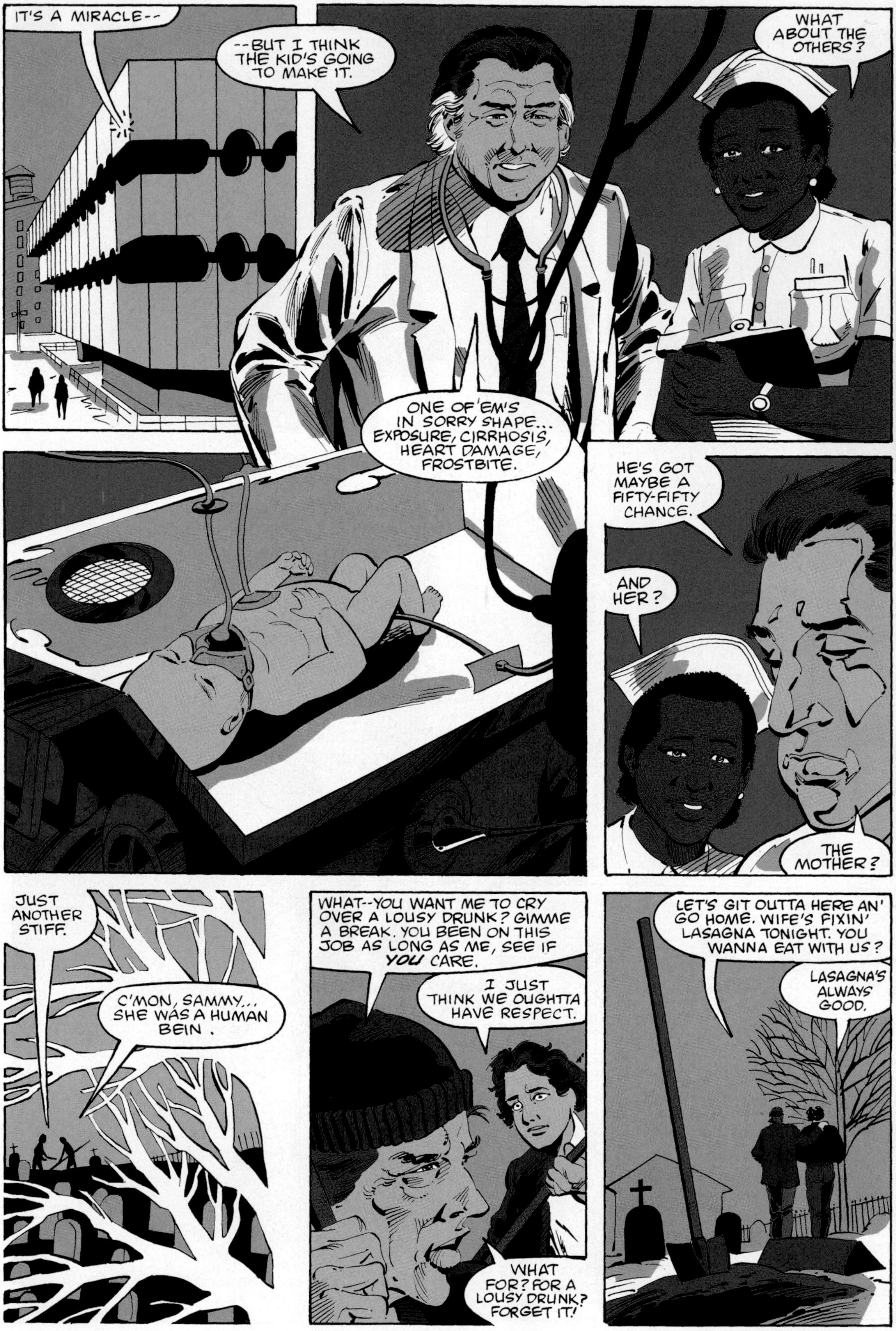
IT'S A MIRACLE--
--BUT I THINK THE KID'S GOING TO MAKE IT.
WHAT ABOUT THE OTHERS?
ONE OF 'EM'S IN SORRY SHAPE... EXPOSURE, CIRRHOSIS, HEART DAMAGE, FROSTBITE.
HE'S GOT MAYBE A FIFTY-FIFTY CHANCE.
AND HER?
THE MOTHER?
JUST ANOTHER STIFF.
C'MON, SAMMY... SHE WAS A HUMAN BEIN .
WHAT--YOU WANT ME TO CRY OVER A LOUSY DRUNK? GIMME A BREAK. YOU BEEN ON THIS JOB AS LONG AS ME, SEE IF YOU CARE.
I JUST THINK WE OUGHTTA HAVE RESPECT.
WHAT FOR? FOR A LOUSY DRUNK? FORGET IT!
LET'S GIT OUTTA HERE AN' GO HOME. WIFE'S FIXIN' LASAGNA TONIGHT. YOU WANNA EAT WITH US?
LASAGNA'S ALWAYS GOOD.

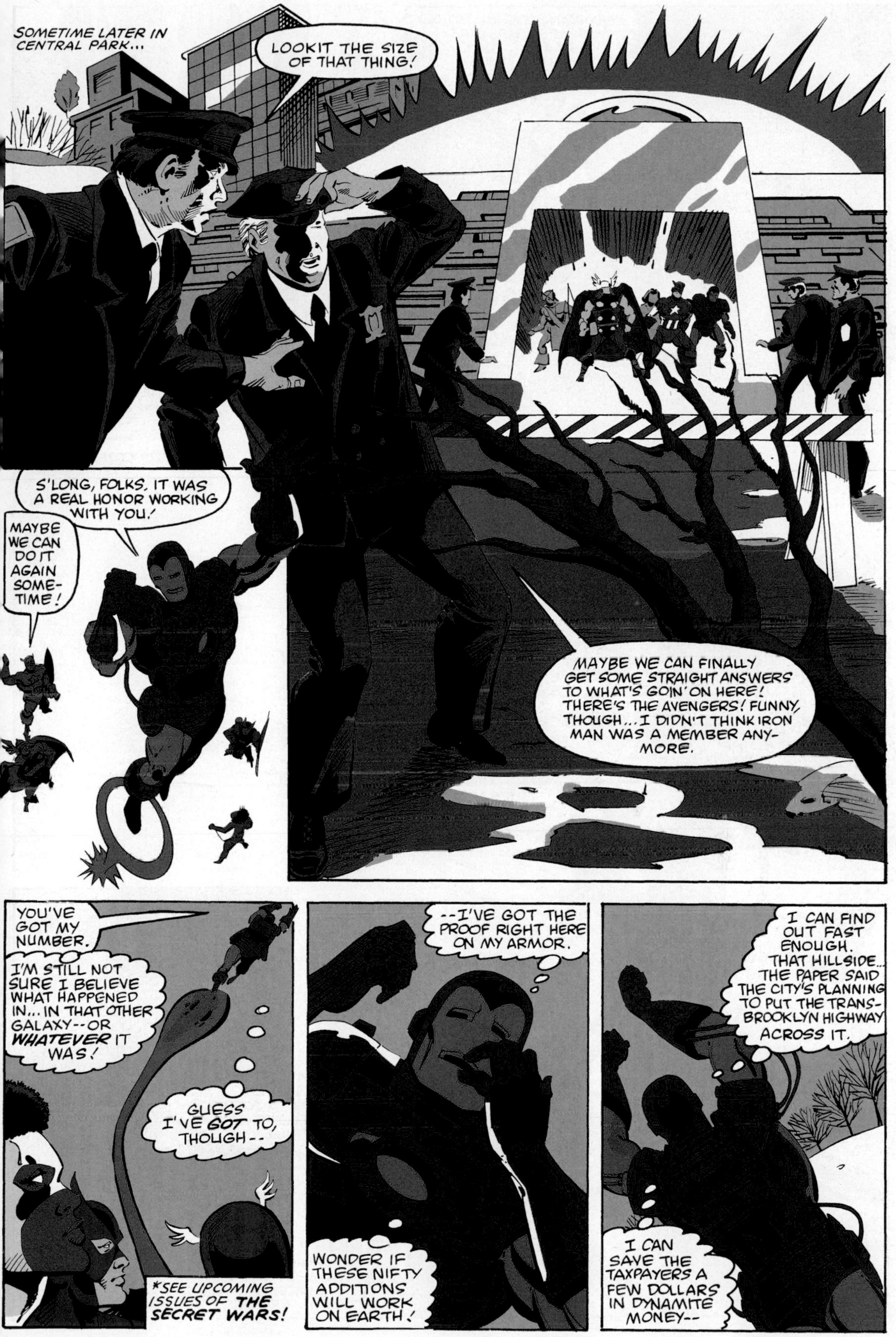
SOMETIME LATER IN CENTRAL PARK...
LOOKIT THE SIZE OF THAT THING!
MAYBE WE CAN FINALLY GET SOME STRAIGHT ANSWERS TO WHAT'S GOIN' ON HERE! THERE'S THE AVENGERS! FUNNY, THOUGH... I DIDN'T THINK IRON MAN WAS A MEMBER ANY-MORE.
S'LONG, FOLKS. IT WAS A REAL HONOR WORKING WITH YOU!
MAYBE WE CAN DO IT AGAIN SOME-TIME!
YOU'VE GOT MY NUMBER.
I'M STILL NOT SURE I BELIEVE WHAT HAPPENED IN... IN THAT OTHER GALAXY--OR WHATEVER IT WAS!
GUESS I'VE GOT TO, THOUGH--
*SEE UPCOMING ISSUES OF THE SECRET WARS!
--I'VE GOT THE PROOF RIGHT HERE ON MY ARMOR.
WONDER IF THESE NIFTY ADDITIONS WILL WORK ON EARTH!
I CAN FIND OUT FAST ENOUGH. THAT HILLSIDE... THE PAPER SAID THE CITY'S PLANNING TO PUT THE TRANS-BROOKLYN HIGHWAY ACROSS IT.
I CAN SAVE THE TAXPAYERS A FEW DOLLARS IN DYNAMITE MONEY--

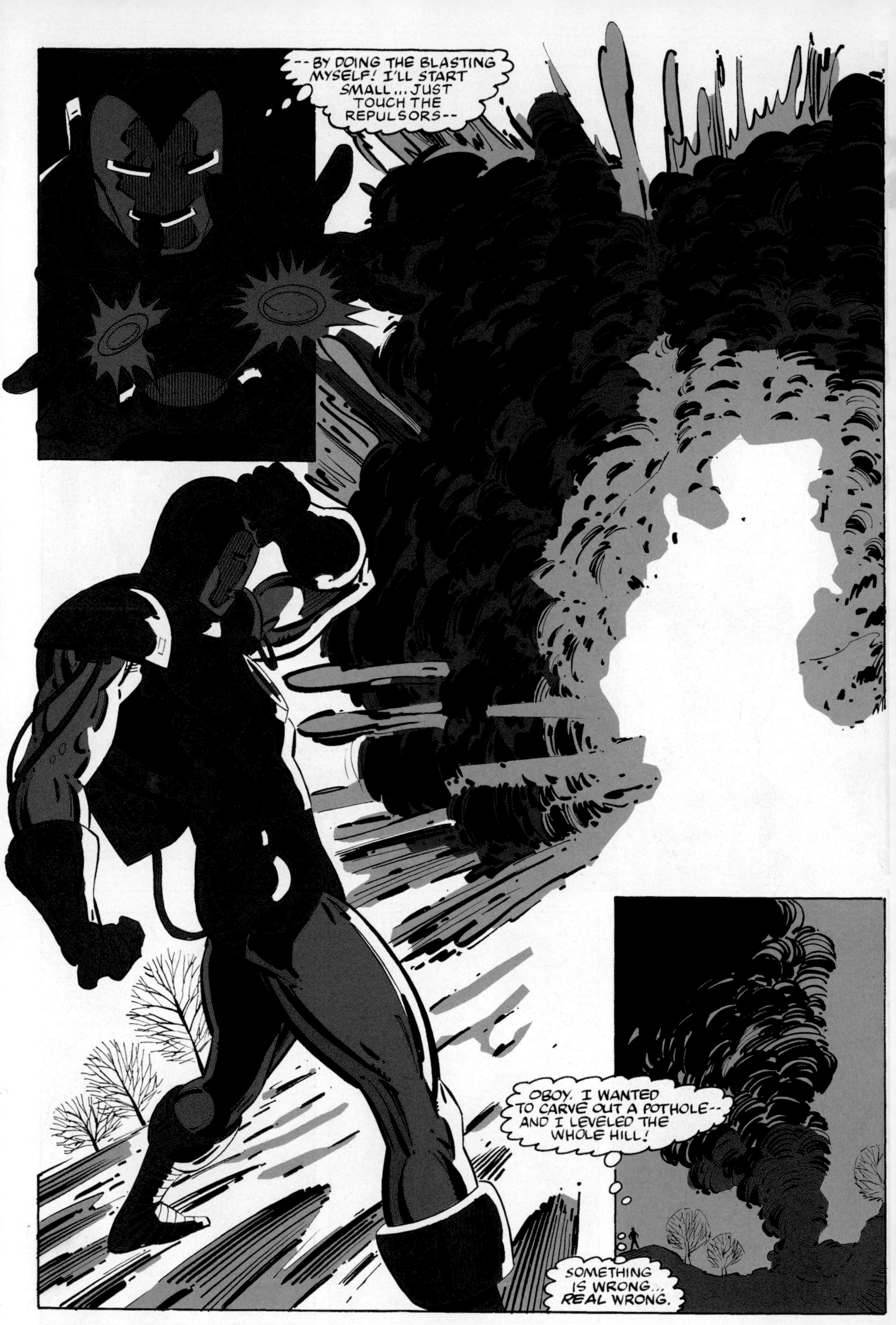
--BY DOING THE BLASTING MYSELF! I'LL START SMALL... JUST TOUCH THE REPULSORS--
OBOY. I WANTED TO CARVE OUT A POTHOLE--AND I LEVELED THE WHOLE HILL!
SOMETHING IS WRONG... REAL WRONG.

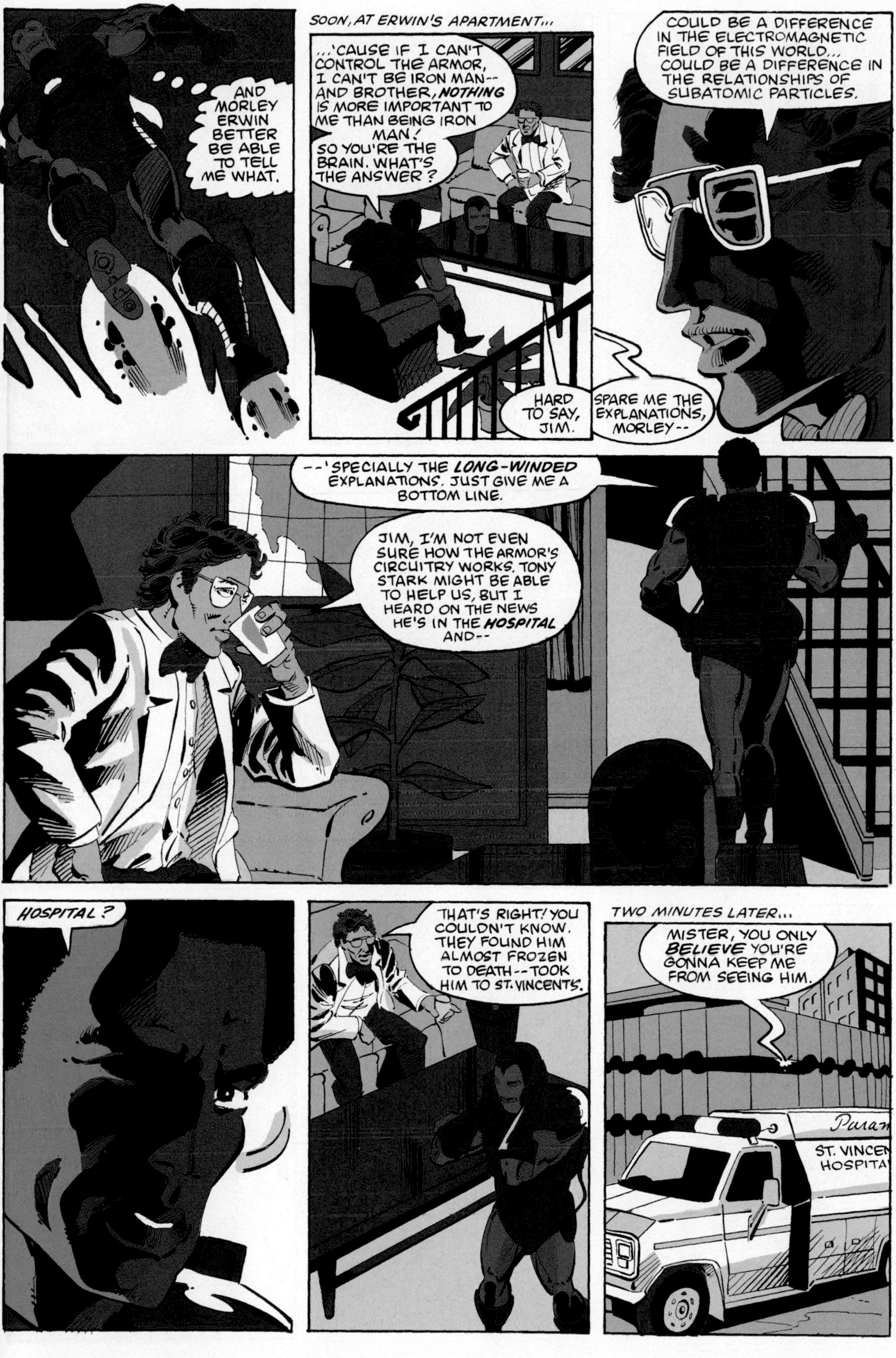
AND MORLEY ERWIN BETTER BE ABLE TO TELL ME WHAT.
SOON, AT ERWIN'S APARTMENT...
...'CAUSE IF I CAN'T CONTROL THE ARMOR, I CAN'T BE IRON MAN-- AND BROTHER, NOTHING IS MORE IMPORTANT TO ME THAN BEING IRON MAN! SO YOU'RE THE BRAIN. WHAT'S THE ANSWER?
COULD BE A DIFFERENCE IN THE ELECTROMAGNETIC FIELD OF THIS WORLD... COULD BE A DIFFERENCE IN THE RELATIONSHIPS OF SUBATOMIC PARTICLES.
HARD TO SAY, JIM.
SPARE ME THE EXPLANATIONS, MORLEY--
--'SPECIALLY THE LONG-WINDED EXPLANATIONS. JUST GIVE ME A BOTTOM LINE.
JIM, I'M NOT EVEN SURE HOW THE ARMOR'S CIRCUITRY WORKS. TONY STARK MIGHT BE ABLE TO HELP US, BUT I HEARD ON THE NEWS HE'S IN THE HOSPITAL AND--
HOSPITAL?
THAT'S RIGHT! YOU COULDN'T KNOW. THEY FOUND HIM ALMOST FROZEN TO DEATH--TOOK HIM TO ST. VINCENT'S.
TWO MINUTES LATER...
MISTER, YOU ONLY BELIEVE YOU'RE GONNA KEEP ME FROM SEEING HIM.
ST. VINCEN
HOSPITA

-- BUT YOU *CAN* CHANGE YOUR MIND, CAN'T YOU?

IT'S CHANGED, IT'S CHANGED...

NURSE, HOW IS HE?

TONY, TONY... HOW'D YOU COME TO THIS? *YOU*-- OF ALL PEOPLE! YOU HAD THE WHOLE PACKAGE... MONEY, BRAINS, WOMEN... EVERYTHING THE AMERICAN MALE WOULD SELL HIS SOUL FOR...

*DOES* SELL HIS SOUL FOR SOMETIMES.

IS ANY OF THIS *MY* FAULT? DID YOU NEED SOMETHING I COULDN'T GIVE YOU? *WOULDN'T* GIVE YOU? MAYBE I ENVIED YOU-- SECRETLY *WANTED* YOU TO FAIL...

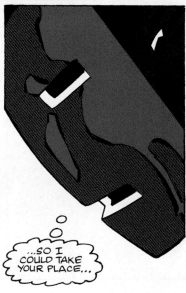

...SO I COULD TAKE YOUR PLACE...

DON'T DIE, TONY. DON'T BURDEN ME WITH THAT. THAT'D BE MORE THAN I COULD HANDLE.

THERE'S ANOTHER REASON, TONY.

YOU'RE MY FRIEND, THE BEST I EVER--

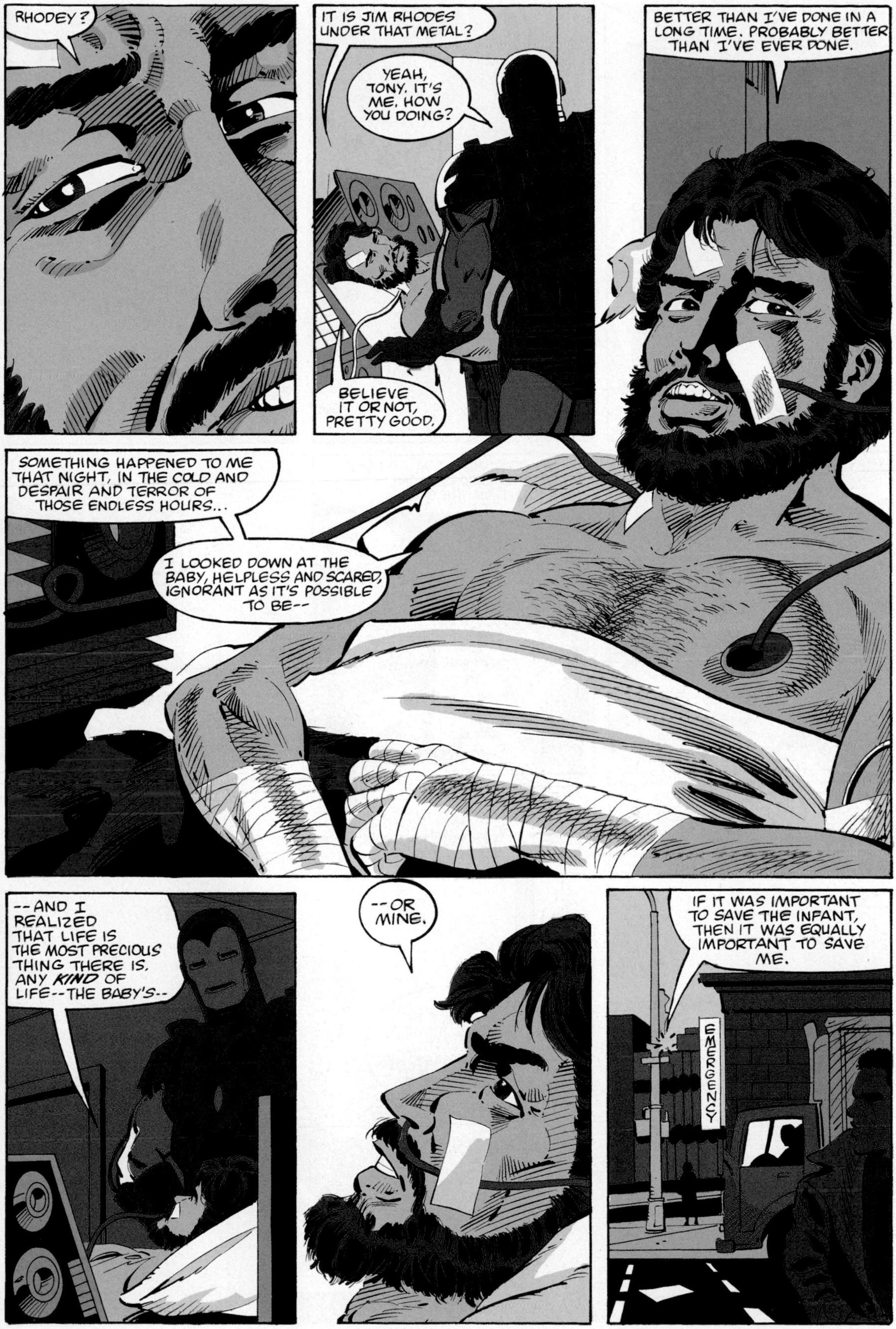
RHODEY?
IT IS JIM RHODES UNDER THAT METAL?
YEAH, TONY. IT'S ME. HOW YOU DOING?
BELIEVE IT OR NOT, PRETTY GOOD.
BETTER THAN I'VE DONE IN A LONG TIME. PROBABLY BETTER THAN I'VE EVER DONE.
SOMETHING HAPPENED TO ME THAT NIGHT, IN THE COLD AND DESPAIR AND TERROR OF THOSE ENDLESS HOURS...
I LOOKED DOWN AT THE BABY, HELPLESS AND SCARED, IGNORANT AS IT'S POSSIBLE TO BE--
--AND I REALIZED THAT LIFE IS THE MOST PRECIOUS THING THERE IS. ANY KIND OF LIFE--THE BABY'S--
--OR MINE.
IF IT WAS IMPORTANT TO SAVE THE INFANT, THEN IT WAS EQUALLY IMPORTANT TO SAVE ME.
EMERGENCY

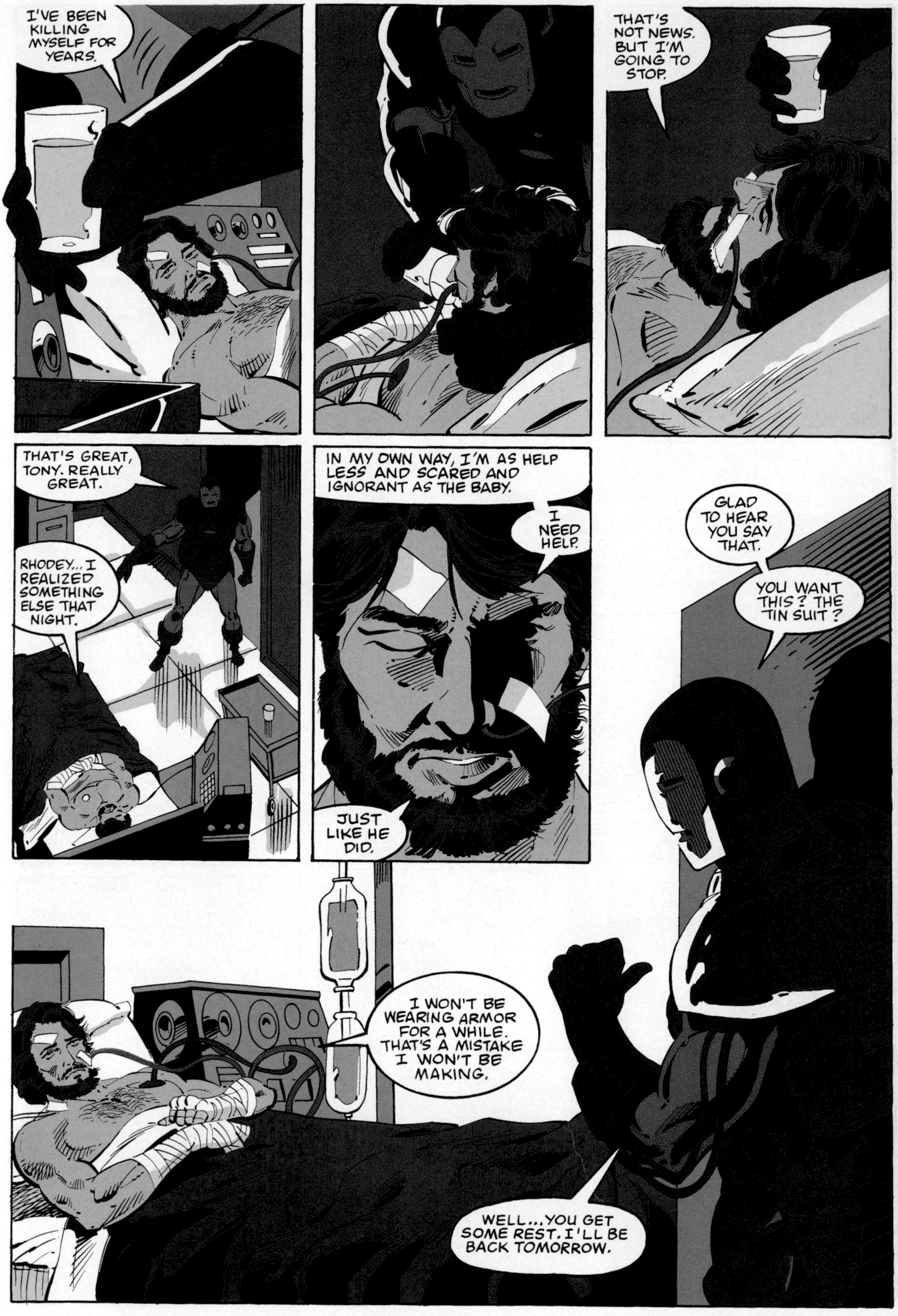
I'VE BEEN KILLING MYSELF FOR YEARS.
THAT'S NOT NEWS. BUT I'M GOING TO STOP.
THAT'S GREAT, TONY. REALLY GREAT.
RHODEY... I REALIZED SOMETHING ELSE THAT NIGHT.
IN MY OWN WAY, I'M AS HELP LESS AND SCARED AND IGNORANT AS THE BABY.
I NEED HELP.
JUST LIKE HE DID.
GLAD TO HEAR YOU SAY THAT.
YOU WANT THIS? THE TIN SUIT?
I WON'T BE WEARING ARMOR FOR A WHILE. THAT'S A MISTAKE I WON'T BE MAKING.
WELL... YOU GET SOME REST. I'LL BE BACK TOMORROW.

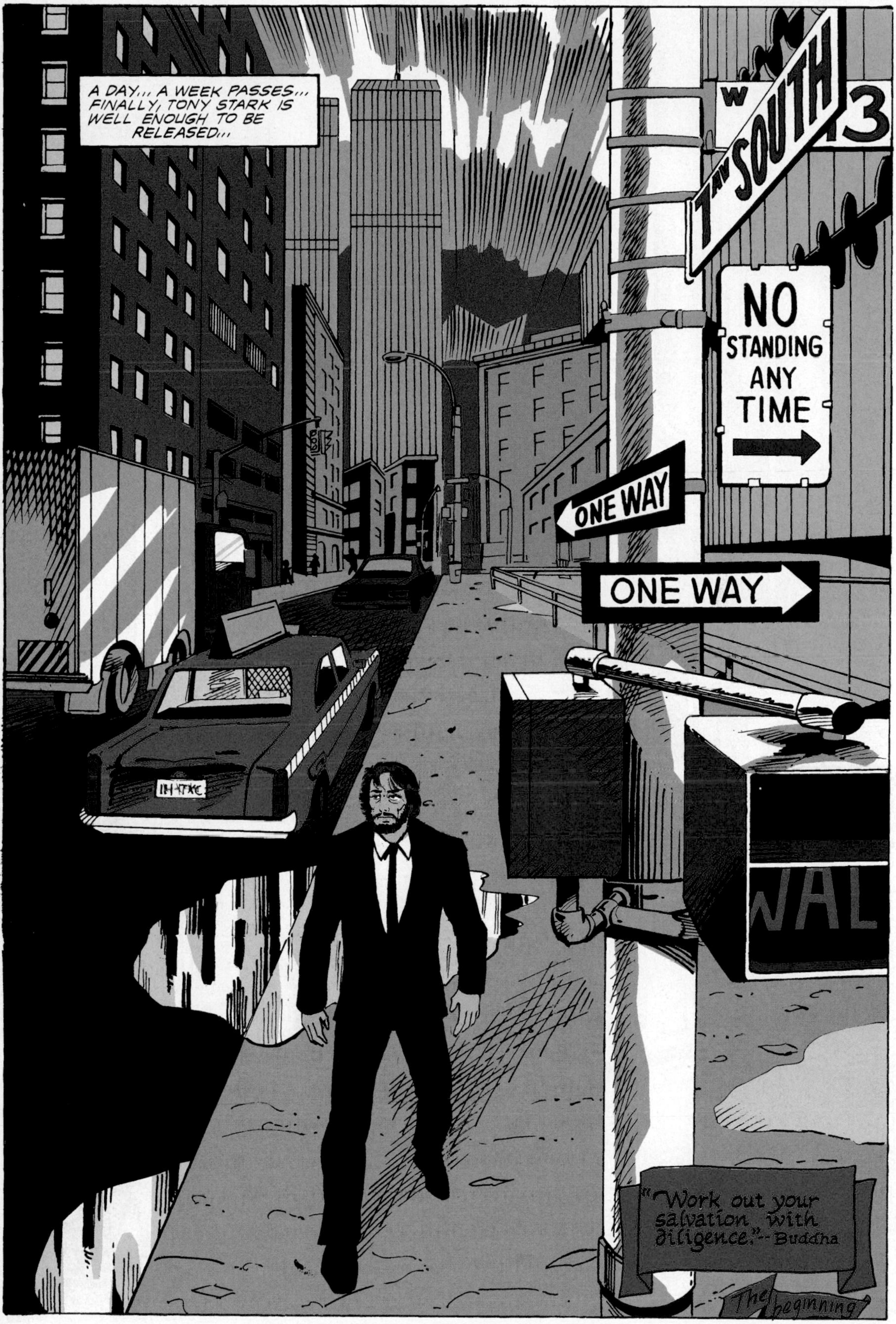

A DAY... A WEEK PASSES... FINALLY, TONY STARK IS WELL ENOUGH TO BE RELEASED...
W 7TH SOUTH 3
NO STANDING ANY TIME
ONE WAY
ONE WAY
"Work out your salvation with diligence." -- Buddha
The beginning

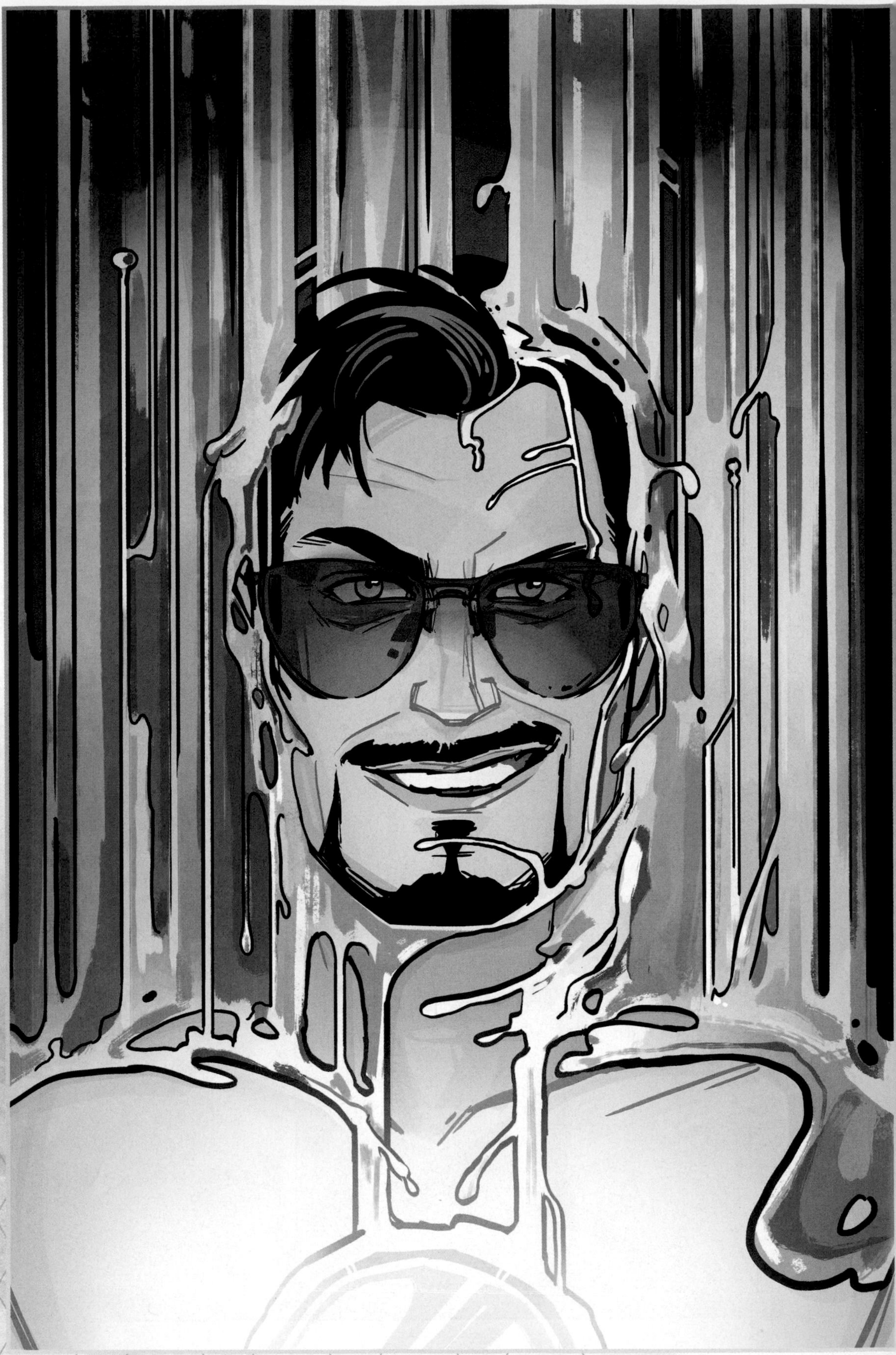

#6 WOMEN OF MARVEL DESIGN VARIANT
BY ANNIE WU

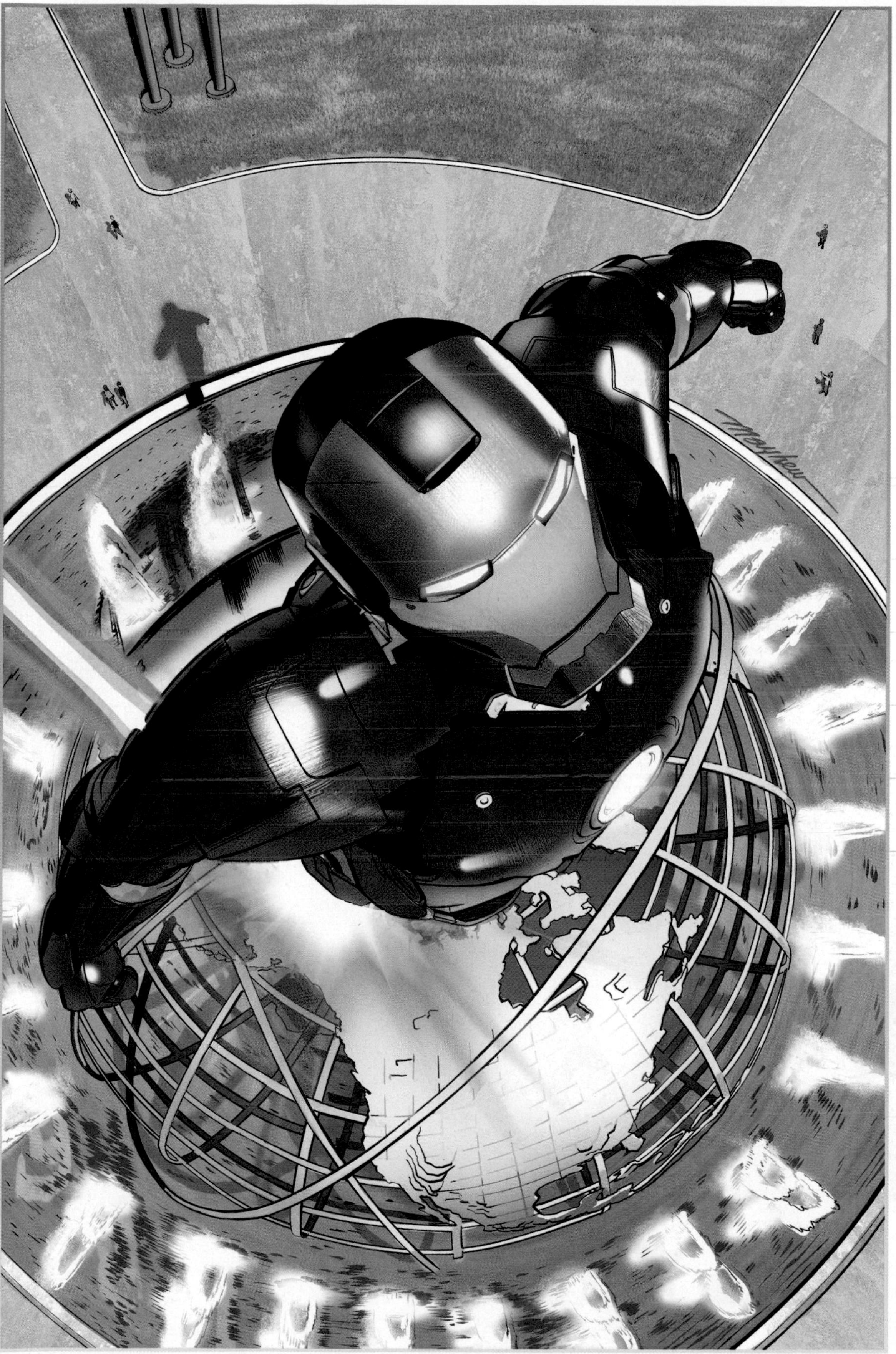

#9 NYC VARIANT
BY MIKE MAYHEW

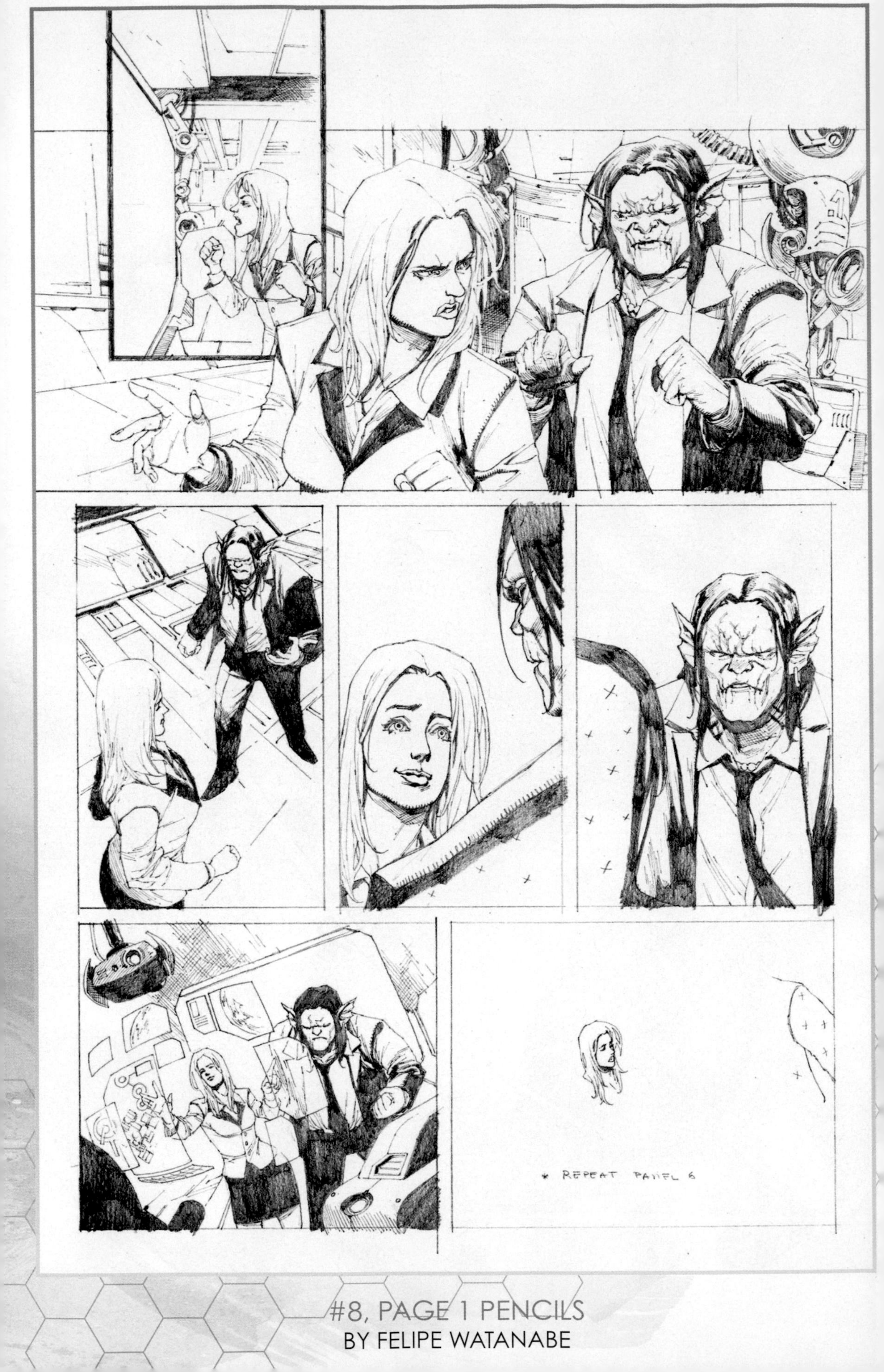
* REPEAT PANEL 6

#8, PAGE 1 PENCILS
BY FELIPE WATANABE

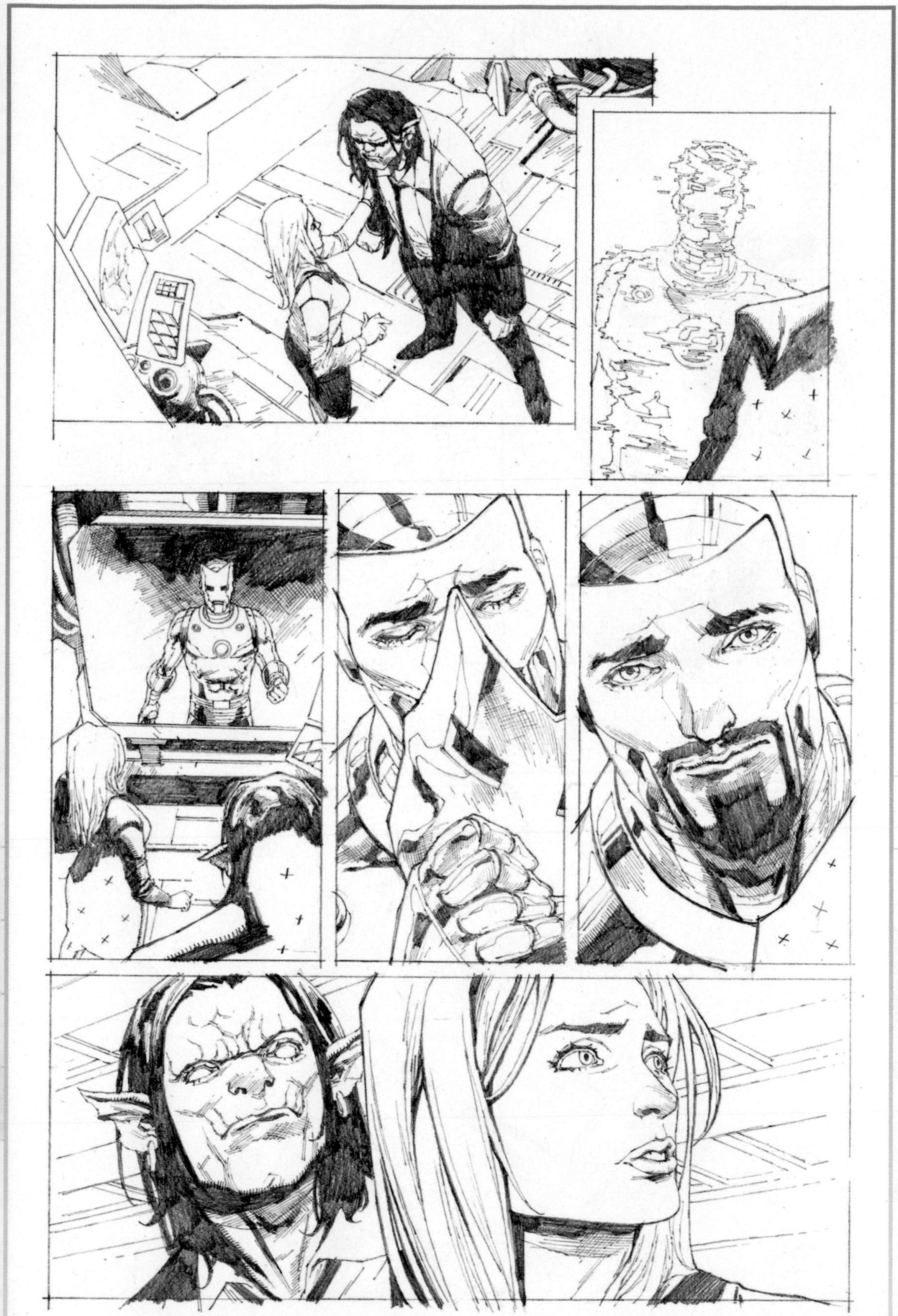

#8, PAGE 2 PENCILS
BY FELIPE WATANABE

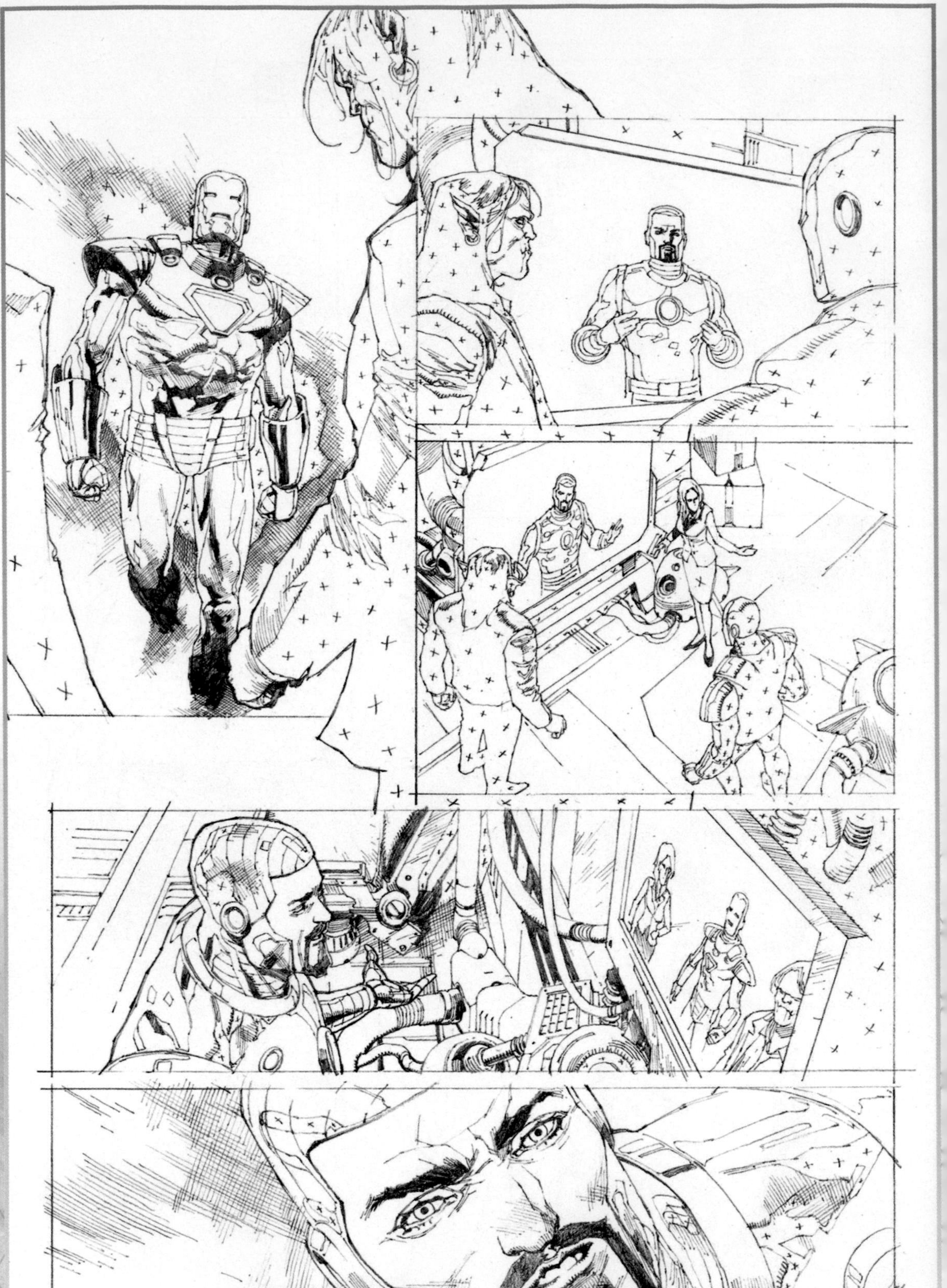

#8, PAGE 3 PENCILS
BY FELIPE WATANABE

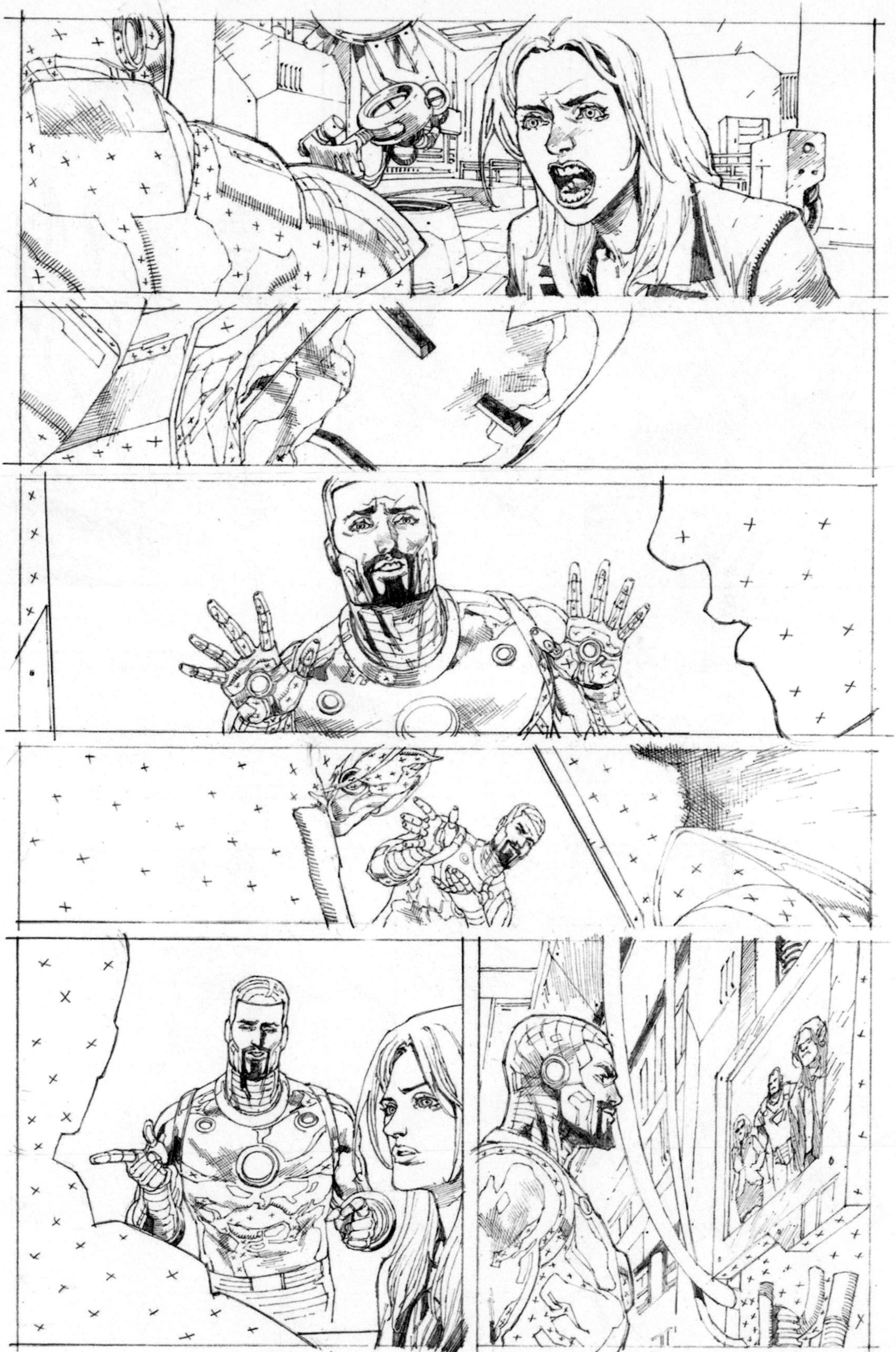

#8, PAGE 4 PENCILS
BY FELIPE WATANABE

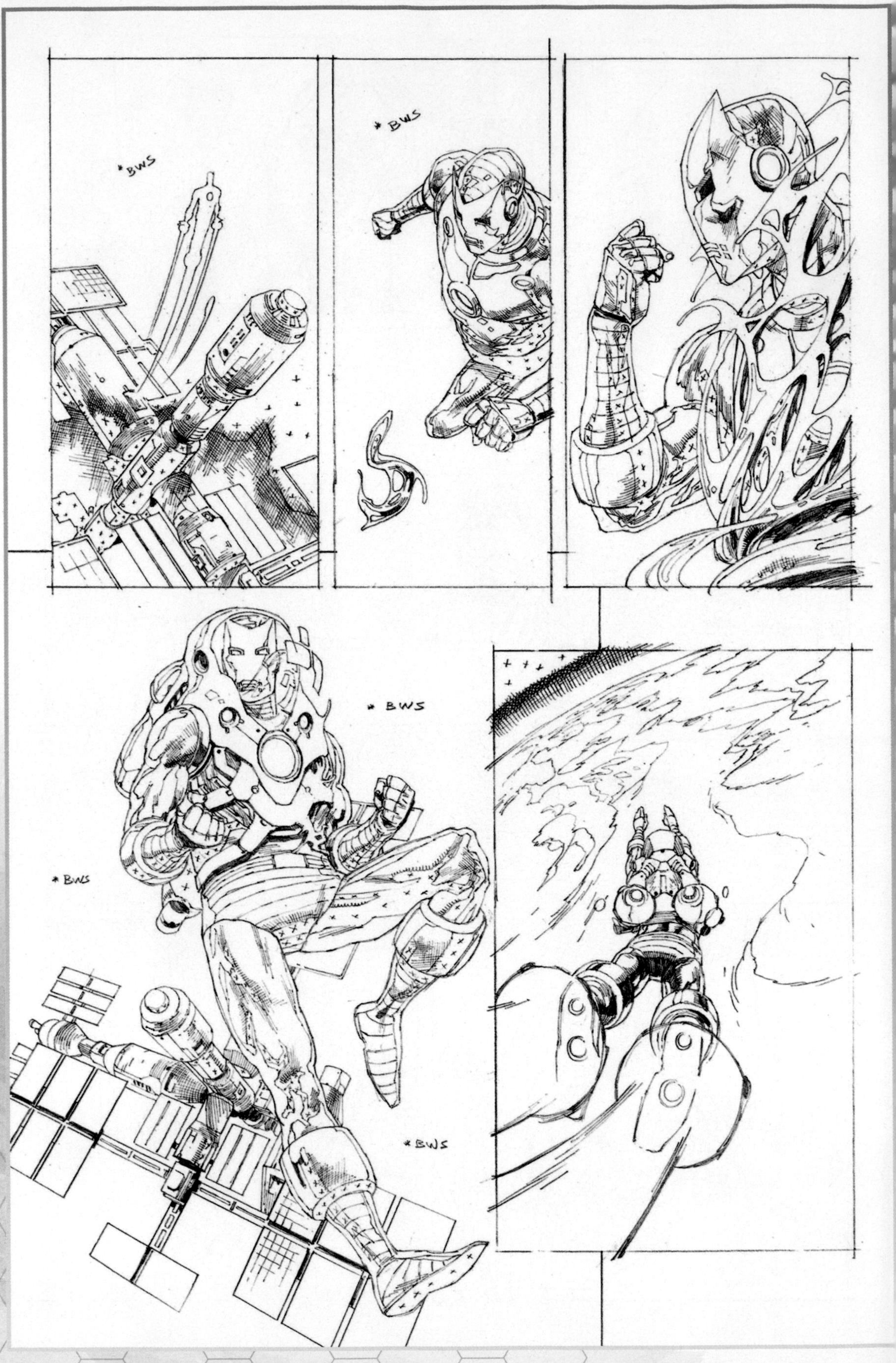
*BWS
*BWS
*BWS
*BWS
*BWS

#8, PAGE 5 PENCILS
BY FELIPE WATANABE

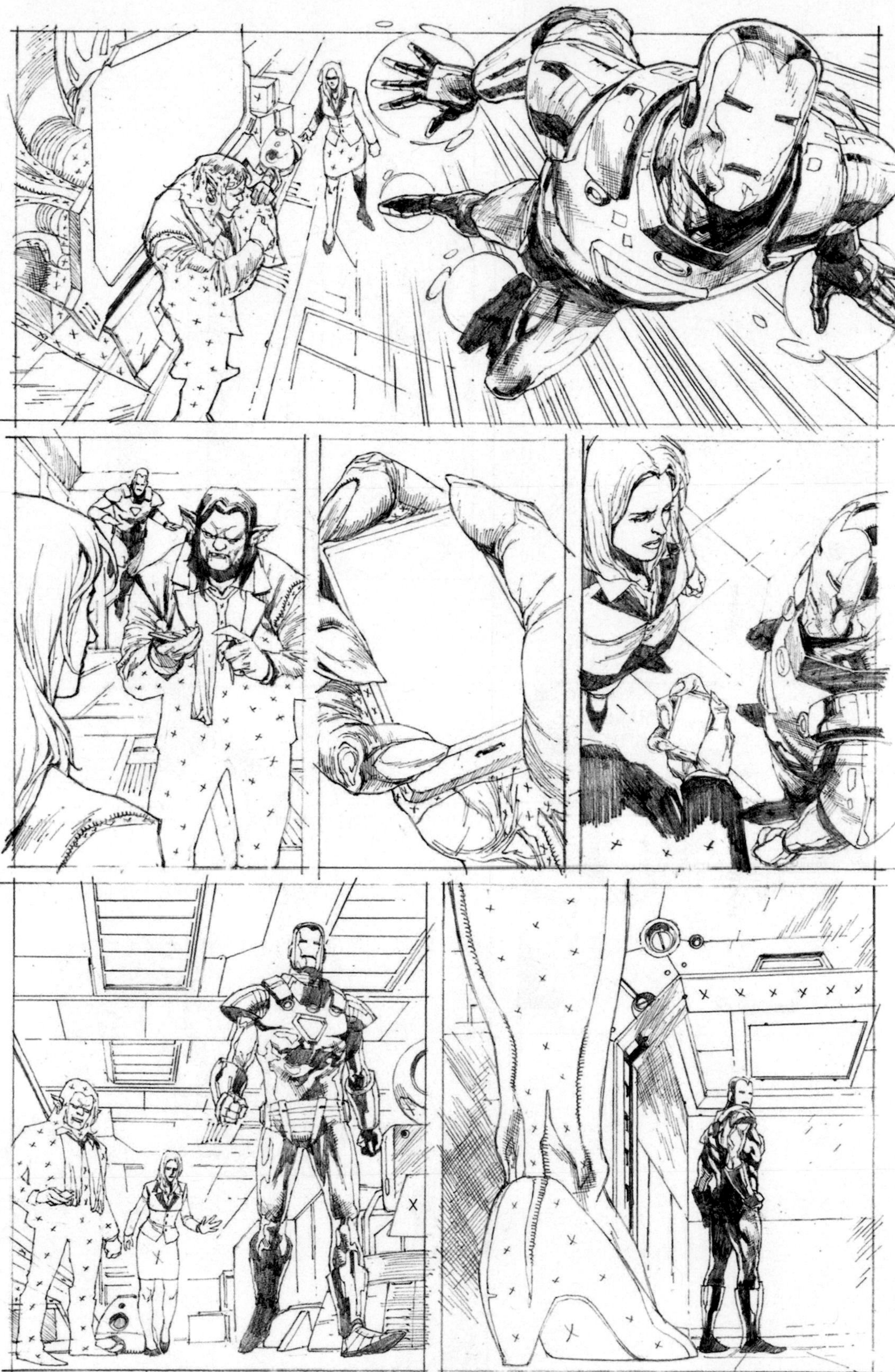

#8, PAGE 6 PENCILS
BY FELIPE WATANABE

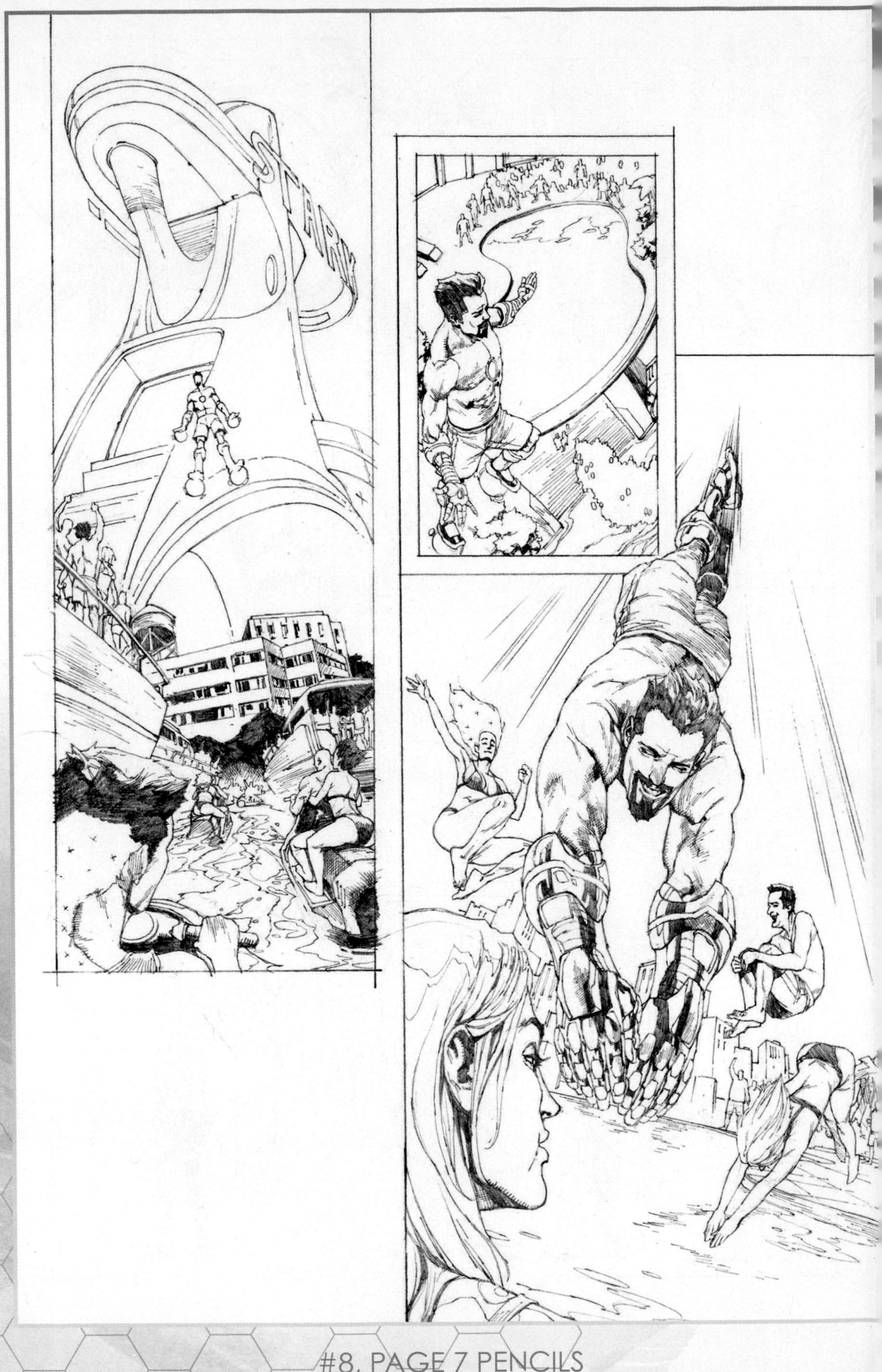
STARK

#8, PAGE 7 PENCILS
BY FELIPE WATANABE

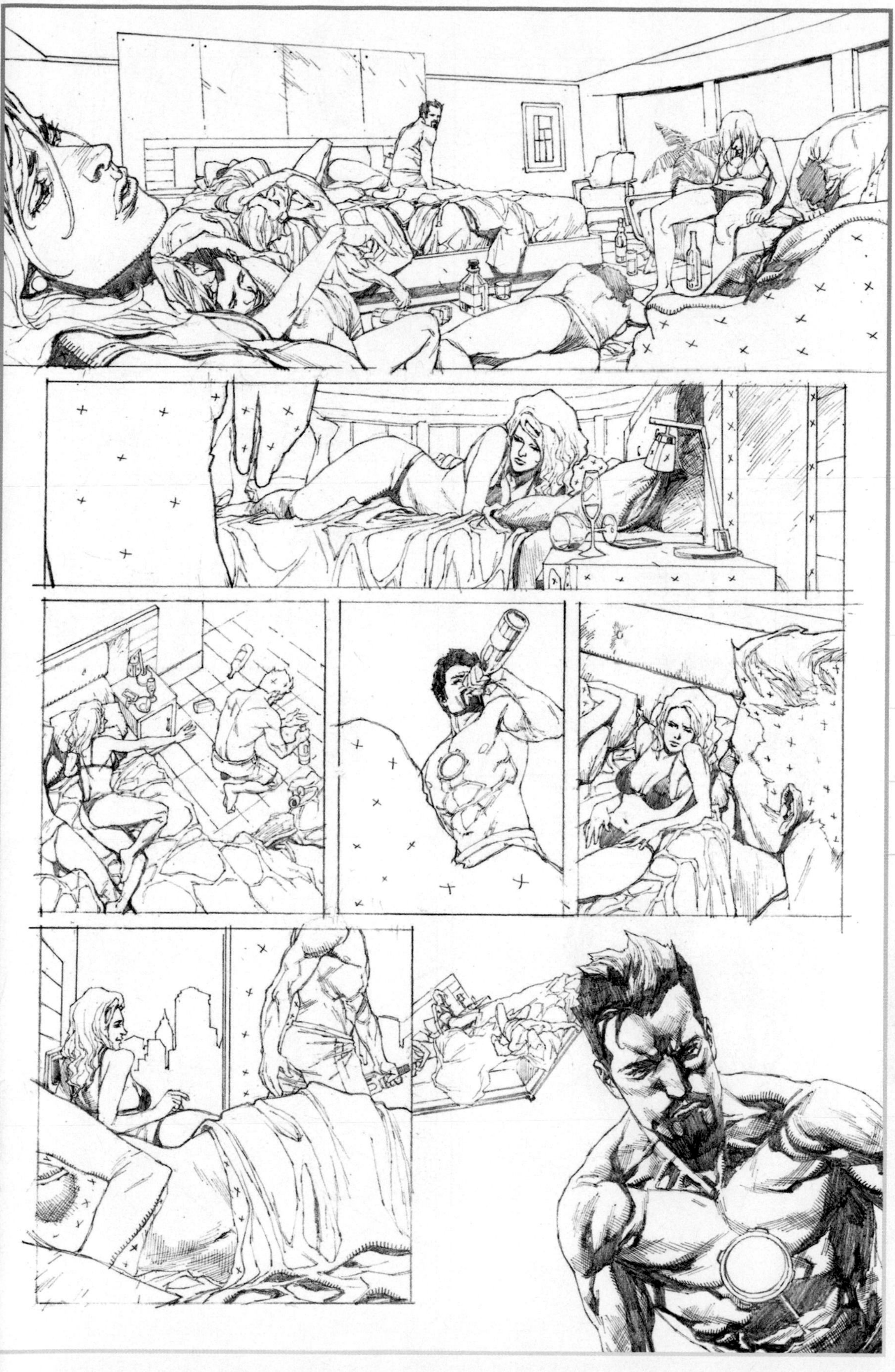

#8, PAGE 8 PENCILS
BY FELIPE WATANABE

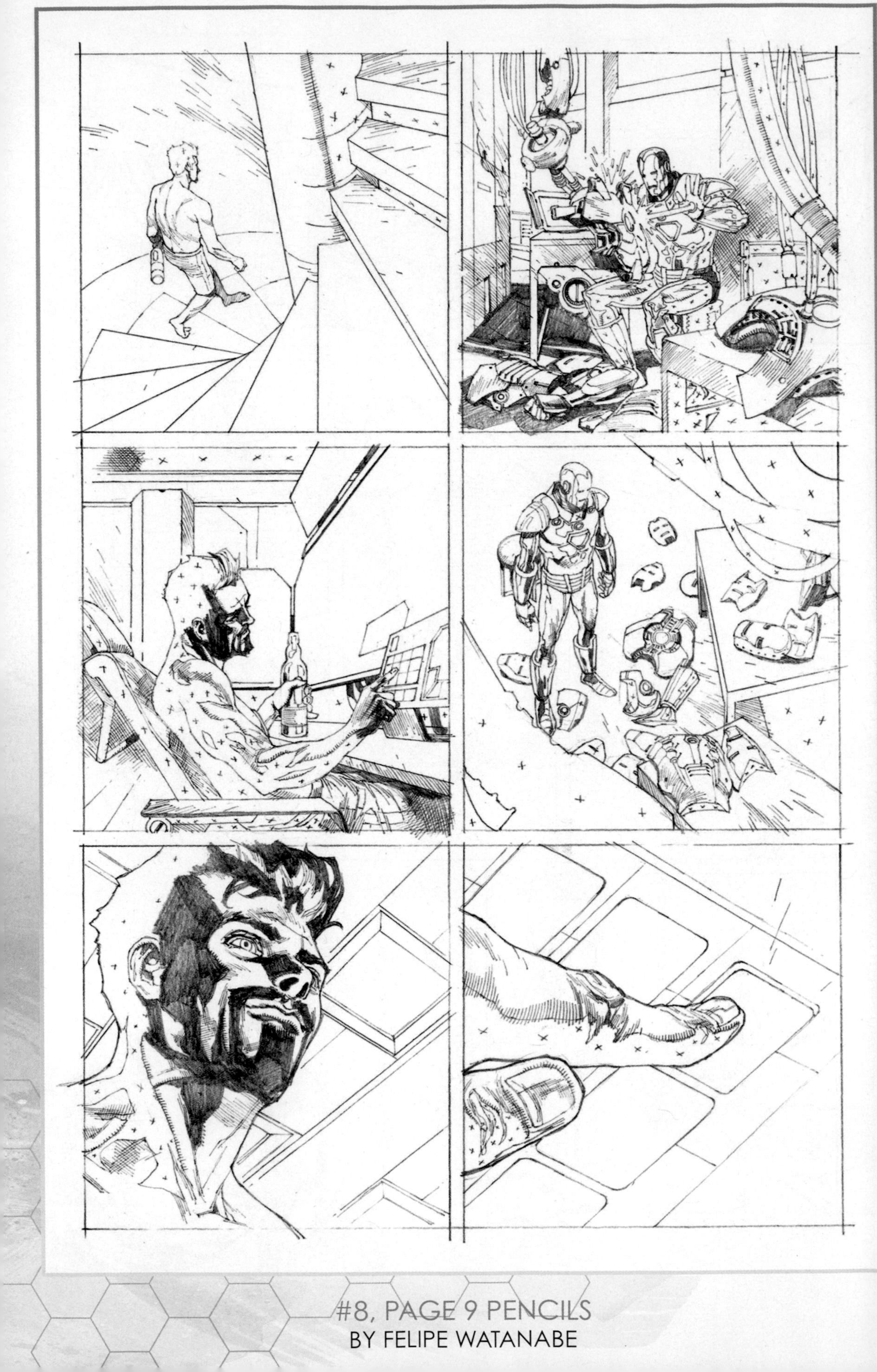

#8, PAGE 9 PENCILS
BY FELIPE WATANABE

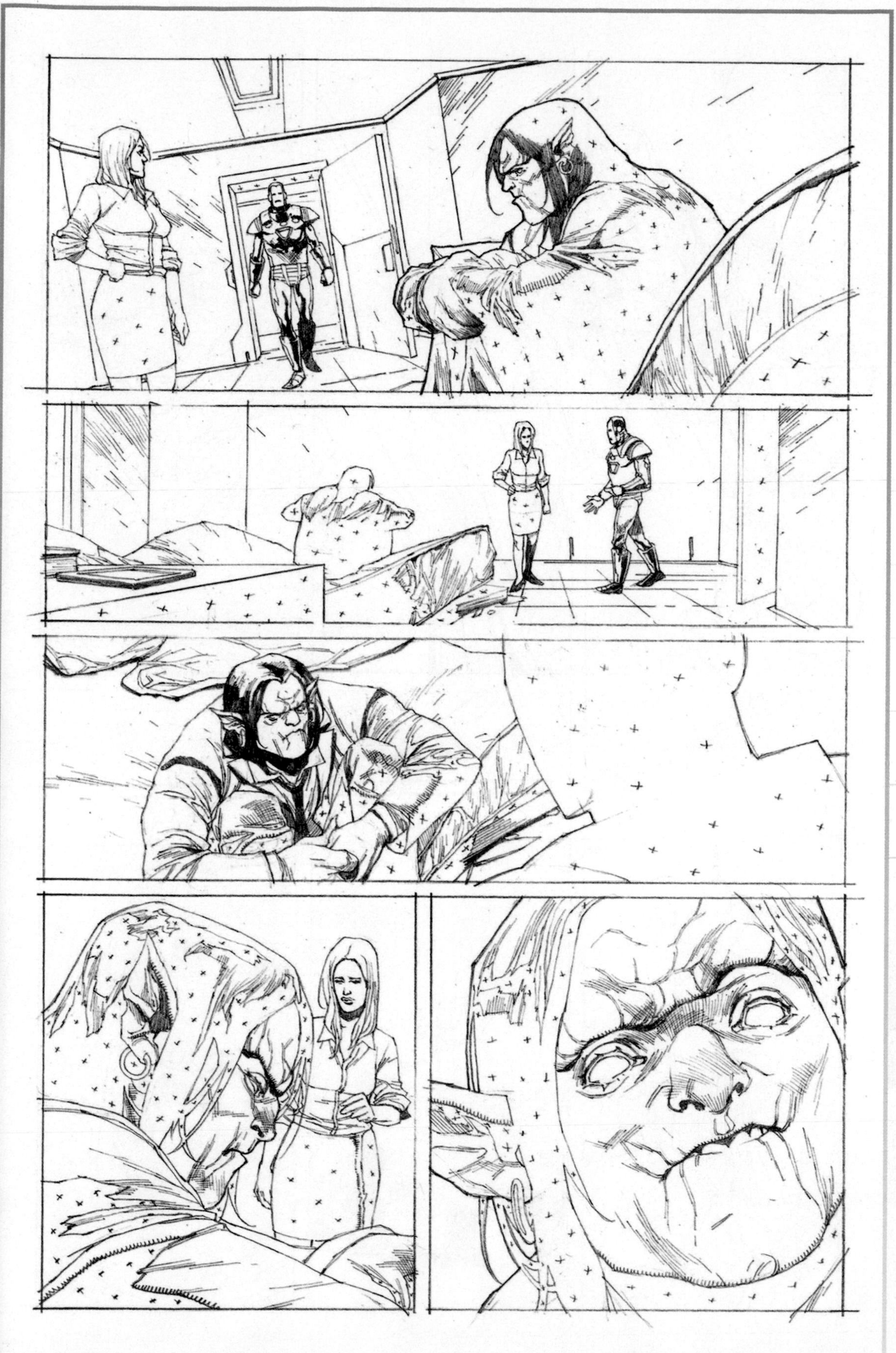

#8, PAGE 11 PENCILS
BY FELIPE WATANABE

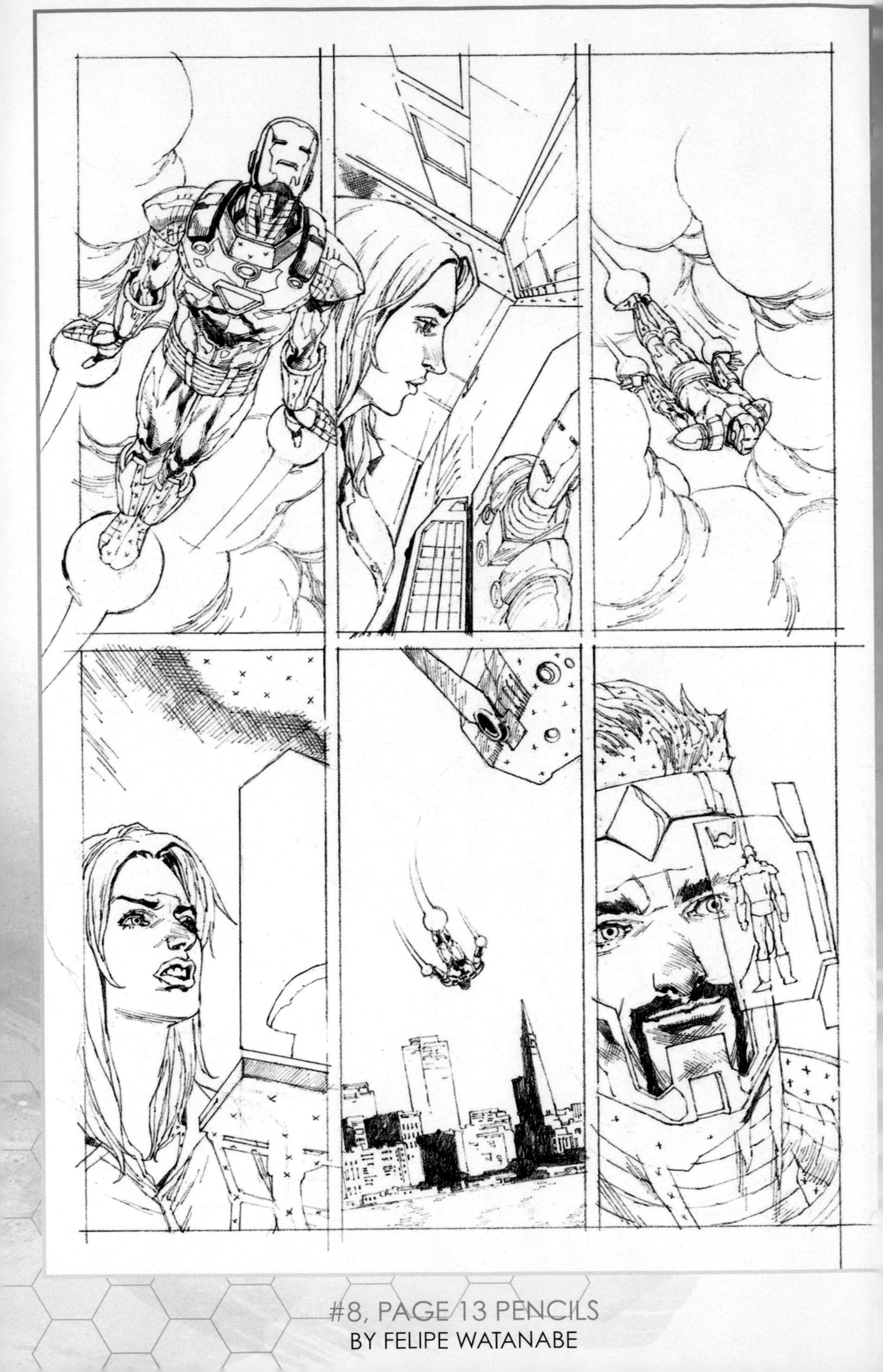

#8, PAGE 13 PENCILS
BY FELIPE WATANABE

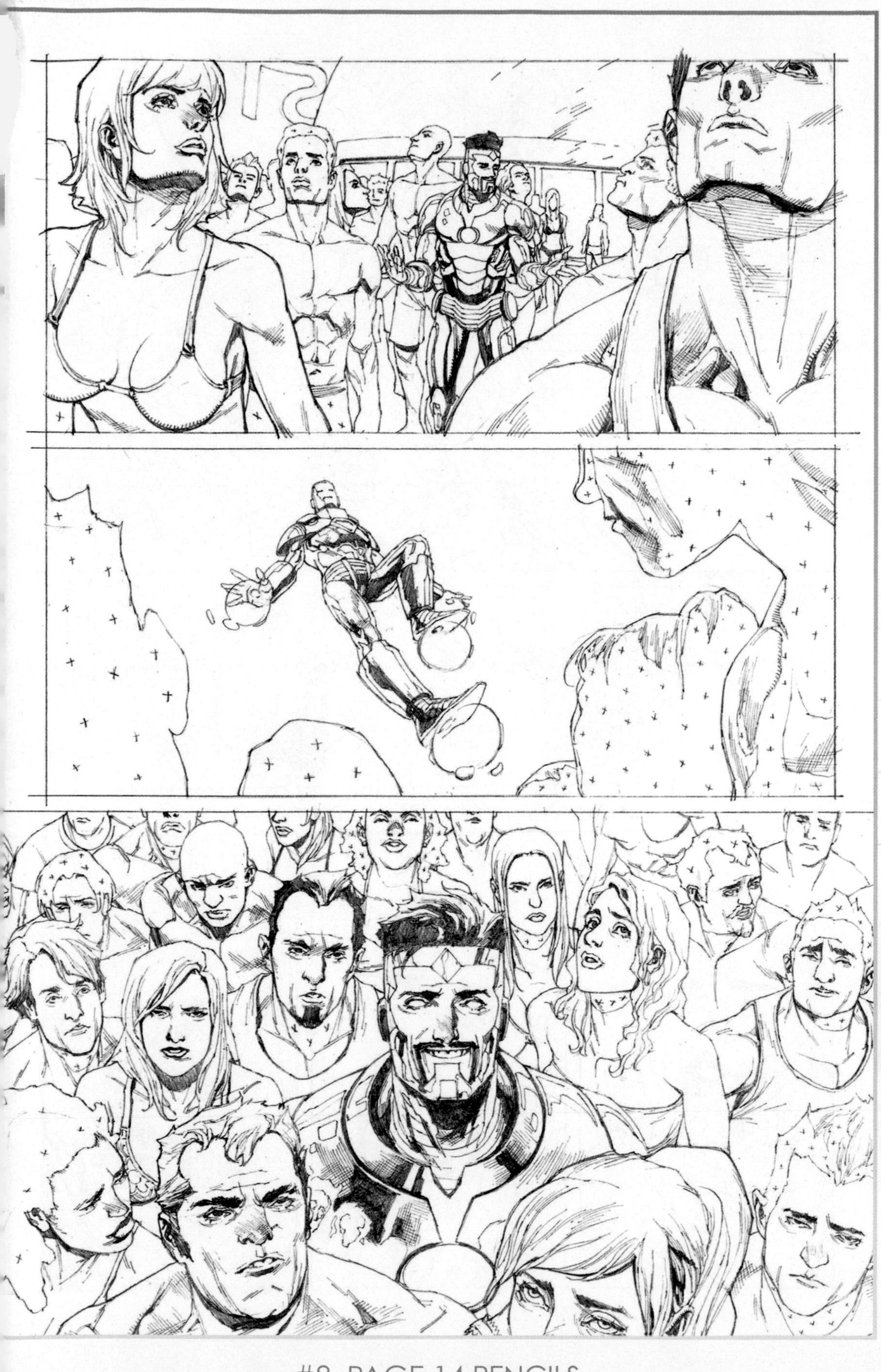

#8, PAGE 14 PENCILS
BY FELIPE WATANABE

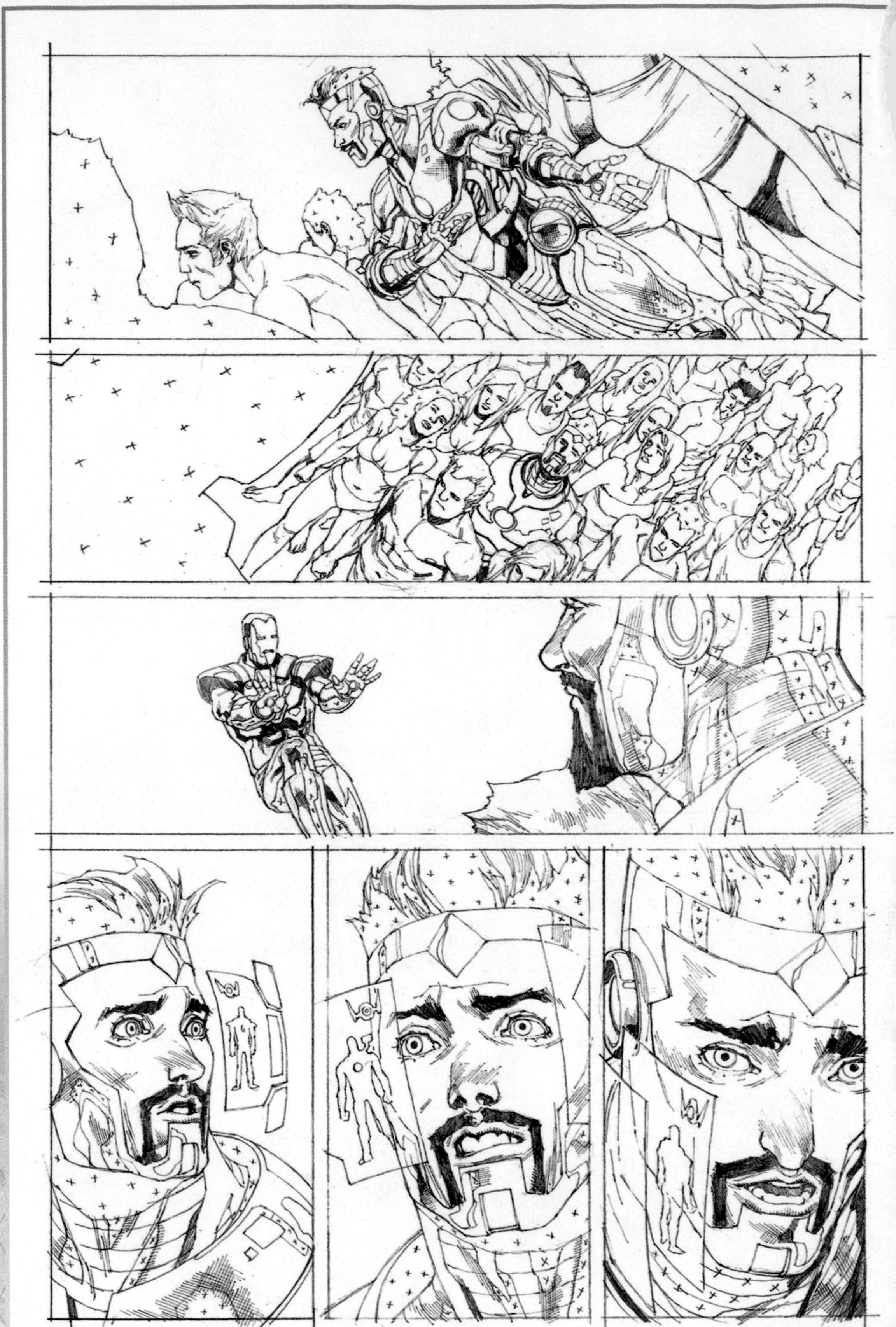

#8, PAGE 15 PENCILS
BY FELIPE WATANABE

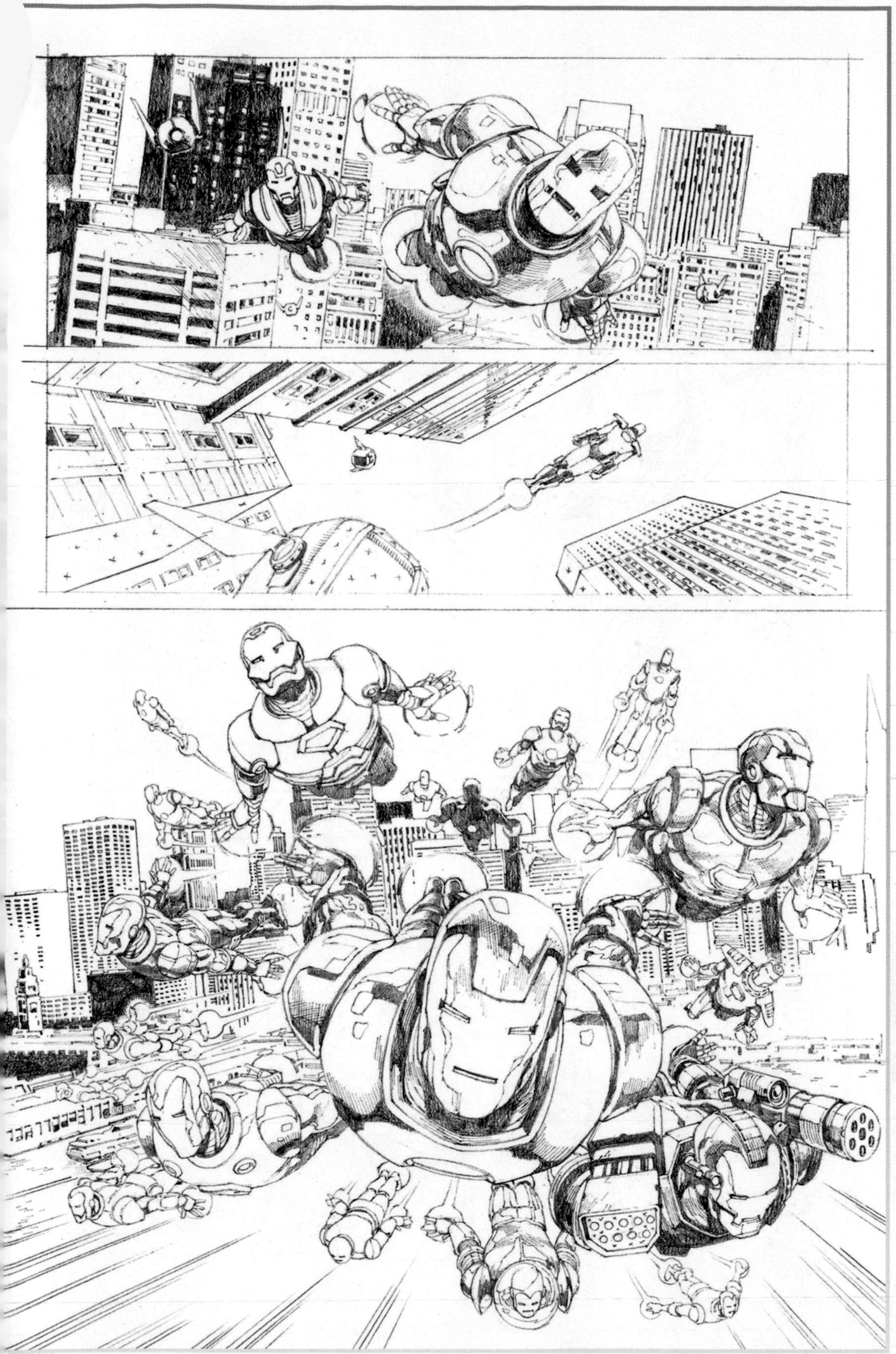

#8, PAGE 16 PENCILS
BY FELIPE WATANABE

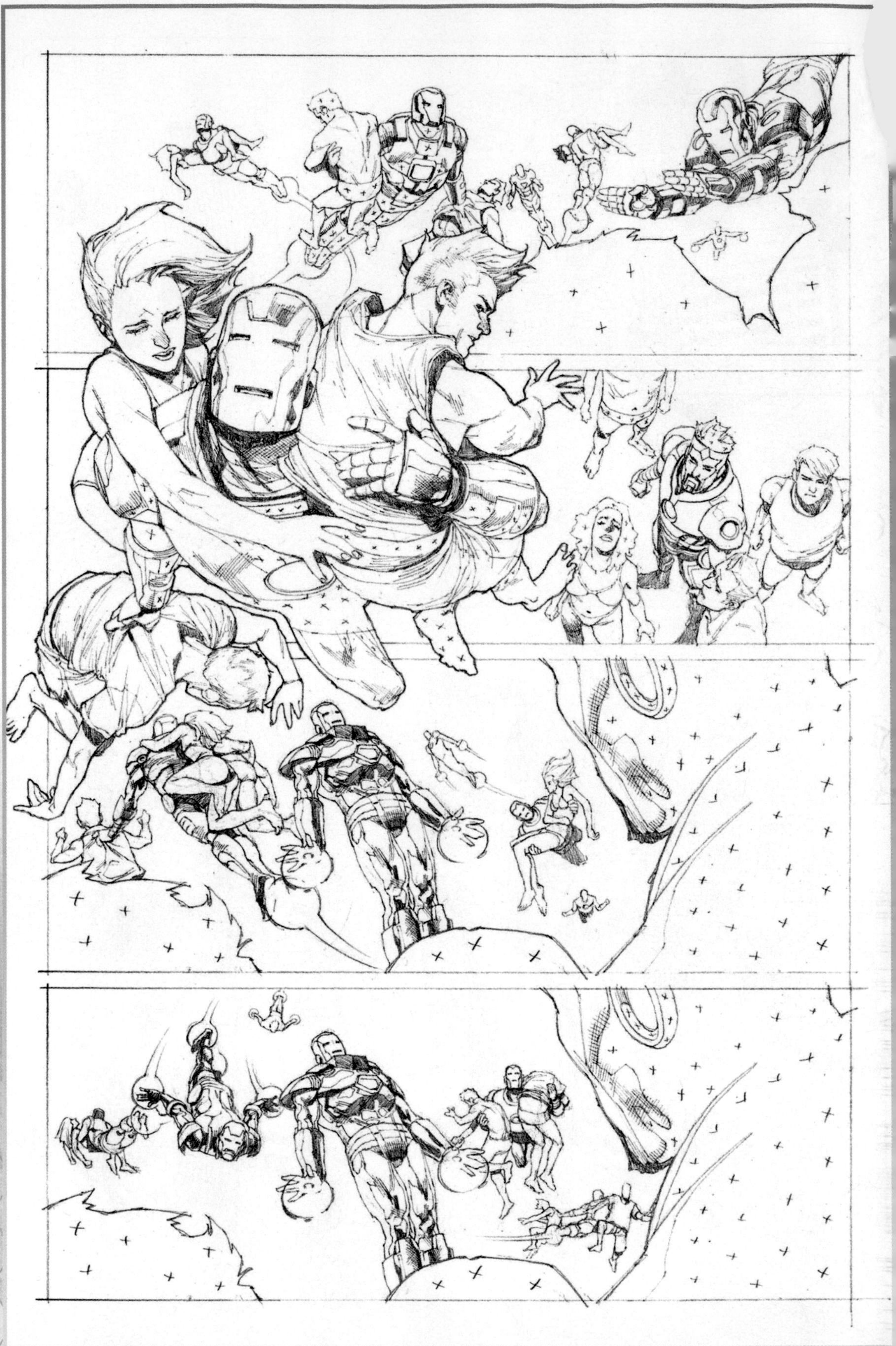

#8, PAGE 17 PENCILS
BY FELIPE WATANABE

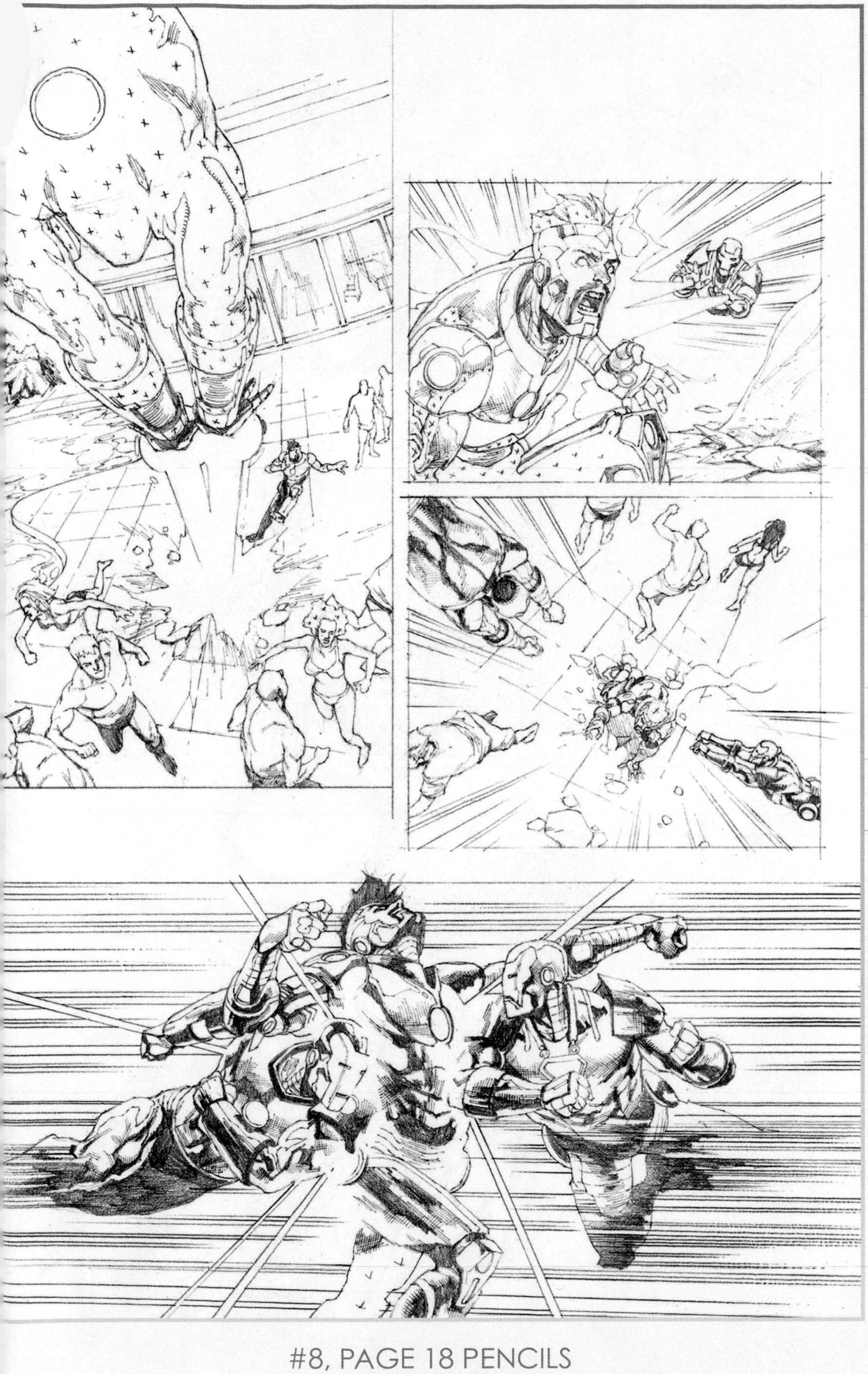

#8, PAGE 18 PENCILS
BY FELIPE WATANABE

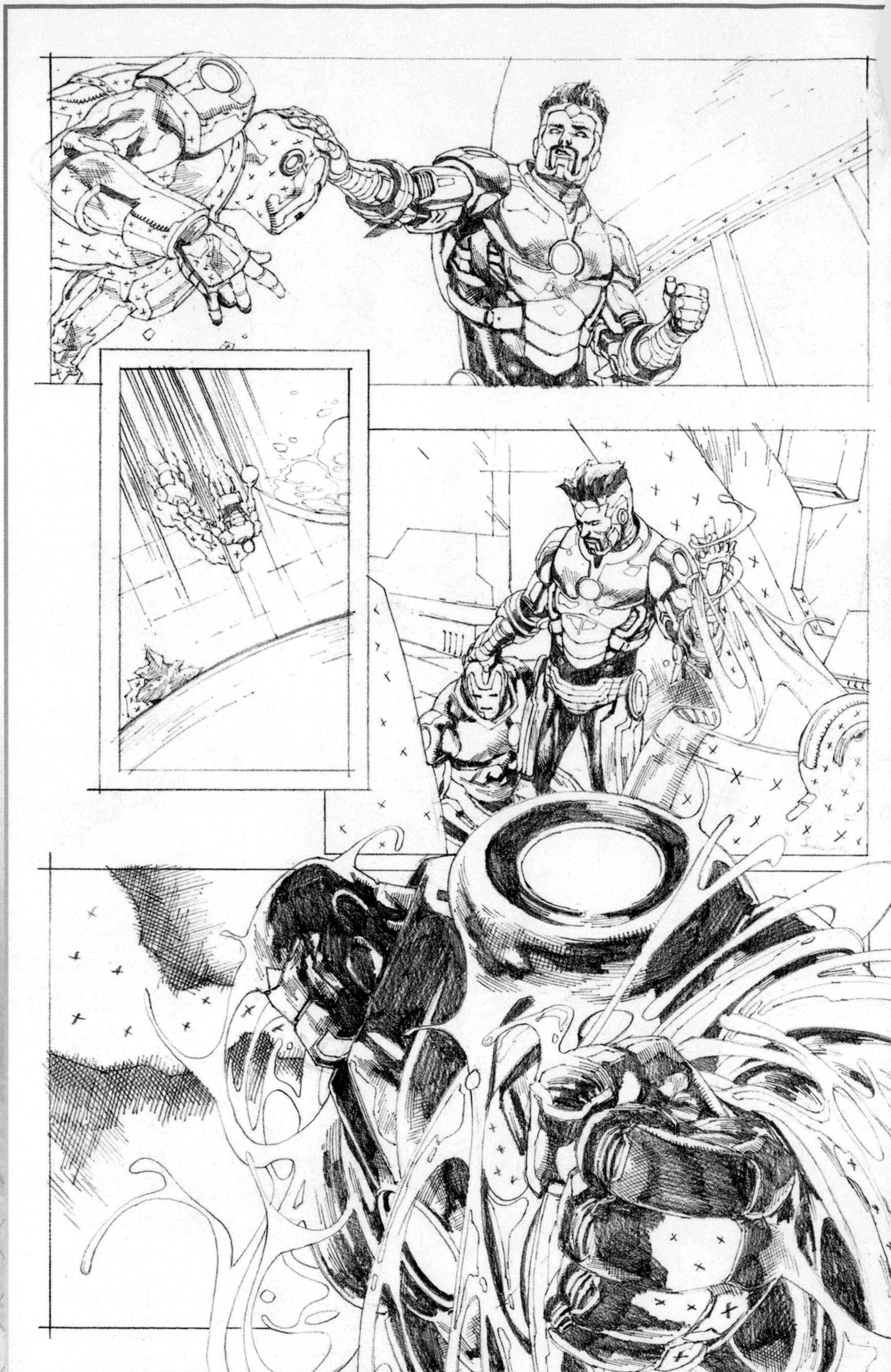

#8, PAGE 19 PENCILS
BY FELIPE WATANABE

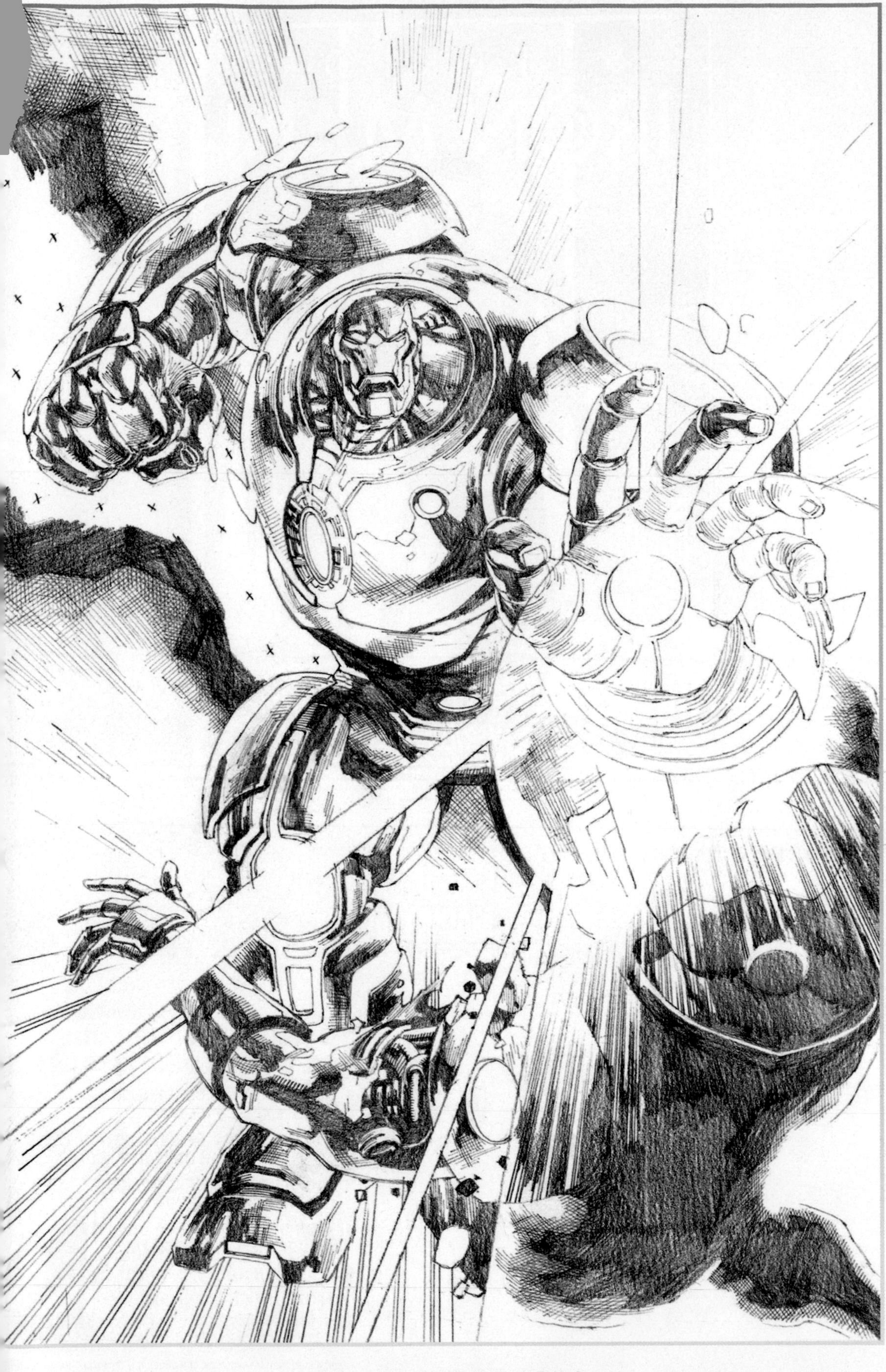

#8, PAGE 20 PENCILS
BY FELIPE WATANABE

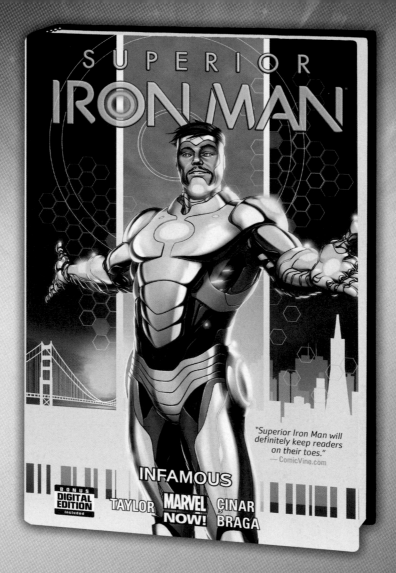

SUPERIOR
IRON MAN
"Superior Iron Man will definitely keep readers on their toes."
— ComicVine.com
INFAMOUS
BONUS DIGITAL EDITION included
TAYLOR
MARVEL NOW!
ÇINAR
BRAGA



TMALVICUWJ89

## TO REDEEM YOUR CODE FOR A FREE DIGITAL COPY:

1. GO TO MARVEL.COM/REDEEM. OFFER EXPIRES ON 9/9/17.
2. FOLLOW THE ON-SCREEN INSTRUCTIONS TO REDEEM YOUR DIGITAL COPY.
3. LAUNCH THE MARVEL COMICS APP TO READ YOUR COMIC NOW!
4. YOUR DIGITAL COPY WILL BE FOUND UNDER THE *MY COMICS* TAB.
5. READ & ENJOY!

YOUR FREE DIGITAL COPY WILL BE AVAILABLE O

MARVEL COMICS APP FOR APPLE® iOS DEVICES

MARVEL COMICS APP FOR ANDROID™ DEVICES